HOW TO BEAT THE DEMOCRATS

HOW TO BEAT
THE DEMOCRATS

and Other Subversive Ideas

DAVID HOROWITZ

Spence Publishing Company · Dallas
2002

Published in the United States by
Spence Publishing Company
111 Cole Street
Dallas, Texas 75207

Library of Congress Control Number: 2002106954

Printed in the United States of America

Contents

PREFACE
The Importance of Stories:
How George W. Bush Won
vii

ACKNOWLEDGMENTS
x

I
HOW THE LEFT UNDERMINED
AMERICA'S SECURITY
3

II
HOW TO BEAT THE DEMOCRATS
A Strategy Guide
49

III

The War Room

An Election Manual

93

IV

The Unrepentant Left

1 *An Open Letter to Anti-War Protesters*   157
2 *The Ayatollah of Anti-American Hate*   160
3 *A 1960s Terrorist Cult and 9/11*   185
4 *The President's Pardoned Bombers*   193
5 *Representative McKinney's Bizarre Mission* 204
6 *Scheer Lunacy at the* Los Angeles Times   209
7 *Progressive Narcissism: The Clinton Left*   223

Notes   239
Index   253

The Importance of Stories:
How George W. Bush Won

WHEN I SPEAK BEFORE REPUBLICAN GROUPS these days, I usually begin with a story I was told by the former congressman Jim Rogan, now a member of the Bush Administration: A man in a hot air balloon realized he was lost. Reducing his altitude, he spotted a woman on the ground below and asked for help. "Excuse me," he said when she was within earshot. "Can you help me? I don't know where I am and I promised a friend I would meet him an hour ago."

The woman looked up at him and said, "Sure. You are in a hot air balloon, about thirty feet above the ground. Your location is between 40 and 41 degrees north latitude and 59 and 60 degrees west longitude."

Hearing this, the man in the balloon became irritated. Looking down at her he asked, "Are you a Republican?"

"Yes," she replied. "How did you know?"

"*Well*," he snapped, "the information you've given me is probably technically correct, but I haven't the foggiest idea what to do with it. I'm still lost, my friend is still waiting for me, and frankly you haven't been any help at all."

"Are you a Democrat?" the woman asked.

"Yes," he said. "How did you know?"

"Easy," she answered. "You don't know where you are, and you don't know where you're going. You've risen to your present position on a large quantity of hot air, you've made promises you have no idea how to keep, and you expect me to solve your problem. Moreover, you're in the same position as when we met, but you've found a way to blame your predicament on me." Republicans laugh at this joke, even though it's on them. The purpose of this book is to change the attitude that inspires the laugh and the behavior behind it.

What the joke tells us is that politics is about stories—and human aggression. The purpose of the stories is to arouse emotions that work in your favor and against your opposition. The stories work for you if you are the victim or if you are helping someone who is perceived to be a victim. Americans like heroes who care, and they identify with underdogs. Aggression is an emotion associated with justice, with getting satisfaction for those who deserve it. In politics, stories work for you if you are the compassionate warrior helper. They work against you if you are the cause of someone's distress.

Democrats are clever at making up stories in which they are the victims and Republicans are the bad guys—the ones you know to blame. Republicans are not story driven at all; they are fact oriented. They are policy wonks who know about latitudes and longitudes, but not how to speak to people who don't. Republicans are abstract and cerebral, rather than visceral and concrete. Nobody understands them except those who share their cultural limitations. As a result, they feel injured and misunderstood, but nobody cares.

Why did George Bush win the presidential election in 2000? He had two stories to tell that reversed these stereotypes and inspired powerful emotions. The first story was that he is a Republican who cares about the weak and the helpless. He was "going to provide a helping hand to every willing heart." He was "not going to leave any child behind."

The second story was perhaps even more important. It is a reason not only why George Bush won the presidency in 2000, but why he will win the presidency again in 2004. This is the promise he made to restore dignity to the White House. If there is one thing that every American voter knew about George W. Bush by the end of the presidential race, it was the words he repeated almost every time he spoke: "If you make me your president, I will restore dignity and honor to the White House."

This was meant, of course, as a reference to Bill Clinton and his transformation of the Oval Office into a site of squalid scandal, casual prevarication, and reckless behavior. Talk show host Chris Matthews, a Democrat, was one of Clinton's toughest but most appreciative critics during the impeachment debate. Matthews himself had once worked as a young staffer in the White House. He had been impressed by the reverence that those who worked there had felt for "the people's house." As a result, Matthews could never understand why the White House had failed to reform the juvenile delinquent in Bill Clinton. "I do not understand," Matthews wrote when it was over, "why a man like Bill Clinton, blessed as he is with extraordinary political skills, did not use those same political skills to become not just president, but a great president. Instead he contented himself with a reign as the country's prom king."[1]

Americans love a rogue, and for a while it looked as though Americans would love a rogue president, too. But the poll numbers during the 2000 election campaign said something different. Clinton's approval ratings as president hovered near 60 percent throughout the campaign. But his personal approval ratings stayed just as firmly at an abysmal level of 30 percent. Put another way, 70 percent of the American people disapproved of Bill Clinton the man and the way he had abused his high office. Somewhere deep down they suspected that the good times the country seemed to be enjoying might be built on foundations of sand. The lying and the irresponsibility were piling up debts that one day would have to be paid, and it was the people who eventually would have to pay them.

What George Bush was saying through his story about dignity and honor was this: The President is the nation's commander in chief. He is accountable for the safety and security of us all. George Bush was saying to the American people, "Send me to the White House and I will honor your trust. I will be your commander in chief. I will be responsible for each and every one of you." What George Bush was saying was "I care about you and your children, and the dangers that may lie ahead."

Everyone who heard George Bush speak during that election campaign heard his message. And everyone who lived through September 11, 2001, understands what he meant.

ACKNOWLEDGMENTS

I WISH TO THANK House Majority Leader Tom DeLay for sponsoring my *War Room* and for standing behind me through tough battles; Bruce Hooper for backing me in in these wars and making possible the publication of "How To Beat The Democrats" in pamphlet form; Congressmen David Dreier, J. C. Watts, Jack Kingston, Ed Royce, and J. D. Hayworth, California Republican Party chair Shawn Steel, David Keene, and Marc and Karen Rotterman for supporting my efforts and being good friends; Cleta Mitchell, Tom Gammon, Susan Arceneaux, Rebecca Bernier, and Amy Sponaugle for gearing up my "machine"; Scott Rubush for providing editorial assistance and research; and my campaign partner April for her love and support.

I

How the Left Undermined America's Security

While the nation was having a good laugh at the expense of Florida's hanging chads and butterfly ballots, Mohammed Atta and Marwan al Shehhi were there, in Florida, learning to drive commercial jetliners [and ram them into the World Trade Center towers]. It will take a novelist to paint that broad canvas properly. It will take some deep political thinking to understand how the lackadaisical attitude toward government and the world helped leave the country so unready for the horror that Atta and Shehhi were preparing.

Michael Oreskes
New York Times, October 21, 2001

T HE SEPTEMBER 11 ATTACKS on the Pentagon and the World Trade Center marked the end of one American era and the beginning of another. Like Pearl Harbor, the September tragedy awakened Americans from their insular slumbers and made them aware of a world they could no longer afford to ignore. Like Franklin Roosevelt, George W. Bush condemned the attacks as acts of war and mobilized a nation to action. It was a sharp departure from the policy of his predecessor, Bill Clinton, who in characteristic self-absorption had downgraded a series of similar assaults—including one on the World Trade Center itself—to criminal matters involving only individuals.

The differences between the September 11 attacks and Pearl Harbor were also striking. The latter was a military base situated on an island three thousand miles from the American mainland. New York, on the other hand, is America's greatest population center, the portal through which immigrant generations of all colors and ethnicities come to seek a better life. The World Trade Center is the hub of the American economy, and its victims were targeted for participating in the most productive, tolerant, and generous society human beings have created. In responding to the attacks, President Bush took note of this: "America was targeted for attack," he told Congress on September 20, "because we're the brightest beacon for freedom and opportunity in the world. And no one will keep that light from shining."

In contrast to Pearl Harbor, the assault on the World Trade Center was hardly a "sneak attack" that American intelligence agencies had little idea was coming. The towers had already been bombed eight years earlier—and by the same enemy. The terrorists themselves were already familiar to government operatives, their aggressions frequent enough that several commissions had been appointed to investigate. Each had reached the same conclusion. It was not a matter of *whether* the United States was going to be the target of a major terrorist assault; it was a matter of *when*.[1]

In fact, the al-Qaeda terrorists responsible for the September 11 attacks had first engaged U.S. troops as early as 1993 in Somalia. The Americans' purpose in being there was humanitarian: to feed the starving citizens of this Muslim land. But these goodwill ambassadors were ambushed by al-Qaeda forces. In a fifteen-hour battle in Mogadishu, eighteen Americans were killed and eighty wounded. A dead U.S. soldier was dragged through the streets in an act calculated to humiliate his comrades and his country. The Americans' offense was not that they had brought food to the hungry. Their crime was who they *were*—"unbelievers," emissaries of "the Great Satan," in the political religion of the enemy they now faced.

The defeat in Mogadishu was not only a blow to American charity; it was a blow to American power and American prestige. Nonetheless, under the leadership of Bill Clinton, there was no military response to the humiliation. The greatest superpower the world has ever seen did nothing. It turned tail and ran.

THE WAR

On February 26, 1993, eight months prior to the Mogadishu attack, al-Qaeda terrorists had struck the World Trade Center for the first time. Their truck bomb made a crater six stories deep, killed six people, and injured more than a thousand. The planners' intention had been to cause one tower to topple the other and kill tens of thousands of innocent people. It was not only the first major terrorist act ever to take place on U.S. soil, but—in the judgment of a definitive account of the event—"the most ambitious terrorist attack ever attempted, anywhere, ever."[2]

Six Palestinian and Egyptian conspirators responsible for the attack were tried in civilian courts and got life sentences like common criminals, but its mastermind escaped. He was identified as Ramzi Ahmed Yousef, an Iraqi intelligence agent. This was a clear indication that the atrocity was no mere criminal event and that it involved more than individual terrorists: it involved hostile terrorist states.

Yet, once again, the Clinton Administration's response was to absorb the injury and accept defeat. The president did not even visit the bomb crater or tend to the victims. Instead, America's commander in chief warned against "overreaction." In doing so, he sent a clear message to our nation's enemies: We are unsure of purpose and unsteady in hand; we are self-indulgent and soft; we will not take risks to defend ourselves; we are vulnerable.

The al-Qaeda terrorists were listening. In a 1998 interview, Osama bin Laden told ABC news reporter John Miller: "We have seen in the last decade the decline of the American government and the weakness of the American soldier who is ready to wage Cold Wars and unprepared to fight long wars. This was proven in Beirut when the Marines fled after two explosions. It also proves they can run in less than 24 hours, and this was also repeated in Somalia. We are ready for all occasions. We rely on Allah."[3]

Among the terrorist entities that supported the al-Qaeda terrorists were Yasser Arafat's Palestine Authority and the Palestine Liberation Organization. The PLO had created the first terrorist training camps, invented suicide bombings of civilians and been the chief propaganda machine behind the idea that terrorist armies were really missionaries for "social justice." Yet, among foreign leaders Arafat was Clinton's most frequent White House guest. Far from treating Arafat as an enemy of civilized order and an international pariah, the Clinton Administration was busily cultivating him as a "partner for peace." For many Washington liberals, terrorism was not the instrument of political fanatics and evil men, but the product of social conditions—poverty, racism, and oppression—for which Western democracies, including Israel, were always ultimately to blame.

The idea that terrorism has "root causes" in social conditions whose primary author is the United States is, in fact, an organizing theme of the contemporary political left. "Where is the acknowledgment that this was not a 'cowardly' attack on 'civilization' or 'liberty' or 'humanity' or 'the free world'"—declared the writer Susan

Sontag, speaking for this faction—"but an attack on the world's self-proclaimed superpower, undertaken as a consequence of specific American alliances and actions? How many citizens are aware of the ongoing American bombing of Iraq?"[4] (Was Susan Sontag unaware that Iraq was behind the first World Trade Center attack? That Iraq had attempted to swallow Kuwait and was a regional aggressor and sponsor of terror? That Iraq had expelled UN arms inspectors—in violation of the terms of its peace—who were there to prevent it from developing chemical, biological, and nuclear weapons? Was she unaware that Iraq was a sponsor of international terror and posed an ongoing threat to others, including the country in which she lived?)

During the Clinton years, the idea that America was somehow responsible for global distress had become an all too familiar refrain among left-wing elites. It had particular resonance in the institutions that shaped American culture and policy—universities, the mainstream media, and the Oval Office. In March 1998, two months after Monica Lewinsky became a White House thorn and a household name, Clinton embarked on a presidential hand-wringing expedition to Africa. With a large delegation of African-American leaders in tow, the President made a pilgrimage to Uganda to apologize for the crime of American slavery. The apology was offered though no slaves had ever been imported to America from Uganda or any East African state; though slavery in Africa preceded any American involvement by a thousand years; though America and Britain were the two powers responsible for ending the slave trade; and though America had abolished slavery a hundred years before—at great human cost—while slavery has persisted in Africa, without African protest, to the present day.

Four months after Clinton left Uganda, al-Qaeda terrorists blew up the U.S. embassies in Kenya and Tanzania.

Root Causes

Clinton's continuing ambivalence about America's role in the world was highlighted in the wake of September 11, when he suggested that America actually bore some responsibility for the attacks. In November 2001, even as the new Bush administration was launching America's military response, the former president made a speech at Georgetown University in which he admonished citizens who were descended "from various European lineages" that they were "not blameless,"[5] and that America's past involvement in slavery should humble them as they confronted their attackers. Characteristically, President Clinton took no responsibility for his own failure to protect Americans from the attacks.[6]

The idea that there are "root causes" behind campaigns to murder innocent men, women and children, and terrorize civilian populations was examined shortly after the Trade Center events by a writer in the *New York Times*. Columnist Edward Rothstein observed that while there was much hand-wringing and many mea culpas on the left after September 11,[7] no one had invoked "root causes" to defend Timothy McVeigh after he blew up the Oklahoma City federal building in 1995, killing 187 people. "No one suggested that this act had its 'root causes' in an injustice that needed to be rectified to prevent further terrorism."[8] The silence was maintained though McVeigh and his collaborators "asserted that their ideas of rights and liberty were being violated and that the only recourse was terror."[9]

The reason no one invoked "root causes" to explain the Oklahoma City bombing was simply that Timothy McVeigh was not a leftist. Nor did he claim to be acting in behalf of "social justice"— the historical code for totalitarian causes. In an address to Congress that defined America's response to September 11, President Bush observed, "We have seen their kind before. They are the heirs of all the murderous ideologies of the twentieth century. By sacrificing human life to serve their radical visions, by abandoning every value except the will to power, they follow in the path of fascism, Nazism, and totalitarianism."

Like Islamic radicalism, the totalitarian doctrines of communism and fascism are fundamentalist creeds. "The fundamentalist does not believe [his] ideas have any limits or boundaries . . . [therefore] the goals of fundamentalist terror are not to eliminate injustice but to eliminate opposition."[10] That is why the humanitarian nature of America's mission to Mogadishu made no difference to America's al-Qaeda foe. The terrorists' goal was not to alleviate hunger. It was to eliminate America. It was to defeat "The Great Satan."

Totalitarians and fundamentalists share a conviction that is religious and political at the same time. Their mission is social redemption through the power of the state. Using political and military power they intend to create a "new world" in their own image. This revolutionary transformation encompasses all individuals and requires the control of all aspects of human life: "Like fundamentalist terror, totalitarian terror leaves no aspect of life exempt from the battle being waged. The state is felt to be the apotheosis of political and natural law, and it strives to extend that law over all humanity. . . . No injustices, separately or together, necessarily lead to totalitarianism and no mitigation of injustice, however defined, will eliminate its unwavering beliefs, absolutist control and unbounded ambitions."[11]

In 1998 Osama bin Laden explained his war aims to ABC: "Allah ordered us in this religion to purify Muslim land of all non-believers."[12] As the *New Republic*'s Peter Beinart commented, bin Laden is not a crusader for social justice but "an ethnic cleanser on a scale far greater than the Hutus and the Serbs, a scale that has only one true Twentieth Century parallel."

In the 1990s America mobilized its military power to go to the rescue of Muslims in the Balkans who were being ethnically cleansed by Serbian communists. This counted for nothing in al-Qaeda's calculations, any more than did America's support for Muslim peasants in Afghanistan fighting for their freedom against the Red Army invaders in the 1980s. The war against radical Islam is not about what America has done, but about what America is. As bin Laden told the world on October 7, the day America began its military response, the war is between those of the faith and those outside the faith, between those who submit to the believers' law and those who are infidels and do not.[13]

While The Clinton Administration Slept

After the first World Trade Center attack, President Clinton vowed there would be vengeance. But as with so many of his presidential pronouncements, the strong words were followed neither by deeds nor by measures necessary to defend the country against the next series of attacks.

. After the victory in Mogadishu and at the 1993 World Trade Center bombing, al-Qaeda made unsuccessful attempts to blow up the Lincoln and Holland Tunnels and other populated targets, including a massive terrorist incident timed to coincide with the millennium celebrations of January 2000. Another scheme to hijack commercial airliners and use them as "bombs," according to plans close to those eventually used on September 11, was thwarted in the Philippines in 1995. The architect of this effort was the Iraqi intelligence agent Ramzi Yousef.

The following year, a terrorist attack on the Khobar Towers, a U.S. military barracks in Saudia Arabia, killed nineteen American soldiers. The White House response was weak, and the case (in the words of FBI director Louis B. Freeh) "remains unresolved."[14] Two years later al-Qaeda agents blew up the U.S. embassies in Kenya and Tanzania killing 245 people and injuring five thousand. (One CIA official told a reporter, "Two at once is not twice as hard. It is a hundred times as hard."[15]) On October 12, 2000 the warship USS Cole was bombed while refueling in Yemen, yet another Islamic country aligned with the terrorist enemy.[16] Seventeen U.S. sailors were killed and thirty-nine injured.

These were all acts of war, yet President Clinton and his cabinet refused to recognize them as such.[17]

Clinton's second-term national security advisor, Sandy Berger, described the official White House position towards these attacks as "a little bit like a Whack-A-Mole game at the circus. They bop up and you whack 'em down, and if they bop up again, you bop 'em back, down again."[18] Like the administration he represented, the national security advisor lacked a proper appreciation of the problem. Iraq's dictator was unimpressed by sporadic U.S. strikes against his regime. He remained defiant, expelling UN weapons inspectors, firing at U.S. warplanes, and continuing to build his arsenal of mass destruction. But "the Administration held no clear and consistent view of the Iraqi threat and how it intended to address it," observed *Washington Post* correspondent Jim Hoagland.[19] The disarray of Clinton's security policy flowed from the signature problem of the Clinton years, the "Administration's growing inability to tell the world—and itself—the truth."[20]

Underlying the Clinton security failure was the fact that the Administration was made up of people who for twenty-five years had discounted or minimized the totalitarian threat, opposed America's armed presence abroad, and consistently resisted the deployment of America's military forces to halt communist expansion. National Security Advisor Sandy Berger was himself a veteran of the 1960s "anti-war" movement, which abetted the communist victories in Vietnam and Cambodia, and created the "Vietnam War syndrome" that made it so difficult afterwards for American presidents to deploy the nation's military forces.

Berger had also been a member of Peace Now, the leftist movement seeking to pressure the Israeli government to make concessions to Yasser Arafat's PLO terrorists. Clinton's first national security advisor, Anthony Lake, was a protégé of Berger who had introduced him to Clinton. All three had met as activists in the 1972 McGovern presidential campaign, whose primary issue was opposition to the Vietnam War, taking the view that the "arrogance of American power" was responsible for the conflict rather than communist aggression.[21]

Anthony Lake's own attitude towards the totalitarian threat in Southeast Asia was displayed in a March 1975 *Washington Post* article, "At Stake in Cambodia: Extending Aid Will Only Prolong the Killing."[22] Lake's article was designed to rally Democratic opposition to a presidential request for emergency aid to the Cambodian regime. The aid was required to contain the threat posed by Communist leader Pol Pot and his insurgent Khmer Rouge forces.

At the time, Republicans warned that if the aid was cut, the regime would fall and a "bloodbath" would ensue. This fear was solidly based on reports that had begun accumulating three years earlier concerning "the extraordinary brutality with which the Khmer Rouge were governing the civilian population in areas they controlled."[23] But Anthony Lake and the Democratic-controlled Congress dismissed these warnings as so much "anti-communist hysteria" and voted to deny the aid.

In his *Post* article, Lake advised fellow Democrats to view the Khmer Rouge not as a totalitarian force, but as a coalition embracing "many Khmer nationalists, Communist and non-Communist," who only desired independence. It would be a mistake, he wrote, to alienate Pol Pot and the Khmer Rouge lest we "push them further into the arms of their Communist supporters."[24] Lake's myopic left-wing views prevailed among the Democrats, and the following year the new president, Jimmy Carter, rewarded Lake with an appointment as policy planning director of the State Department.

The prediction contained in Lake's title proved to be exactly wrong, not a small mistake for someone who in 1992 would be placed in charge of America's national security apparatus. In Cambodia, the termination of U.S. aid led immediately to the collapse of the government allowing the Khmer Rouge to seize power within months of the congressional vote. The victorious revolutionaries proceeded to implement their plans for a new Communist utopia by systematically eliminating their opposition. In the next three years they killed nearly two million Cambodians, a campaign universally recognized as one of the worst genocides ever.

WARNINGS IGNORED, OPPORTUNITIES MISSED

For nearly a decade before the World Trade Center disaster, the Clinton Administration was aware that Americans were increasingly vulnerable to attacks which might involve biological or chemical weapons, or even nuclear devices bought or stolen from the former Soviet Union. This was the insistent message of Republican speeches in Congress and was reflected in the warnings of several government commissions, as well as Clinton's own secretary of defense, William Cohen.

In July 1999, Cohen wrote an op-ed piece in the *Washington Post* predicting a terrorist attack on the American mainland. "In the past year, dozens of threats to use chemical or biological weapons in the United States have turned out to be hoaxes. Someday, one will be real." But the warnings led to little action by the commander in chief. Meanwhile, the media looked the other way. As the president of the

Council on Foreign Relations told the *New Yorker*'s Joe Klein, he "watched carefully to see if anyone followed up on [Cohen's warning]. But none of the television networks and none of the elite press even mentioned it. I was astonished."[25]

The following year, the National Commission on Terrorism, chaired by former Reagan counter-terrorism head Paul Bremer, issued a report with the eerily foreboding image of the Twin Towers in a cross-hair on its cover. Jon Kyl and Dianne Feinstein led a bipartisan effort to attach the recommendations of the panel to an intelligence authorization bill. But Senator Patrick Leahy, who had distinguished himself in the 1980s by opposing the government's efforts to halt the communist offensive in Central America "said he feared a threat to 'civil liberties' in a campaign against terrorism and torpedoed the effort. After the bombing of the USS Cole, Kyl and Feinstein tried again. This time, Leahy was content with eviscerating the proposals instead of defeating them outright. The weakened proposals died as the House realized 'it wasn't worth taking up.'"[26]

After the abortive plot to blow up commercial airliners in the Philippines, Vice President Gore was tasked with improving airline security. A commission was formed, but under his leadership it also focused on civil liberties and profiling, liberal obsessions that diluted any efforts to strengthen security measures in the face of a threat in which all of the known terrorists were Muslims from the Middle East and Asia. The commission concluded that, "no profile [of passengers] should contain or be based on . . . race, religion, or national origin." According to journalist Kevin Cherry, the FAA also decided in 1999 to seal its passenger screening system from law enforcement databases, thus preventing the FBI from notifying airlines that suspected terrorists were on board."[27]

In 1993, the FBI identified three charities connected to the Palestinian terrorist organization Hamas that were being used to finance terrorist activities, sending as much as twenty million dollars a year to America's enemies.[28] According to presidential adviser Dick Morris, "at a White House strategy meeting on April 27, 1995—two weeks after the Oklahoma City bombing—the President was urged to create a 'President's List' of extremist/terrorist groups, their members and donors 'to warn the public against well-intentioned donations which might foster terrorism.' On April 1, 1996, he was again advised to 'prohibit fund-raising by terrorists and identify terrorist organizations.'"[29] Hamas was specifically mentioned.

Clinton ignored these recommendations. Why? FBI agents have stated that they were prevented from opening either criminal or national security cases because of a fear that it would be seen as profiling Islamic charities. While Clinton was politically correct, Hamas flourished.[30]

In failing to heed the signs that America was at war with a deadly adversary, overcome the ideological obstacles created by the liberal biases of his administration,[31] and arouse an uninformed public to concern, it was the commander in chief who bore primary responsibility. As one former administration official told reporter Joe Klein "Clinton spent less concentrated attention on national defense than any another President in recent memory."[32] Clinton's political advisor Dick Morris flatly charged, "Clinton's failure to mobilize America to confront foreign terror after the 1993 attack [on the World Trade Center] led directly to the 9-11 disaster." According to Morris, "Clinton was removed, uninvolved, and distant where the war on terror was concerned."[33]

By Clinton's own account, Monica Lewinsky was able to visit him privately more than a dozen times in the Oval Office. But according to a *USA Today* investigative report, the head of the CIA could not get a single private meeting with the president, even after the World Trade Center bombing of February 26, 1993, or the killing of eighteen American soldiers in Mogadishu on October 3 of the same year. "James Woolsey, Clinton's first CIA director, says he never met privately with Clinton after their initial interview. When a small plane crashed on the White House grounds in 1994, the joke inside the White House was, 'that must be Woolsey, still trying to get an appointment.'"[34]

In 1996, an American-Muslim businessman and Clinton supporter, Mansoor Ijaz, opened up an unofficial channel between the government of the Sudan and the Clinton Administration. At the same time, "the State Department was describing bin Laden as 'the greatest single financier of terrorist projects in the world' and was accusing the Sudan of harboring terrorists."[35] According to Mansoor, who met with Clinton and Sandy Berger, "President Omar Hassan Ahmed Bashir, who wanted terrorism sanctions against Sudan lifted, offered the arrest and extradition of bin Laden and detailed intelligence data about the global networks constructed by Egypt's Islamic Jihad, Iran's Hezbollah and the Palestinian Hamas. Among the members of these networks were the two hijackers who piloted commercial airliners into the World Trade Center. The silence of the Clinton administration in responding to these offers was deafening."[36]

President Bashir sent key intelligence officials to Washington in February 1996. Again, according to Mansoor, "the Sudanese offered to arrest bin Laden and extradite him to Saudi Arabia or, barring that, to 'baby-sit' him—monitoring all his activities and associates." But the Saudis didn't want him. Instead, in May 1996 "the Sudanese capitulated to U.S. pressure and asked bin Laden to leave, despite their feeling that he could be monitored better in Sudan than elsewhere. Bin Laden left for Afghanistan, taking with him Ayman Awahiri, considered by the U.S. to be the chief planner of the September 11 attacks." One month later, the US military housing complex in Saudi Arabia was blown apart by a five thousand-pound truck bomb. Clinton's failure to grasp the opportunity, concludes Mansoor, "represents one of the most serious foreign policy failures in American history."[37]

According to a London *Sunday Times* account, based on a Clinton Administration source, responsibility for this decision "went to the very top of the White House."[38] Shortly after the September 11 disaster, "Clinton told a dinner companion that the decision to let bin Laden go was probably 'the biggest mistake of my presidency.'" But according to the *Times* report, which was based on interviews with intelligence officials, this was only one of three occasions on which the Clinton Administration had the opportunity to seize bin Laden and failed to do so.

When the president's affair with Monica Lewinsky became public in January 1998, and his adamant denials made it a consuming public preoccupation, Clinton's normal inattention to national security matters became part of a general executive paralysis. In Dick Morris's judgment, the United States was effectively "without a president between January 1998 until April 1999," when the impeachment proceedings concluded with the failure of the Senate to convict.[39] It was in August 1998 that al-Qaeda truck bombs blew up the embassies in Kenya and Tanzania.

THE FAILURE TO TAKE SECURITY SERIOUSLY

Yet this was only half the story. During its eight years, the Clinton Administration *was* able to focus enough attention on defense to hamstring the intelligence services in the name of civil liberties, to shrink the U.S. military in the name of economy,[40] and to prevent the Pentagon from adopting (and funding) a "two-war" strategy, because "the Cold War was over." In the White House's judgment there was no military threat in the post-communist world that might make fighting wars on two fronts necessary. Inattention to defense did not prevent the Clinton Administration from pursuing massive social experiments in the military in the name of gender and diversity reform, which included requiring "consciousness-raising" classes for military personnel, rigging physical standards women were unable to meet, and in general undermining the meritocratic benchmarks that are a crucial component of military morale.

While budget cuts forced some military families to go on food stamps, the Pentagon spent enormous sums to reequip ships and barracks to accommodate co-ed living.[41] All these efforts further reduced the Pentagon's ability to put a fighting force in the field—a glaring national vulnerability dramatized by the war in Kosovo. This diminished the crucial elements of fear and respect for American power in the eyes of adversaries waiting in the wings.[42]

The Democrats' insistence that American power was somehow the disturber—rather than the enforcer—of international tranquility prompted the White House during the Clinton years to turn to multilateral agencies for leadership, particularly the discredited United Nations. While useful in limited peacekeeping operations, the UN was in large part a collection of theocratic tyrannies and brutal dictatorships which regularly indicted and condemned the world's most tolerant democracies, specifically the United States, England, and Israel, while supporting the very states providing safe harbors for America's al-Qaeda enemy. Just prior to the World Trade Center attacks, the UN's "Conference on Racism" engaged in a ritual of America bashing over reparations for slavery and support for Israel. The agenda had been set by an Arab coalition led by Iran.

During the 1990s, Bill Clinton's most frequent foreign guest was Yasser Arafat, whose allegiance to Iraq and betrayal of America during the Gulf War could not have been more brazen. Following the defeat of Iraq, a "peace process" was launched in the Arab-Israeli conflict that predictably failed through Arafat's failure to renounce the terrorist option. But why renounce terror if there is no price exacted for practicing it?

It is true that the Clinton White House was able, during its eight-year tenure, to shed some of the Democrats' normal aversion to the use of American military might. (In 1990, for example, only six Democratic senators voted to authorize the Gulf War against Iraq.) But the Clinton deployments of American forces were often non-military: a "democracy-building" effort in Haiti that failed, or flood relief and "peacekeeping" operations that were more appropriately the province of international institutions. Even the conflict Clinton belatedly engaged in the Balkans was officially characterized as a new kind of "humanitarian war," as though the old kinds of war for national interest and self-defense were somehow tainted. While the Serbian dictator Milosevic was toppled, "ethnic cleansing," the casus belli of the Western intervention, continues, except that the Christian Serbs in Kosovo have now become victims of the previously persecuted Albanian Muslims.

Among Clinton's deployments were also half-hearted strikes using cruise missiles against essentially defenseless countries like the Sudan or the sporadic bombing of Iraq when Saddam violated the terms of the Gulf peace. Clinton's strikes failed in their primary objective—to maintain the UN inspections. On the other hand, a negative result of this "Whack-A-Mole" strategy was the continual antagonizing of Muslim populations throughout the world.

The most notorious of these episodes was undoubtedly Clinton's ill-conceived and ineffectual response to the attacks on the African embassies. At the time, Clinton was preoccupied with preparing his defense before a grand jury convened because of his public lies about the Lewinsky affair. Three days after Lewinsky's grand jury appearance, without consulting the Joint Chiefs of Staff or his national security advisors, Clinton launched cruise missiles into two Islamic countries, which he identified as being allied to the terrorists and their leader Osama bin Laden. One of these missiles hit and destroyed a pharmaceutical factory in the Sudan, killing one individual. Since the factory was the sole plant producing medicines for an impoverished African nation, there were almost certainly a number of collateral deaths.

The incident, which inflamed anti-American passions all over the Islamic world, was—in conception and execution—a perfect reflection of the distorted priorities and reckless attitudes of the Clinton White House. It also reflected the irresponsibility of congressional Democrats who subordinated the safety concerns of their constituents to provide unified support for the presidential misbehavior at home and abroad.

The Partisan Nature of the Security Problem

More than one hundred Arabic operatives participated in the attack on the World Trade Center. They did so over a period of several years. They were able to enter the United States with and without passports, seemingly at will. They received training in flying commercial airliners at American facilities despite clear indications that some of them might be part of a terrorist campaign. At the same time, Democrats pressed for greater relaxation of immigration policies and resisted scrutiny of foreign nationals on the grounds that to do so constituted "racial profiling." To coordinate their terrorist efforts, the al-Qaeda operatives had to communicate with each other electronically on channels that America's high-tech intelligence agencies normally intercept. One reason they were not detected was that the first line of defense against such attacks was effectively crippled by powerful figures in the Democratic Party who considered the CIA the problem and not America's enemies.

Security controls that would have prevented adversarial agents from acquiring encryption devices that thwarted American intelligence efforts were casually lifted on orders from the highest levels of government.[43] Alleged abuses by American intelligence operatives became a higher priority than the abuses of the hostile forces they were attempting to contain.[44] Reporter Joe Klein's inquiries led him to conclude "there seems to be near unanimous agreement among experts: in the ten years since the collapse of the Soviet Union almost every aspect of American national-security—from military operations to intelligence gathering, from border control to political leadership—has been marked by . . . institutional lassitude and bureaucratic arrogance."[45]

The Democrats' cavalier attitude towards American security in the years preceding September 11 was dramatized in a series of annual amendments to cut intelligence funds sight unseen, which was introduced every year of the Clinton Administration (except 2000) by Independent Bernie Sanders.

The Sanders amendment was initially proposed in 1993, after the first al-Qaeda attack on the World Trade Center. In that year, the Democrat-controlled House Intelligence Committee had voted to reduce President Clinton's own authorization request for the intelligence agencies by 6.75 percent. But this was insufficient for Sanders. So he introduced an amendment that required a *minimum* reduction in financial authorization for each individual intelligence agency of at least 10 percent.[46]

Sanders refused even to examine the intelligence budget he proposed to cut: "My job is not to go through the intelligence budget. I have not even looked at it."[47] According to Sanders the reasons for reducing the intelligence budget were that "the Soviet Union no longer exists," and that "massive unemployment, that low wages, that homelessness, that hungry children, that the collapse of our educational system is perhaps an equally strong danger to this Nation, or may be a stronger danger for our national security."[48]

Irresponsible? Incomprehensible? Ninety-seven Democrats in all voted for the Sanders cuts, including House Armed Services Committee chair Ron Dellums and the House Democratic leadership. Moreover, between a third and more than half the Democrats in the House voted in favor of the Sanders amendment over the years. As the terrorist attacks on America intensified year by year during the 1990s, Sanders steadfastly reintroduced his amendment. In 1995, 1996, and 1997, Barney Frank introduced a similar amendment that would cut the intelligence funds by less, but cut them still.[49] In 1997, 158 Democrats voted for the Frank amendment. That same year a majority voted for a modified Sanders amendment to cut intelligence funds by 5 percent.

According to a study by political consultant Terry Cooper, "Dick Gephardt (D-MO), the House Democratic leader, voted to cut on five of the seven amendments on which he was recorded. He appears to have 'taken a walk' on two other votes. David Bonior (D-MI), the number-two Democratic leader who as Whip enforces the party position, voted for every single one of the ten cutting amendments. Chief Deputy Whips John Lewis (D-GA) and Rosa DeLauro (D-CT) voted to cut intelligence funding every time they voted. Nancy Pelosi (D-CA), just elected to replace Bonior as Whip when Bonior leaves early in 2002, voted to cut intelligence funding three times, even though she was a member of the Intelligence Committee and should have known better. Two funding cut amendments got the votes of every single member of the elected House Democratic leadership.

In all, members of the House Democratic leadership supported the Saunders and Franks funding cut amendments 56.9 percent of the time."

Many of the Democrats whose committee positions give them immense say over our national security likewise voted for most or all of the funding cut amendments. Ron Dellums (D-CA), the top Democrat on the Armed Services Committee from 1993 through 1997, cast all eight of his votes on funding cut amendments in favor of less intelligence funding.[50] Three persons who chaired, or were ranking Democrats on, Armed Services subcommittees for part of the 1993-99 period—Pat Schroeder (D-CO), Neil Abercrombie (D-HI), and Marty Meehan (D-MA)—also voted for every fund-cutting amendment that was offered during their tenures. Dave Obey (D-WI), the senior Democrat on the Appropriations Committee that holds the House's keys to the federal checkbook, voted seven out of eight times to reduce intelligence funding.[51]

In 1994, Republican Porter Goss, a former CIA official and member of the House Intelligence Committee, warned that the cuts proposed in the intelligence budget amounted to 16 percent of the 1992 budget and were 20 percent below the 1990 budget. Yet this did not dissuade Dellums, Bonior and a hundred or more Democrats from continuing to lay the budgetary axe to America's first line of defense. Ranking Republican Larry Combest warned that the cuts endangered "critically important and fragile capabilities, such as in the area of human intelligence."[52] In 1998, Osama bin Laden and four radical Islamic groups connected to al-Qaeda issued a *fatwa* condemning every American man, woman, and child, civilian and military. Sanders responded by enlisting Oregon Democrat Peter DeFazio to author an amendment cutting the intelligence authorization again.[53]

The Republicans and National Security

When Republicans took control of the House in 1994, Republican Floyd Spence expressed his outrage at the Democrats' handiwork in words that were eerily prescient:

> We have done to our military and to our intelligence agencies what no foreign power has been able to do. We have been decimating our own defenses. . . . In this day and time you do not have to be a superpower to raise the horrors of mass destruction warfare on people. It could be a Third World country, a rogue nation, or a terrorist group. . . . These weapons of mass destruction are chemical, biological, bacteriological. . . . Anthrax could be released in the air over Washington, D.C. . . . That could happen at any time and people are talking about cutting back on our ability to defend against these things or to prevent them from happening. It is unconscionable to even think about it. It borders on leaving our country defenseless.[54]

Yet the warning signs continued right up to the disaster. Before and after the 1999 *Washington Post* article by Defense Secretary Cohen, "there was a series of more elaborate reports about grand terrorism, by assorted blue-ribbon task forces, which warned of chemical, biological, and nuclear attacks." A report by former senators Hart and Rudman called for a huge "homeland security" campaign that would include—in Joe Klein's summation for the *New Yorker*—"intensive municipal civil defense and crisis response teams, new anti-terrorist detection technology," and a new cabinet level position of Secretary of Homeland Security, which was established by the Bush Administration shortly after the attack.[55]

Klein—a liberal Democrat and former "anti-war" activist—refused to draw the obvious conclusion from these events, and place the responsibility where it belonged—squarely on the shoulders of the Democrats. Instead he wrote: "There can't be much controversy here. Nearly everyone—elected officials, the media, ideologues of every stripe—ignored these reports."[56]

This is a falsehood so self-serving as to be almost understandable. Fortunately there is an extensive public record attesting to the intense and ongoing concern of Republican officials and the conservative media over the nation's security crisis, and their determined if unsuccessful efforts to expose and remedy it. There is an equally extensive public record of the Democrats' resistance to strengthening the nation's defenses and of the liberal media's efforts to minimize, dismiss, and ridicule attempts by Republicans to do so. The national press's negative treatment of Representative Dan Burton's and Senator Fred Thompson's committee investigations into the efforts by Communist China to influence the 1996 presidential election is a dramatic instance, particularly since the liberal media have made campaign finance reform one of their highest priorities.

In fact, the Chinese poured hundreds of thousands of dollars—legal and illegal—into the Clinton-Gore campaigns in 1992 and 1996. The top funder of the 1992 Clinton-Gore campaign was an Arkansas resident and Chinese banker named James Riady, whose relationship with Clinton went back twenty years. Riady is the scion of a multi-billion dollar financial empire whose throne room in Jakarta is adorned with two adjacent portraits of Clinton and Chinese leader, Li Peng, the infamous "butcher of Tiananmen Square." Though based in Indonesia, the Riady empire has billions of dollars invested in China and is in a working economic and political partnership with China's military and intelligence establishments. The Riadys gave 450,000 dollars to Clinton's 1992 presidential campaign and another six hundred thousand dollars to the Democratic National Committee and Democratic state parties—and that was just the tip of the iceberg.[57]

The question that Democratic obstructions prevented the Thompson and Burton committees from answering was whether these payments resulted in the transfer of U.S. weapons technologies to Communist China. China is known to have transferred such sensitive military technologies to Iran, Libya, North Korea, and Iraq. Beginning in 1993, the Clinton Administration systematically lifted security controls at the Department of Commerce, which had previously prevented the transfer of sensitive missile, satellite, and computer technologies to China and other nuclear proliferators. At the beginning of 1993, Clinton appointed John Huang, an agent of the Riady interests as well as Communist China, to a senior position at the Commerce Department with top security clearance. Clinton later sent Huang to the Democratic National Committee to take charge of fundraising for his 1996 campaign.[58]

In May 1999, a bipartisan House committee, headed by Representative Christopher Cox, released a report which was tersely summarized by the *Wall Street Journal* in these harrowing words: "The espionage inquiry found Beijing has stolen U.S. design data for nearly all elements needed for a major nuclear attack on the U.S., such as advanced warheads, missiles and guidance systems."[59] Among the factors contributing to these unprecedented losses—most of which took place during the Clinton years—the report identified lax security by the Clinton Administration.

Two committees of Congress headed by Dan Burton and Fred Thompson attempted to get to the bottom of the matter to see if there was any connection between these problems and the Riady-Huang fundraising efforts, particularly the illegal contributions by foreign agents of the Chinese military and intelligence establishments. The investigations failed because the Republicans were stonewalled by the Clinton Administration, their Democratic colleagues, and the witnesses they called. In all, 105 of these witnesses either took the Fifth Amendment or fled the country to avoid cooperating with investigators. They did this not only with the tacit acquiescence of the Clinton Administration, but the active help of Clinton officials.[60]

Dozens of Republican congressmen—leaders of military, intelligence, and government oversight committees—attempted to sound the alarm and expressed publicly (as well as to me, personally) their distress at being unable to reach the broad American electorate with their concerns because of the indifference of the liberal media and the partisan rancor of the Democrats.[61]

In the year prior to the World Trade Center attack, I met in the Capitol with more than a dozen Republican members of the House—including members of the Armed Services Committee—to discuss how the security issue could be brought before the American public. Given the President's talent for political doubletalk and the lockstep submission of congressional Democrats to his most reckless agendas, and without the possibility of media support for such an effort, not a single member present thought that raising these issues would be effective. Even attempting to raise them, they felt, exposed them to damaging political risks. These risks included attacks by Democrats and liberal journalists who would label them "mean-spirited partisans," "right–wing alarmists," "xenophobes" and, of course, "Clinton bashers."

While the liberal media put up a wall of opposition, journalists in the conservative media worked to make the issues public. Bill Gertz, Ken Timperlake, and William C. Triplett III wrote books based on military and intelligence sources and data collected by the Thompson and Burton committees that would have shaken any other administration to its roots, but received little attention outside conservative circles. Other conservative journalists including the *Washington Times*'s Rowan Scarborough and various writers for the *Wall*

Street Journal's editorial pages, *National Review,* and the *Weekly Standard* pursued the story but were also unable to reach a broad enough audience to make any impact. The conservative side of the ideological spectrum has no apologies to make for disarming the nation in the face of security threats. The Democratic Party and its subsidiary institutions, the liberal press and the left-wing academy, do.

The Lobby against America's Intelligence Services

One of the obvious causes of the many security lapses preceding the World Trade Center attack was the post-Vietnam crusade against U.S. intelligence and defense agencies dating from the Church Committee reforms in the mid-1970s and led by "anti-war" Democrats and other partisans of the American left. A summary episode reflecting this mood involved CIA operative Robert Baer, described by national security reporter Thomas Powers as "a twenty-year veteran of numerous assignments in Central Asia and the Middle East whose last major job for the agency was an attempt to organize Iraqi opposition to Saddam Hussein in the early 1990s—shuttling between a desk in Langley and contacts on the ground in Jordan, Turkey, and even northern Iraq." According to Powers,

> that assignment came to an abrupt end in March 1995 when Baer, once seen as a rising star of the Directorate of Operations, suddenly found himself "the subject of an accusatory process." An agent of the FBI told him he was under investigation for the crime of plotting the assassination of Saddam Hussein. The investigation was ordered by President Clinton's national security adviser, Anthony Lake, who would be nominated to run the [CIA] two years later. [Lake's appointment was successfully resisted by the intelligence community.]. . . . Eventually, the case against Baer was dismissed . . . but for Baer the episode was decisive. "When your own outfit is trying to put you

in jail," he told me, "it's time to go." Baer's [was] one of many resignations [in the Directorate of Operations] in recent years.[62]

Hostility to the CIA during the Clinton years ran so high that intelligence professionals refer to it as the "*Shia* era in the agency," Powers reported. The term referred to the Islamic sect that stresses the sinfulness of its adherents. "We all had to demonstrate our penance," a former CIA chief of station in Jordan told Powers. "Focus groups were organized, we 're-engineered' the relationship of the Directorate of Operations and the Directorate of Intelligence," which meant introducing "uniform career standards" that would apply indiscriminately to analysts and covert operators in the field. This meant high-risk assignments in target countries resulted in no greater advancement up the bureaucratic ladder than sitting at a computer terminal in Langley. "In the re-engineered CIA," comments Powers, "it was possible for Deborah Morris to be appointed the DO's deputy chief for the Near East. [The DO is the department of covert operations.] "She worked her way up in Langley," an operative told Powers. "I don't think she's ever been in the Near East. She's never run an agent, she doesn't know what the Khyber Pass looks like, but she's supposed to be directing operations [in the field]."[63]

The end of the Cold War in 1991 inspired the anti-intelligence reformers to close down all the counterespionage groups in the CIA because their expertise was no longer "needed." Spies were passé. "The new order of the day was to 'manage intelligence relationships.'" After interviewing many operatives who had left the CIA in disgust during this period, Powers concluded that the Agency had become more and more risk averse as the result of "years of public criticism, attempts to clean house, the writing and rewriting of rules, . . . efforts to rein in the Directorate of Operations, . . . catch-up hiring of women and minorities [and] public hostility that makes it hard to recruit at leading colleges."[64]

A post-9/11 article by Peter Beinart, editor of the liberal *New Republic* amplified Powers's observations.[65] Beinart speculated that the CIA's lapses may have occurred because of a fundamental mediocrity that had overtaken the institution. This mediocrity was the direct result of the attacks on the Agency (and on America's global purposes) by the political left, and the culture of hostility towards the American government that had been successfully implanted in America's elite universities, once the prime recruiting grounds for the intelligence services.

Beinart began with a description of the recent assassination of Abdul Haq in Afghanistan. Haq was potentially the most important leader of the internal opposition to the ruling Taliban. Yet the CIA had failed to provide him with protection. A key element in this disaster was the fact that the CIA did not have a single operative who could communicate with Haq in his native tongue, Dari. Nor did the CIA have a single operative who spoke Pashto, the language of the Taliban, even though al-Qaeda's base had been Afghanistan for years. The problem of reading intercepted intelligence transcripts in Pashto was "solved" by sending the transcripts to Pakistan to be translated by Pakistani intelligence officials—who were also sponsors of the Taliban. Some CIA officials believe it was Pakistani intelligence officials who warned Osama bin Laden to get out of Khost before U.S. missiles were launched into Afghanistan after the embassy bombings in 1998.[66]

The Abdul Haq assassination exposed the enormous human intelligence gap that has developed within the agency during the post-Vietnam years. As much as 90 percent of America's intelligence budget was being spent on technology, electronic decryption, and eavesdropping systems for the National Security Agency, rather than human intelligence based on agents in the field. Without human language skills much of this information itself remains useless. In

September 2001, the House Permanent Select Committee on Intelligence concluded: "At the NSA and CIA, thousands of pieces of data are never analyzed or are analyzed 'after the fact'. . . . Written materials can sit for months and sometimes years before a linguist with proper security clearance and skills can begin a translation."[67]

According to a 1998 article in the *Atlantic Monthly* written by a former CIA official, "Not a single Iran-desk chief during the eight years I worked on Iran could speak or read Persian. Not a single Near East Division chief knew Arabic, Persian or Turkish, and only one could get along even in French."[68] These deficiencies become intelligible only when one understands what happened to Middle Eastern studies in American universities in the post-Vietnam era.

UNIVERSITIES AGAINST THE NATION'S SECURITY

The story of the university left's subversion of the field of Middle Eastern studies is recounted in a recent book by Martin Kramer, editor of the *Middle East Quarterly*.[69] As a reviewer summarized Kramer's argument, "In the late seventies, the radical students of the 1960s began to enter the professoriate. The way was cleared for them to wrest power from the Middle East studies establishment when Edward Said's *Orientalism* (1978) crystallized a new understanding of the field."[70] Said was a member of the ruling council of Yasser Arafat's PLO and quickly became one of the most powerful academics in America, eventually heading the Modern Language Association, whose forty thousand members make it the largest professional association of academics. On November 21, 1993, eight months after the first World Trade Center bombing, Said wrote an article for the *New York Times Sunday Magazine* with the revealing title "The Phony Islamic Threat." Said's title summarized the intellectual shift in Middle East studies during the previous decade. The new perspective that came to dominate the field was that perceptions of a terror-ist threat from Islamic radicals were expressions of "Eurocentric" or racist attitudes by their Western oppressors.

In his book *Orientalism*, Said argued that all previous scholar-ship on the Middle East was hopelessly biased because it was writ-ten by white Europeans and thus "racist." According to Said, "All Western knowledge of the East was intrinsically tainted with impe-rialism." In one stroke Said thus discredited all previous scholarship in the field, paving the way for its replacement by Marxist radicals like himself. With the help of his left-wing academic allies, Said's extremist viewpoint created the climate and context for a revolution in Middle Eastern studies.[71] This was accelerated by the "multi-culturalist" attitudes of the university and racial preference policies in faculty hiring, which involved the widespread recruitment of po-litical leftists from the Islamic theocracies of the Middle East. Be-fore Said, "3.2 percent of America's Middle East area specialists had been born in the region. By 1992, the figure was nearly *half*. This demographic transformation consolidated the conversion of Middle Eastern studies into leftist anti-Americanism."[72]

In a statement issued ten days after the World Trade Center attack, the Middle East Studies Association—the professional or-ganization representing the field—refused to describe the perpetra-tors of the attack as "terrorists" and preemptively opposed any U.S. military response.[73] Georgetown professor John Esposito, a former president of the Middle East Studies Association and an academic star in the field, made his name after the first World Trade Center attack by following Said's example and disparaging concerns about Islamic terrorism as thinly veiled anti-Muslim prejudice. He was rewarded by being made a foreign affairs analyst for the Clinton State Department and assigned to its intelligence department.[74]

The language deficiency at the CIA—to which the political take-over of the academic profession greatly contributed—proved crucial at the operational level. But it was only a reflection of the more profound problem that afflicted the intelligence community because of the universities' leftward turn. In Beinart's words, "Today's CIA is a deeply mediocre institution. Its problems aren't legal or financial; they're intellectual. The agency needs a massive infusion of brainpower." How massive an infusion was indicated in an article Beinart cited: "According to a 1992 *New York Times* story, applicants for the CIA's 'Undergraduate Student Trainee Program' needed only a combined SAT score of 900 and a grade point average of 2.75." This compares to the average requirements for entrance into top ranked schools like Harvard or Princeton, which require SAT scores above 1300 and grade point averages of 4.0.

The only places the CIA can recruit its missing brainpower— "the only institutions able to supply the world-class linguists, biologists, and computer scientists it currently lacks—are America's universities." But the universities have long since become the political base of a left that has not given up its fantasies of social revolution and is deeply antagonistic to America and its purposes. The root cause of the nation's security problem is that, beginning in the 1960s, the political left aimed a dagger at the heart of America's security system, and from a vantage of great power in the universities, the media and the Democratic Party were able to press the blade home for three decades prior to the World Trade Center disaster.

The main reason the CIA no longer recruits agents from top-ranked schools is because it can't. "The men and women who teach today's college students view the CIA with suspicion, if not disdain," as Beinart put it. The formulation is, in fact, too mild. The left hates the CIA and regards it as an enemy of all that is humane and decent.

To make their case, academic leftists drill the nation's elite youth in a litany of "crimes" alleged to have been carried out by the CIA since the late 1940s—the rigging of the Italian and French elections of 1948 against popular communist parties (whose aim, unmentioned in this academic literature, was to incorporate Western Europe into Stalin's satellite system), the overthrow of Mossadegh in Iran in 1951 (whom they fail to identify as a Soviet asset who would have delivered Iranian oil reserves to Stalin), the overthrow of the Arbenz regime in Guatemala (whom the left portrays as a democrat but who was in fact a communist fellow-traveler who chose to spend his exile years as a privileged guest in Castro's police state), the "Bay of Pigs" (which was the CIA's failed effort to overthrow the most oppressive communist regime in the hemisphere), and the "Phoenix Program" in Vietnam (which was an attempt to prevent a communist front set up by the Hanoi dictatorship from overthrowing the Saigon government and establishing a communist police state in the south.)[75]

In the perverse view of the academic left, the CIA is an agency of torture, death, and oppression for innocent masses all over the world that otherwise would be "liberated" by progressive totalitarian forces. Utilizing the powerful resources of the academy, the left has created a vast propaganda apparatus to establish what is essentially the view of the CIA held by America's fiercest enemies. The anti-American propaganda is itself disseminated under the imprint of America's most prestigious university presses including Harvard, California, Duke, and Princeton.

University administrations have caved in to these leftists so consistently as to leave themselves little room for maneuver. "When the president of the Rochester Institute of Technology took a brief leave to work for the CIA in 1991," recalls Beinart, "many students and faculty demanded that he resign. Last year, when the government tried to establish a program under which college students would receive free language instruction in return for pursuing a career in intelligence, the University of Michigan refused. As assistant professor Carol Bardenstein told *Time*, "We didn't want our students to be known as spies in training." For caving in to these pressures, the president of the University of Michigan, Claude Bollinger, was rewarded by being appointed president of Columbia University shortly after the September 11 bombing.

As Beinart points out, there can be reasonable concerns about the proper functions of a university and the appropriate relationship of government agencies to private institutions of learning (although the University of Michigan is a state-financed school). "But most of the squeamishness about training, and encouraging students to work for the CIA doesn't have anything to do with the mission of the academy; it has to do with ideological hostility to the instruments of American power."[76] This ideology is enforced by political correctness in the university hiring process, a bias that virtually excludes conservative academics from obtaining positions at most schools. At Ivy League schools, for example, a study by the Luntz Companies showed that only 3 percent of the professors identify themselves as Republicans and the overwhelming majority have views well to the left of the American center.[77]

CONGRESSMAN DELLUMS AND THE DEMOCRATS' FIFTH COLUMN CAUCUS

Given the role of universities in shaping the culture, the same powerful anti-American, anti-military, anti-CIA sentiments have prevailed in the left wing of the Democratic Party for the last thirty years. The size of this group can be partially gauged by the fifty-eight congressional Democrats who describe themselves as members of its "Progressive [socialist] Caucus." But its actual influence is far greater.

No political career symbolizes the Democrats' acceptance of radical ideas better than the twenty-seven-year tenure of Congressman Ron Dellums who came to the House in the 1970s as the first 1960s radical to penetrate the political mainstream, and was able—with the encouragement and cooperation of his colleagues—to establish himself as a power player on both the Armed Services and Intelligence committees overseeing the nation's security policy.

A militant Berkeley leftist, Dellums was an ardent admirer of Fidel Castro's Marxist dictatorship and a relentless opponent of American military power. On his election to Congress in 1970, Dellums went out of his way to announce his radical commitments and pledged to remain faithful to his anti-American roots. "I am not going to back away from being a radical," he said. "My politics are to bring the walls down [in Washington]."

During his long career Dellums has worked hand in glove with Soviet front groups, proposed scrapping all U.S. "offensive weapons," and opposed every U.S. effort to block the spread of communist rule. In the 1980s, he even turned over his congressional office to a Cuban intelligence "asset" organizing a network of "solidarity committees" on U.S. campuses to support communist guerrilla movements in Central America. When Jimmy Carter attempted in 1979 to reinstitute the draft and increase America's military preparedness after the Soviet invasion of Afghanistan, Dellums joined a "Stop the Draft" rally of Berkeley leftists, denounced American "militarism," and condemned Carter's White House as "evil."[78]

Dellums's attitude towards America's intelligence services has reflected his consistent support for America's international enemies. Just before the 1980 presidential election, with Soviet invasion forces flooding into Afghanistan, with the American embassy held hostage by the new radical Islamic regime in Iran, and with crowds chanting

"Death to America" in the streets of Tehran, Dellums told the same Berkeley rally: "We should totally dismantle every intelligence agency in this country piece by piece, nail by nail, brick by brick."[79]

Yet, despite these views, Dellums has been no marginalized backbencher in the Democratic House. With the full approval of the Democratic Party leadership and its House caucus, Dellums was made a member of the Armed Services Committee on which he served throughout the 1980s and 1990s. In the midst of a hot war with Central American communists seeking to establish a Soviet military base in the Western hemisphere, Democrats made Dellums chairman of the House Subcommittee on U.S. Military Installations worldwide, where he enjoyed top security clearance. This was done with the specific imprimatur of the Democratic chair of the Armed Services Committee, Les Aspin.

Nor was Dellums alone. Clinton appointed an anti-military, environmental leftist, Hazel O'Leary, to be secretary of energy, the department in charge of the nation's nuclear weapons labs. O'Leary promptly surrounded herself with other political leftists (including one self-described "Marxist-Feminist") and anti-nuclear activists, appointing them as assistant secretaries with responsibility for the nuclear labs. In one of her first acts, O'Leary declassified eleven million pages of nuclear documents, including reports on 204 U.S. nuclear tests, describing the move as an act to safeguard the environment and a protest against a "bomb-building culture."[80] Having made America's nuclear weapons' secrets available to the whole world, including the al-Qaeda network, O'Leary then took steps to relax security precautions at the nuclear laboratories under her control. She appointed Rose Gottemoeller, a former Clinton National Security Council staffer with extreme anti-nuclear views, to be her director in charge of national security issues. Gottemoeller had been previously nominated to fill the post, long vacant in the Clinton Administration, of assistant secretary of defense for international security policy. The appointment was successfully blocked, however, by congressional Republicans alarmed by her radical disarmament views. The Clinton response to this rejection was to put her in charge of security for the nation's nuclear weapons labs.[81]

Democrats also appointed George Crockett to head the House Subcommittee on Western Hemisphere Affairs in the 1980s, when the United States was fighting a fierce battle of the Cold War in Central America. Crockett had strong ties to the Communist Party and to pro-communist organizations. He had begun his career as a lawyer for the Communist Party in Detroit and was so loyal to its agenda that he was the only House member to refuse to sign a resolution condemning the Soviet Union for its unprovoked shooting down of a commercial Korean airliner (KAL 007) and the only member to vote against a House resolution condemning the Soviet Union for denying medical aid to U.S. Army major Arthur Nicholson. (Nicholson had been shot in East Germany and the Communists had denied him medical aid for forty-five minutes while he bled to death.)[82]

Crockett's appointment came at a time when the Sandinista dictatorship in Nicaragua was engaged in supplying military aid to communist guerrillas in Guatemala and El Salvador and was building a major Soviet military base on its territory. Dellums and Crockett were the most prominent and probably the most extreme supporters of the communists, but they had powerful allies, like David Bonior and senators Patrick Leahy and Chris Dodd, in their efforts to protect the Sandinista regime and the communist guerrillas. Appointed to head the Senate Judiciary Committee in 2001, Leahy became the leader of Democrats' opposition to Bush Administration attempts to strengthen domestic anti-terrorism legislation after the September 11 attacks.[83]

In 1991, Democratic Speaker of the House Tom Foley appointed Dellums and five other left-wing party members to the sensitive House Intelligence Committee, with oversight over the CIA and other U.S. intelligence agencies. Two years later, Bill Clinton appointed Les Aspin, the left-wing Democrat behind Dellums's rise, to be his first secretary of defense. As Aspin's protégé, Dellums became the chair of the Armed Services Committee, and thus the most important member of the House in overseeing U.S. military defenses, controlling their purse strings, and acting as the chief House advisor on military matters to the President himself.

The vote among members of the Democratic caucus to confirm this determined opponent of American power as chairman of the Armed Services Committee was 198 to 10. In other words, 198 congressional Democrats including its entire leadership saw nothing wrong in placing America's defenses in the hands of one of its most implacable foes. They saw nothing problematic in Dellums's statement that as head of the Armed Services Committee he would (in the words of the *Los Angeles Times*) "favor a faster reduction of the armed forces and billions more for economic conversion," calling for a "tripling" of the billions that he would actively seek to be moved out of the defense sector.[84]

The vote to confirm Dellums's new position and authority took place on January 17, 1993.[85] Exactly one month later, on February 26, al-Qaeda terrorists bombed the World Trade Center. On his retirement four years afterwards in a ceremony in the Capitol, Dellums was presented by Bill Clinton's third secretary of defense, William Cohen, with the highest honor for "service to his country" that the Pentagon can bestow on a civilian.

The Party of Blame America First

How could the Democratic Party have become host to—and pro-mote—legislators whose commitment to America's security was so defective and whose loyalties were so questionable? How could a party that led the fight against Hitler, that organized a Cold War alliance to save Europe from Stalin's aggression, that under John F. Kennedy led the greatest expansion of America's military power in peacetime, reach a point where so many of its leaders seemed to re-gard America itself as the world's problem, rather than "the bright-est beacon"—as President Bush put it—"for freedom and opportunity in the world."

The transformation of the congressional Democrats into a party of the left can be traced to the turbulent decade of the Vietnam War and the 1972 presidential candidacy of Senator George McGovern, whose campaign slogan, "America Come Home," is self-explana-tory. George McGovern had been a World War II hero who com-pleted more than thirty bomber missions. But he emerged from combat traumatized by the killing he had witnessed and transformed into a kind of premature peacenik.

In 1948, he entered politics as an activist in the Progressive Party presidential campaign of Henry Wallace, who was running as an "anti-war" candidate for the pro-Soviet left. Wallace had once been FDR's vice president, but in 1948 he left the Democratic Party to protest Harry Truman's "Cold War" policy of opposing Stalin's con-quest of Eastern Europe.[86] Although Wallace himself was not a com-munist, the Progressive Party was a creation of the American Communist Party and under its political control. The Communist Party was controlled by the Kremlin, which had instructed its Ameri-can supporters to create the campaign in order to weaken America's opposition to Soviet expansion.[87]

Like Wallace, George McGovern was not a communist or even a radical. But like many otherwise patriotic Americans, then and since, he was seduced by the appeasement politics of the left and became permanently convinced that the United States was co-responsible with Stalin for the Cold War because Washington had failed to understand the "root causes" of the conflict in Soviet fears of invasion. In McGovern's view the Cold War could have been averted if Truman had been more accommodating to the Soviet dictator and his designs on Eastern Europe.[88] This anti-anti-communist naivete was a permanent aspect of McGovern's foreign policy agendas throughout his political career.

At the end of the 1960s, the radicals who had bolted the Democratic Party in 1948 began to return under circumstances that made the party particularly vulnerable to their agendas. In 1968, the Democrats' presidential candidate was Hubert Humphrey, a liberal but also a staunch anti-communist who wanted to stay the course and prevent a communist victory in Vietnam. At the Democratic convention to nominate Humphrey, the anti-war radicals staged an event that destroyed Humphrey's chances of becoming president.

The anti-Humphrey plan was the brainchild of radical leader Tom Hayden, who had met with the Vietnamese communists in Czechoslovakia the previous year and gone on to Hanoi to collaborate with the communist enemy.[89] In the late spring of 1968, Hayden proceeded to plan, and then to organize, a riot at the Democratic Party convention in the full glare of the assembled media.[90] The negative fallout from the chaos in the streets of Chicago and the Democrats' heavy-handed reaction to the "anti-war" rioters effectively elected the Republican candidate Richard Nixon the following November.

After Nixon's election, the "anti-war" radicals turned their attention to the Democratic Party with the intention of seizing control of its political machinery.[91] Humphrey's defeat fatally weakened the political power of the anti-communist forces that had supported him. A series of internal rule changes pressed by the radicals paved the way for the ascension of the anti-Humphrey left. Their agenda was to remake the party into a left-wing organization like the Progressive Party of 1948, which would not stand in the way of Communist expansion. The figure around whom they rallied their forces was George McGovern, who had been put in charge of the committee to reform the party's rules. The left's immediate agenda was to end the Democratic Party's support for the anti-communist war.

During the 1960s, radicals were intent on making a "revolution in the streets." They were led back into electoral politics by figures like Hayden himself, and his wife to be, Jane Fonda. Through Hayden's auspices, Fonda had traveled to Hanoi to make anti-American war propaganda for Hanoi, inciting American troops to defect and also aiding the Vitenamese communists in covering up their torture of John McCain and other American POWs.[92] On their return, Hayden and Fonda, gave "anti-war" lectures in the Capitol to the House Democratic Caucus. Although radicals like Hayden had previously condemned the Democrats and deliberately destroyed the party's presidential candidate, their energies were now directed towards infiltrating the party and shaping its agendas. This compromise of political principle was made painless by McGovern's campaign slogan —"America Come Home"—implying that America's military power was the source of the Cold War conflict with communism, instead of its solution.

Radicals became Democratic Party regulars and—in the case of Hillary Clinton and others—eventually party leaders.[93] Among the more famous activists elected to Congress as Democrats in this period were Ron Dellums, Bella Abzug, Elizabeth Holtzman, Robert Drinan, David Bonior, Pat Schroeder, and Bobby Rush, a former

Black Panther. Hayden himself failed to win a congressional seat but became a Democratic state assemblyman and then a Democratic state senator in California. Following the Watergate scandal and the resignation of Nixon the newly radicalized Democrats voted to cut off all economic aid to the anti-communist governments of Cambodia and South Vietnam. (The United States had already withdrawn its armies from Indochina after signing the truce of 1973). Both regimes fell within months of the vote leading to the mass slaughter in both countries of approximately two and half million peasants at the hands of their new communist rulers.

McGovern's presidential campaign was an electoral disaster: he carried only one state, Massachusetts.[94] But the internal party reforms the McGovernites were able to put in place *after* the election established the left as a power inside the Democratic Party. From this newfound position of strength, the left was able to shape the Carter presidency (1977-1981), following Nixon's Watergate debacle. Notwithstanding that Jimmy Carter was a southerner, a Navy man, and a self-described conservative—all factors that made him electable—his foreign policy reflected the leftward tilt of the party he inherited.

Of his secretary of state, Cyrus Vance, it was said "he was the closest thing to a pacifist that the U.S. has ever had as a secretary of state, with the possible exception of William Jennings Bryan."[95] Carter himself warned of Americans' "inordinate fear of communism."[96] At the end of Carter's term in 1980, his foreign policy performance was summed up by former secretary of state Henry Kissinger in these words: "The Carter Administration has managed the extraordinary feat of having, at one and the same time, the worst relations with our allies, the worst relations with our adversaries, and the most serious upheavals in the developing world since the end of the Second World War."[97]

Among these "serious upheavals" were the Soviet aggression in Afghanistan (the first crossing of an international border by the Red Army since 1945) and the Sandinista coup in Nicaragua (when the Carter Administration stood by while a group of pro-Castro Marxists subverted a democratic revolution, joined the Soviet bloc, and began arming communist insurgencies in Guatemala and El Salvador). A third debacle was the loss of Iran to Islamic fundamentalists in a 1979 revolution led by the Ayatollah Khomeni.

This event transformed Iran into the first radical Islamicist state and thus launched the forces that eventually came together in the World Trade Center attack. Because of its bias to the left, the Carter White House had bungled the defense of the previous Iranian regime, led by the dictatorial but modernizing Shah. Among the Shah's achievements that incited the hatred of the Ayatollah's rebels, was the lifting of the veil and the education of women. Despite the misogynist and reactionary agendas of the Khomeni revolution, the American left cheered the seizure of power by anti-American radicals, as a Third World liberation.[98]

The utopian illusion was short-lived, however. "Khomeini lost no time in installing a fundamentalist Islamic Republic, executing homosexuals and revoking, among other security laws, the statute granting women the right to divorce and restricting polygamy." American leftists and liberals had pressured Carter to abandon the Shah because of his repressive police apparatus, the SAVAK. But "Khomeini's regime executed more people in its first year in power than the Shah's SAVAK had allegedly executed in the previous 25 years."[99] The advent of the Khomeni regime was the real beginning of the current war between the West and Islamic radicals.

Partisan Agendas and "Root Causes"

On November 7, 2001—one month to the day after America began its response to the al-Qaeda attack on the World Trade Center—the man most responsible for our national security failures gave a speech to college students at Georgetown that may rank as the most disgraceful ever to pass the lips of a former American president.[100] Without any acknowledgment of his own responsibility, Bill Clinton joined America's enemies in attempting to transfer the blame for the atrocities to his own country. "Those of us who come from various European lineages are not blameless," he explained, expressing the sentiments of American appeasers since the 1948 Wallace campaign.

Although Europeans in America were the creators of a political democracy that had declared all men equal and had separated church from state (so that it did not identify a category of people as "infidels," let alone wage wars against them), Clinton linked the terror of the Islamo-fascists to their victims by recalling a crime committed by Christian crusaders against Jews and Muslims a thousand years before. "In the first Crusade when the Christian Soldiers took Jerusalem, they first burned a synagogue with 300 Jews in it," he said, then mentioned that the crusaders killed some Muslims as well. "I can assure you that that story is still being told today in the Middle East and we are still paying for it."

Even this version of the past neglected to mention the Muslim invasions that provoked the crusades. Did Clinton seriously intend to suggest, moreover, that the al-Qaeda fundamentalists would be outraged by the story of the martyred Jews rather than wishing the crusaders had perhaps killed three *million* instead of three hundred? This genocidal passion is the reality in today's Middle East. But what was the point of the Clinton story? The Crusades took place a thousand years ago. It is the Muslim world that still hasn't learned to separate the religious from the secular, and God from the state. Or to live with those who do not share their religious beliefs. It is the Muslim world that is still conducting "holy wars." What Christian church in modern America or in any modern European country would sanction the religious murder of "infidels"?

As though the attempt to establish a moral equivalence between the terrorists and their victims was not obscene enough, Clinton then threw in the equally absurd, but increasingly popular, example of black slavery. "Here in the United States," he continued his ethnic insult, "we were founded as a nation that practiced slavery." What version of American history is this but the standard ideological libel by the anti-American left?

In point of historical fact the United States was founded as a nation dedicated to equality and thus to ending slavery and did so at an enormous cost of half a million American lives. Some of these American lives were also sacrificed to end the Atlantic slave trade and the slave systems that persisted in Africa itself, which were conducted by Muslims and black Africans. The ex-president's idea that Osama bin Laden and the fanatical Islamicists at war with America should care in the slightest about the plight of black slaves today—let alone more than a century ago—is itself a lunatic anti-Americanism in view of the fact that one of bin Laden's former allies, the Muslim government of the Sudan still practices slavery against blacks, while the descendants of slaves in America have the highest standard of living and the most generous and secure civil rights of any blacks anywhere in the world today.[101]

One point Clinton failed to make is that the current leaders of America's war against Islamic racism are two African-Americans, Colin Powell and Condoleeza Rice. This fact is of world significance, since there is no example comparable among other states great or small of minorities entrusted with a nation's security. It would be hard to sum up in a more succinct image the historic impact America has had on the liberation of ethnic minorities, of the world's "huddled masses," of those still forgotten in the princely kingdoms of the Muslim world—its role as "a beacon of freedom and opportunity," to use the words of the Republican president who appointed them. Because of the skill with which they have managed America's war against al-Qaeda, the leadership roles of Powell and Rice have made all of our citizens the beneficiaries of America's progressive influence in world affairs. They symbolize the extent to which our ex-president—like our enemies—has turned matters upside down.

Clinton's attempt to smear his own country in order to exonerate himself and hide his national security failures is itself a symbol of how this nation is under threat not only from the external forces of a theocratic radicalism but from the radical nihilists and self-doubters, whose political locus is the Democratic Party.

No Excuses

In August 1998, the chair of the National Commission on Terrorism, Paul Bremer, wrote in the *Washington Post*, "The ideology of [terrorist] groups makes them impervious to political or diplomatic pressures . . . We cannot seek a political solution with them." He then proposed that we, "defend ourselves. Beef up security around potential targets here and abroad. . . . Attack the enemy. Keep up the pressure on terrorist groups. Show that we can be as systematic and relentless as they are. Crush bin Laden's operations by pressure and disruption. The U.S. government further should announce a large reward for bin Laden's capture—dead or alive."

Bremer was not alone. Given these warnings, as Andrew Sullivan observes, "Whatever excuses the Clintonites can make, they cannot argue that the threat wasn't clear, that the solution wasn't proposed, that a strategy for success hadn't been outlined. Everything necessary to prevent September 11 had been proposed in private and in public, in government reports and on op-ed pages, for eight long years. The Clinton Administration simply refused to do anything serious about the threat."[102]

On January 20, 2001, George W. Bush was sworn in as the 43rd president of the United States. Within months of taking office, he ordered a new strategy for combating terrorism that would be more than just "swatting at flies," as he described Clinton's policy. The new plan reached the President's desk on September 10, 2001. It was "too late," as columnist Andrew Sullivan wrote, "But it remains a fact that the new administration had devised in eight months a strategy that Bill Clinton had delayed for eight years."[103]

II

How to Beat the Democrats
A Strategy Guide

"POLITICS IS WAR CONDUCTED BY OTHER MEANS."[1] If you didn't understand this before the Democrats tried to overturn the election result in Florida, you probably do now. It doesn't matter whether you think such behavior is proper. If you don't come to the arena ready to fight a political war, the Democrats will. And they will win.

To win in war you need to know your enemy. You need to answer these questions: Who is he? What motivates him? What are his strengths and weaknesses? What is he capable of? Good intelligence is essential to answer these questions. It can provide the winning edge.

The time to start thinking about the next election is now. It doesn't matter whether the vote is next month or next year. Whether the vote is a year away or four, start preparing now, because *the Democrats already are.*

For Democrats, politics is a permanent war. Every conflict is a contest for power; every battle is about burying their enemies. About burying *you.* Not just in this election, but in the next.

That's what half the battle in Florida was about. If Democrats couldn't win by overturning the result, they could damage the winner through a political brawl. "Among . . . pragmatic elected officials, especially members of Congress," observed the *Wall Street Journal,* "it's about tarnishing a Bush presidency and preparing for 2002."[2]

For Democrats, politics is not just about who's in office or which policy will prevail. If it were, Democrats would not be so ruthless in their pursuit of victory. But for them, the political war is about matters of even greater moment. It's about good and evil; it's about control over the future; it's about changing the world. These ends will justify almost any means. That's why Republicans must look at Florida as a wake-up call.

Most Republicans do not share Democrats' attitude toward the political process (and, of course, neither do some moderate Democrats). Republicans think of politics as a way to fix government so that it will work better. They want to preserve the core principles of the Founding Fathers. These are important goals, but they are not as ambitious as their opponents' schemes.

More importantly, Republicans' very pragmatism leads them to believe that sometimes it might be better to lose than to persist in a political conflict. On occasion Republicans have preferred to lose rather than support practices that would hurt the Republic. Republicans pressed their own president to step down after Watergate, and voted to impeach President Clinton despite his high ratings in the polls. These are examples of Republicans' willingness to injure their own cause, or risk electoral defeat, to do what they think is right.

Democrats rarely exhibit such compunction—as their lockstep behavior during the impeachment and win-at-any-cost tactics in Florida show. Their goals—fighting "evil" and changing the world—are too important, their hunger for power too strong, to permit such political restraint. As Florida demonstrated, many Democrats feel morally obligated not only to win elections but to steal them, if they think that is what it will take to make a "better world."[3]

Because the Democrats' need for victory is so strong, they involve themselves in the political battle all day, every day. They are ready to give up normal lives for the privilege of waging the political war. For Democrats, politics is not just about *who* will run the government. It's about the nature of government itself.

For example, Democrats regard the Constitution as a "living" document. To many on the left, in fact, the Constitution is an outdated arrangement, just waiting to be rewritten by judges who will make it suitably "progressive."[4] That's the real meaning of "liberal" court decisions on abortion, prayer, gender relations, crime, punishment, and other matters crucial to the nation's cultural life. Those activist courts were no more "liberal" than the Democrats themselves. "Radical" is the term that actually describes what they achieved.

For Democrats, politics is not about adjusting the framework the Founders devised. It's about inventing a new America—a nation governed by racial and gender preferences, economic entitlements and executive orders; a nation in which property rights are diminished and citizens are placed in the hands of a cradle-to-grave, we-know-what-is-good-for-you guardian state. For Democrats, politics is about who gets to define the American future.

And that's why Republicans must look at political war as a life and death proposition for the republic they love. If you love what the Founders created, start fighting now.

The Idea Is to Win

Politics is about winning. It seems like an obvious fact, but Republicans sometimes forget it. Many seem to think that politics is only about being right: if you espouse good principles and proclaim good policies, you've performed your political task. In one sense, of course, politics *is* about such things. Why engage in political battles if you don't think you are wiser or more principled than your opponent?

But politics is also a war in which almost anything goes. Consequently good principles and good policies are defeated as often as they are implemented.

Every good citizen would like elections to be about the "issues" and not about personalities or catchy sound bites. But real elections almost never are. The public is not willing to pay the necessary attention. If it were, policy debates would be prime-time television events like game shows and football. Even then the public would wander in the political dark. That's because politicians work hard to confuse voters and misrepresent their opponents' case. In an ideal world it wouldn't be that way. But in this one it is.

Those who think they can win elections on superior principles and better issues I call "Gold Star" Republicans. Gold Star Republicans believe that if they show voters they are decent human beings and support good policies, they will be rewarded.

But that's not the way the political war works. Just look at what Democrats did to Clarence Thomas and Robert Bork, whose careers were exemplary before the left went after them. The same politics of personal destruction was on display in the 2000 election. When Democrats weren't defaming George Bush as a mental midget, they were running a multimillion dollar scare-campaign to warn seniors he would bankrupt the Social Security system and take away their pensions. The NAACP and DNC conducted a multimillion dollar ad campaign featuring the daughter of a lynching victim who said she felt George Bush had killed her father "a second time," because he did not support her position on "hate crimes" legislation.

This was one of the most shameful displays in campaign history. Democrats smeared George Bush as a cold hearted racist who would not protect African-Americans against a lynch mob if he were elected president. They did this to a man whose public record is above reproach, a governor who took special pride in having raised the education levels of African-American children in his state. George Bush ran a campaign of "compassionate conservatism" and went out of his way to reach out to African-Americans. But the Democrats tarred him as a racist indifferent to minority concerns. Over 90 percent of African-American voters bought some or all of the Democrats' lies.

Political war is unfair, and you don't get to make the rules. When your opponents are Democrats, hate campaigns are what you can expect. If Democrats don't use gutter tactics to defeat you, it will be because they think they can beat you without them.[5]

To win against Democrats, you don't have to stoop to their shameful level or adopt their disgraceful tactics. But you *do* have to know what you are up against. And you'd better have a plan to fight back when their attacks are directed at *you*.

Politics is not the same as policy; nor is it the same as acting on principle. It's about the *implementation* of policy and about putting principles into *practice*. These are the iron rules: (1) You don't get to make policy unless you win the political battle; (2) You don't get to put your principles into practice if you don't win the political war.

Politics *is* about winning the war. If you're not focused on winning, you're in the wrong place. Go look for something else to do— become a preacher or a missionary. Do charity work. Write books.

FOUR PRINCIPLES OF POLITICS

In order to win the political war, it is necessary to understand its basic principles.[6]

(1) *Politics is a war of emotions.* For the great mass of the public, casting a vote is not an intellectual choice, but a gut decision. It is based on impressions that may be superficial and premises that could be misguided. Political war is about evoking emotions that favor one's

goals. It is the ability to manipulate the public's feelings in support of your agenda, while mobilizing passions of fear and resentment against your opponent.

George W. Bush is a decent man. There is nothing further from his heart than the hateful act of a racial lynching. He would never dream of taking away old people's pensions. Yet millions of voters were manipulated by the Gore Democrats to vote against him because they were persuaded to believe just that.

(2) *Politics is a war of position.* If a majority of the electorate perceives your party to be the party of the people—if you position yourself on their side—you will win. But the same rule holds whether you actually serve their interests or not. It all depends on how you play it.

Just consider all those poor black and Hispanic children whose parents voted for Democrats, but who are trapped in failing government schools that Democrats control. Just think of the inner city with its crumbling housing, dangerous streets, rampaging drug gangs, moral breakdown, and economic decay. In every such community, Democrats control the city councils, the elected school boards, and the administrative agencies. Democrats have shaped the life of America's inner cities for more than half a century. Insofar as Democrats offer policies for the inner cities, they are failed policies. Insofar as they have principles to guide their policies, they are the wrong principles. Yet Democrats invariably win about 90 percent of the inner city vote. That's what shrewd political positioning can achieve.

The art of politics is about getting a majority of voters to identify with you in their gut. To win, it helps if you have good principles and good policies. But having a good image for yourself and attaching a bad image to your opponent is even better.

(3) *Politics is about fear.* To win in politics you must convince a majority of the voters that you are their friend. But almost as important, you must get them to *fear* your opponent as their enemy. "I will fight for you," was Al Gore's battle cry in the election; "I will fight *them*." Who is "them"? The answer is the corporate interests. The answer is the Republican Party, which Democrats identify as the party of the corporate interests.

No matter how much Republicans deplore such tactics, no matter how fervently they wish that electoral contests would turn on good policies and good principles, it is not in their power to change the reality of political war. Anger, fear, and resentment are among the most potent weapons in the Democrat arsenal: resentment of success; anger at the Grinches who cheat the poor and steal old folks' pensions; fear of bigots and lynchers. These are powerful emotions that drive voters to the polls. If they are not countered, these emotions will bury your Gold Stars every time.

When Al Gore was lagging in the presidential race, Democratic leaders said they were not concerned. They said they would "win on the issues." Now that the race is over, even the most complacent Gold Star Republican can see what these Democrats meant. They meant that they would use the issues to distort what Republicans stood for and make the voters fear them. In the Democrats' hands, the issues would become political weapons. They would use the issues to smear Republicans by any means necessary.

As election day approached, Democrats made "hate crimes" a major issue. To Republicans, the "hate crimes" issue was a policy debate over whether there should be such legislation.[7] To Democrats it was a chance to *commit* a hate crime against Republicans, an opportunity to burn the image of a Texas lynching into the psyches of American minorities and stick it to Republicans everywhere.

After the ads had done their work, 92 percent of all African-Americans voted against George W. Bush. This was more African-Americans than had voted against Ronald Reagan or Bob Dole or Richard Nixon. And none of these men had made half the effort George W. Bush did to woo the African-American vote.

Democrats get away with such tactics because they are adept at the war of position. By using minorities who share their politics to launch the race-baiting attacks, Democrats are able to frame Republicans so that they appear to be against minorities, and Democrats appear to be their friends. That explains why Democrats are able to smear Republicans with impunity during political campaigns and why Republicans must come up with an effective response.

(4) *Politics is about hope.* Seeking to win the political center may seem counter to the spirit of political war, but it is really its main idea: to make the Republican Party the party of the majority of the people. The key to the center is hope.[8]

The American people want their leaders to be tough-minded but inclusive, disciplined but tolerant, responsible but caring. That's why in 1996 they elected Bill Clinton on a Republican platform— balanced budgets and welfare reform. They thought of him as a Republican with a heart. They wanted a leader who would impose limits and restraints, but who was also sensitive to their needs. It was the same calculation that enabled George Bush to run neck and neck, as a compassionate Republican, in an election the Democrats should have won in a landslide.

Politics may be a war zone, but the winning issue is hope. Victorious candidates persuade voters that they provide the best hope for a better future and a more united country. Remember Reagan's theme: "It's Morning in America." Fear may be an important weapon in neutralizing a negative campaign ("Al Gore will say anything to be president"), but hope is the emotion that inspires people and wins political elections ("I will leave no child behind.")[9]

While thinking about political war, it is extremely important to remember that independent and swing voters, who are the ultimate arbiters of elections, are not partisans, do not relate to politics as a political war, and can barely tell the difference between the parties— let alone the candidates. This is partly because American politics is not ideological in the European sense. But it is mainly because of the success of America itself.

The much lamented fact that 50 percent of the eligible electorate do not vote at all reflects the great good fortune that most Americans enjoy in the land of opportunity. Americans are too busy getting on with the business of their lives to pay much attention to what looks to them like partisan squabbles. What Americans want are leaders who are uniters. What they want are politicians who offer them hope.

In short, political war is more complex than the real thing, beginning with the battleground itself. The public who decides its outcome does not like to think of it as "war" at all. They want their leaders to govern them, rather than lead them in battle. Often they are not even paying enough attention to know if a battle is being fought in their behalf. They regard most politicians as *fungible* (interchangeable) and available to the highest bidder.

The public's desires are often contradictory. They want their politicians to be "for" them, but they don't want them to be "partisan." They want government programs that benefit them, but they don't want higher taxes. They feel threatened by politics and at the same time would prefer political problems to "go away." Consequently, there are many times when the political battle assumes the aspect of a game of poker rather than a serious conflict. Politicians regularly mask their partisan intentions. "Flying below the radar" and conducting silent attacks are strategies in political war too.

If this seems confusing, here's a way to think about it: Ronald Reagan was a great Cold War leader. When he became president, his first moves in office were to re-arm America and confront the Soviets with overwhelming firepower. While liberals denounced him as a warmonger, Reagan ignored their warnings and called his adversary an "evil empire." He stripped away the Soviets' moral credibility and diminished their political influence. Addressing the last Communist leader from a podium in front of the Berlin Wall, Reagan said: "Mr. Gorbachev, tear down this Wall." But Reagan's next step was not martial at all. From a position of moral and military strength, he extended an olive branch to the isolated Gorbachev and gave him a great big bear hug. And the Wall came tumbling down.

Six Lessons of the Election

Lesson 1: *Strategy Is Decisive.* In a year of economic boom and relative peace, against an administration that registered 60 percent approval ratings with the American public, the Republican victory was something like a political miracle. Academic political scientists, working with models based on the economic climate and presidential elections over the last one hundred years, had predicted that Al Gore would win 55 percent of the popular vote. Al Gore won only 48 percent, a difference that can be attributed to the candidates and to the political strategies with which both campaigns were fought.[10]

This is the first lesson of the election campaign: political strategies are decisive. With the right political battle plan you can win, even when the odds say you can't. It is an especially important lesson for Republicans, who are prone to pessimism. Low expectations are a feature of the conservative outlook. Conservatives are realists. They appreciate human weakness and understand how wishful thinking inspires the illusions of the political left. But because conservative expectations are low, they easily become visions of defeat.

But fatalism is a self-fulfilling prophecy. Conservatives need to remind themselves that they too can make a difference. If the left-wing media and the Democratic Party had had their way during the Cold War, the Soviet Empire would still be with us. Conservatives need to remember the victories they have won against the odds. They could do worse than adopt the motto of Antonio Gramsci, a famous strategist of the left, who said a revolutionary must be guided by "pessimism of the intellect, optimism of the will."

LESSON 2: *Unity in Battle Is the Key to Victory.* In the election, only one percent of Republicans defected to the Buchanan candidacy compared to 3 percent of Democrats who voted for Nader. Without this superior Republican unity, the Republican candidate would have lost.

All political campaigns are about forming and maintaining majority coalitions. The very diversity of the electorate means that the success of national campaigns depends on a united political front. For the Republican Party, achieving this unity is not easy. Its coalition embraces amazing diversity—conservatives and moderates, secularists and religionists, moral absolutists and agnostic libertarians (a fact for which Republicans rarely get the credit they deserve).

During the Cold War, the Republican coalition was unified in the face of the Soviet threat. But the Cold War is over, and maintaining this unity is far more difficult. Republicans need to remind themselves that America's security is still at risk and that its constitutional order is threatened by a political left whose values remain socialist and whose agendas are subversive.

LESSON 3: *There Is No Natural Conservative Majority (But You Can Create One through Political Action)*. The critical role Republican unity played in the election leads to a third lesson: There is no "natural" conservative majority.

The bad news of the election is that nearly half the American people voted for 285 new federal programs, billions in new taxes, and the largest budget expansion since Lyndon Johnson's Great Society. The Republican victory was barely achieved against a campaign that was badly run by a leader widely perceived to lack character and integrity. Al Gore was vice president of the most corrupt and disgraced administration in history. He personally broke election laws, lied to federal investigators, and seemed compulsive in his inability to stay within range of the facts. Yet Al Gore won a plurality of the popular vote.

Nearly half the electorate voted for a Democratic Party that denigrates the military, fiercely defends racial preferences, and believes the U.S. Constitution is an outdated and bigoted document that needs to be rewritten to accord with the left-wing agenda. In a speech to "energize" his African-American base, Al Gore attacked George Bush for promising to appoint Supreme Court justices who would remain faithful to the constitutional text. Said Gore: "I often think of the strictly constructionist meaning that was applied when the Constitution was written, how some people were considered three-fifths of a human being."[11] This was false history used by the vice president to undermine the Constitution's authority and defame America's heritage.[12] It was Gore's contribution to the Democrats' attempt to smear the Republican candidate as a closet racist seeking to turn back the clock on civil rights.

Unfortunately, the negative lesson of the election is one that many Republicans do not want to hear. Days before the vote, two of the brightest editors at *National Review* criticized the strategy of "compassionate conservatism" with which Bush had challenged Gore in his bid for the political center: "If Mr. Bush wins, it will not be because of his personality, compassionate or otherwise. It will be because America remains, in crucial respects, a conservative country that wants energetic conservative leaders."[13]

This can hardly be the case in the sense the authors seem to imply. Al Gore ran a campaign well to the left of the American political center—too *far* to the left according to centrist critics in his own party. If Americans were conservative in the authors' sense, they would have roundly rejected Gore's populist appeal.

Such facts are no cause for conservatives to despair. What they are is a reality-check. If the conservative mission is to restore basic American values, the way conservatives fight the political battle will determine its outcome. There may be no current conservative majority in America, but there is a potential majority, if Republicans have the will and intelligence to create one.

Lesson 4: *Republicans Cannot Rely on Low Voter Turnout.* One of the great strengths of the Democrats' campaign was its ground war—the so-called "knock and drag" effort to get registered Democrats to the polls. Republican expectations of a comfortable margin were thwarted on November seventh by the Democrats' ability to mobilize a higher voter turnout than anyone had predicted. In the crucial battleground of Florida, Democratic organizers increased the African-American turnout by 65 percent over previous years.

Because Gore ran a confusing campaign and his negatives were unusually high, most political consultants were not prepared for the intensity Democrats displayed in fighting the campaign. Understanding the source of this intensity is crucial for the battles to come.

Traditionally, Republican strategies have depended on low voter turnout. In every election cycle of recent years, Republicans have prayed for bad weather and hoped that voter apathy would depress the Democrats' big city numbers. But the 2000 result should teach Republicans that they can no longer depend on this electoral crutch. They can no longer rely on Democrats' complacency to achieve their victories for them.

The reason is obvious. In 1994, Republicans won a majority of the House of Representatives for the first time in forty years. Because the House holds the purse strings of the federal bureaucracy, it is the cockpit of Big Government social policy. Without it, Democrats cannot implement their expansive agenda. That is why Democratic complacency and low voter turnout *ended* with the 1994 result. Having been taken by surprise once, Democrats are not going to make the mistake again of taking victory for granted.

Bottom line: In order to become a majority party, Republicans must mobilize an aggressive ground war and make inroads into the Democrats' urban base.

LESSON 5: *Democrats Rely on Bribery and Fear.* As Alexander Tytler warned in the eighteenth century, "a democracy cannot exist as a permanent form of government. It can only exist until the voters discover that they can vote themselves money from the public treasury. From that moment on the majority always votes for the candidates promising the most money from the public treasury, with the result that a democracy always collapses over loose fiscal policy followed by a dictatorship." The Democratic Party is aptly named in precisely this sense: it runs on the corruption of the people.

Democrats' passion for Big Government is an expression of this corruption. Voters who look to government for entitlements, look to the Democratic Party to supply them. Conversely, the Democratic Party recruits its supporters through taxpayer-funded programs that buy their votes.

Does this mean that Alexander Tytler was right and democracy is doomed? Only pessimists will surrender to the thought. Others will recognize three barriers to this undesirable outcome:

(1) The individualism of the American people, who have already withstood a thirty-year assault on the American identity and the American idea. Despite the left's attacks on America as a "racist," "patriarchal," "imperial" "oppressor," enough citizens still believe in individual rights, limited government, and the market system to have kept America resilient and free.

(2) The impractical nature of the programs Democrats seek to expand. In the long run, Big Government entitlements do not work because there are few limits to what people think they deserve, and even fewer to what they think they need. Such socialist schemes generally make no allowance for individual accountability and provide no incentives to individuals to create and produce. That is why impending bankruptcy—financial and moral—is their normal state.

(3) The Republican Party. Just because Big Government works badly or does not work at all will not discourage Democrats from pursuing an agenda that feeds their hunger for power, and funds their political machine. That is why the third and most important barrier to their designs is the Republican Party itself.

The modern Republican Party is not the "Party of the Establishment" or the "Party of the Rich," as Democrats claim. It is the Party of Reform, infused with middle-class energy and entrepreneurial values, conservative only in the sense that its core principles are inspired by the framework that the Founders devised.

It is only by misrepresenting Republicans and distorting their message that Democrats can maintain their grip on power. This is why Democrats more and more depend on scare tactics to advance their agenda. No one could have said it better than George Bush did, at the Republican Convention in Philadelphia: "[Al Gore] now leads the party of Franklin Delano Roosevelt. But the only thing he has to offer is fear itself."

When Democrats label Republicans racists and even "Nazis," it is not an intellectual claim they are making (since it is so obviously absurd). It is emotional dynamite they are throwing in the direction of Republican bunkers. Their objective is to create an explosion so loud in the minds of ordinary voters that they can no longer hear what Republicans are saying or think clearly about conservative arguments and positions. The most important political task for Republicans is to neutralize these attacks.

Lesson 6: "Compassionate Conservatism" Is a Winning Agenda. In the 2000 presidential race, Republicans unveiled a program to neutralize Democratic fear attacks. George Bush's agenda of "compassionate conservatism" worked. It achieved a Republican victory despite a vicious racial smear campaign and an unfavorable electoral terrain.

By celebrating racial, ethnic, and gender inclusion at the Republican convention, and by contesting the "caring" issues of Social Security, healthcare, and education George Bush and his strategist Karl Rove were able to take away the Democrats' target, deprive them of their advantage, and make decisive inroads into constituencies and states that Democrats traditionally have won. These additions to the conservative base provided the margin of Republican victory when conventional political wisdom predicted a Democratic landslide.

Contesting the caring issues to win the center will be essential to Republicans even in years that are favorable to Republican victory. Since the New Deal (and except on matters of defense), Democrats have been a majority coalition.[14] It is only because Democrats moved sharply to the left on foreign policy during the 1972 McGovern campaign that they consistently lost the White House until the end of

the Cold War.[15] At the same time they continued to prevail on domestic issues, achieving decisive majorities in Congress virtually every year.

To win a national election, it is necessary to capture a majority
among independents who occupy the political middle. It doesn't
matter what Republicans call their strategy to achieve this outcome—
"compassionate conservatism" or something else. For Republicans to
win, it is necessary to compete with Democrats on the caring issues,
to reach beyond the partisan core and expand the conservative base.

WHO THE DEMOCRATS ARE

The first thing to realize about the Democratic Party is that it is no
longer the party of Harry Truman. As Patrick Caddell, a former
pollster for George McGovern, Gary Hart, and Jimmy Carter, put
it: "I'm a liberal Democrat. I started in Florida politics. I worked for
George McGovern. I worked for Jimmy Carter. I've worked for Ted
Kennedy, Mario Cuomo. Nobody can question, I think, my creden-
tials and my convictions. But I have to tell you... my party, the party
that [my family has] belonged to since my great-great-grandfather
... has become no longer a party of principles, but has been hijacked
by a confederacy of gangsters who need to take power by whatever
means and whatever canards they can."[16]

Consider the following: The politics of John F. Kennedy are not
really different from the politics of Ronald Reagan. Kennedy was a
militant anti-communist and a hawk on defense, authorizing the
biggest expansion of the military since World War II. He was in
favor of a balanced budget and a capital gains tax cut, and half the
cabinet he appointed—including his secretaries of state, treasury, and
defense—were Republicans. If JFK were alive today and held the same
views, the media would describe him as a "right-wing" Republican.

This is an indication of how far the Democratic Party has shifted to the left since the 1960s. It is true that Clinton's "New Democrat" strategy temporarily pushed the party towards the center. But, as the Gore campaign shows, without a leader as devious or adroit as Clinton, it will be difficult for this center to hold. The Democratic Party core remains solidly left and almost indistinguishable in outlook from the socialist parties of Europe.[17]

The Democrats' left-wing orientation has deep organizational roots. The party apparatus feeds off the entitlements of the welfare state: social workers, university intellectuals, trial lawyers, government bureaucrats, and government unions are all clients of the Big Government programs the party promotes. As an ex-Democrat observed in the *Wall Street Journal*, her former party is Alexander Tytler's cynical vision come true: "The fundamental motivation for Democrats is their understanding that winning control of government is tied to paychecks, jobs, government grants, public money for private groups and companies, government contracts, union bargaining advantages, rules by which trial lawyers bring lawsuits. . . . The use of government to feed friends and starve enemies is something Democrats know instinctively. Winning elections means getting or keeping a livelihood. Say what you will about trial lawyers, but remember this: They only get paid if their clients win."[18]

To the mix of Boss Tweed operators and patronage pols must be added the progressive missionaries who make up the party's trade union, environmental, and "civil rights" left. These are disciples of the old populist and communist religions, who believe that government power can be used to redeem the world. They are convinced that government policies can reform smokers, rehabilitate criminals, vanquish racists, eliminate poverty, conquer "sexism," and create a world in which there will be no wars, handguns, or combustion engines. In Hillary Clinton's pregnant words, the task of politics is nothing less than "to remold society by redefining what it means to be a human being in the 21st century."[19]

It is well known that the constituencies of the Democratic Party are more conservative than the party's activists. Delegates to Democratic conventions (about a quarter of them from government unions) poll well to the left of Democratic voters. This offers Republicans an opportunity to make inroads into the Democratic base.

But on the battlefield, it is the political left that provides the party with the manpower of its political ground war and the firepower of its political air war.[20] Its search and destroy teams accuse Republicans of racism and sexism, of polluting the environment and of abusing old people, women, and little children.

Marxism may be dead, but a Marxist morality play provides the ordnance for the Democrats' political attacks. The rhetorical artillery of class, race, and gender warfare puts Republicans on the defensive and pins their forces down. Unless this attack from the left can be effectively blunted, Democrats will continue to have the advantage going into combat.

In an article written during the Florida fracas, Clinton-strategist and Gore-advisor Paul Begala revealed the inner thoughts of the Democrats' strike force:

> Yes . . . tens of millions of good people in Middle America voted Republican. But if you look closely at that [electoral] map [showing counties that voted Republican in red] you see a more complex picture. You see the state where James Byrd was lynch-dragged behind a pickup truck until his body came apart—it's red. You see the state where Matthew Shepard was crucified on a split-rail fence for the crime of being gay—it's red. You see the state where right-wing extremists blew up a federal office building and murdered scores of federal employees—it's red. The state where an army private who was thought

to be gay was bludgeoned to death with a baseball bat, and the state where neo-Nazi skin-heads murdered two African Americans because of their skin color, and the state where Bob Jones University spews its anti-Catholic bigotry: they're all red too.[21]

This is the image of Republicans that Democrat activists hold in their hearts: *Republicans are racists and lynchers*. Republicans should study Begala's map, because it offers a glimpse of the sniper on the other end of the gun that is always pointed at them.

One could respond to Begala in like fashion: The state where left-wing extremist, Muslim terrorists blew up the World Trade Center—that's blue. The county where a race riot following a court verdict destroyed 2000 Korean businesses and caused the deaths of 58 people—that's blue, too. The states where Colin Ferguson and Ronald Taylor killed 8 whites and Asians because left-wing race baiters convinced them they were victims of a racial conspiracy—they are blue.[22] The counties, nationwide, where the vast majority of murderers, rapists, and child molesters live and operate—those are blue, too.

But more important than the retort is to understand what Begala's outburst reveals about the left. The passions that motivate them are self-righteousness and hate: *They hate you*. They think you're evil.

Bill Clinton told Dick Morris exactly that. In the 1996 campaign he said: "Bob Dole is evil. The things he wants to do to children are evil. The things he wants to do to poor people and old people and sick people are evil. Let's get that straight."[23] Bob Dole is a war hero. In his career as majority leader of the Senate, he was a gentleman dealmaker. Yet, to Clinton, Bob Dole is "evil." George Stephanopoulos's White House memoir recalls an episode in the Oval Office when Clinton was telling him it was time to get back to the hustings for the next congressional election. What Clinton said was: "It's Nazi time out there. We've got to hit them back."[24]

Republicans are often surprised when Democrats refer to them as "Nazis" and "fascists," the way Representative John Lewis did on the floor of the House during the Medicare debate. Or when they accuse Republicans of taking food out of the mouths of children. When attacked, Republicans become defensive. They worry about whether it was something they said (or perhaps did) to elicit such suspicion and abuse. Republicans think, "If only we were more careful. . . . If only we presented ourselves better."

It's fine for Republicans to put on their best face in public. It's important for persuading those in the middle who are not ideological and whose votes decide elections. But for the Democratic hardcore who are politically left *nothing Republicans can do will make them stop thinking of Republicans as racists and lynchers, or wanting them politically dead.*

If you doubt this, look at what Democrats did to Supreme Court justice Clarence Thomas. When he was nominated to a seat on the Court, Thomas had been an upstanding citizen and civil servant for twenty years. He had risen from circumstances of great adversity without a single blemish on his public record. But this meant nothing to the Democrats. They went straight for his jugular.

They employed the pretext that, in a private conversation ten years before, he had allegedly used improper language *to a Yale civil rights lawyer!* They said this was an outrage against a helpless female who was unable to speak up for herself. They said that Thomas had abused his position and power as her employer. They said he had committed a crime against all women and called for his head in the name of all women. They were unable to defeat his nomination, but they tarnished his reputation and neutralized him as a public force.

A few years later, Bill Clinton had actual sex with a White House employee. This was not a Yale attorney with a portfolio in civil rights law, but a confused intern of college age. It was revealed that Clinton had also groped a widow, demanded a sexual favor from a state employee, and forced himself on a campaign worker. Unlike Thomas, who never attacked the character of his accuser, Clinton and his agents set out to destroy the reputations of each of his female victims when they came forward to speak about the abuse. Clinton even went so far as to lie in court to accomplish this.

But when confronted with Clinton's sexual harassment, the same pack of feminists, liberals, and progressives who had attempted to lynch Thomas said: "It's OK." "He's just a man." "Boys will be boys." They did more than give Clinton a pass. They sprang to his defense. Congressional Democrats who preened themselves on being the social conscience of the nation were willing to go to the wall to keep a guilty male in power. They said: "It's *only* sex."

When the political chips were down, the Democrats' principles didn't matter. What mattered was that Clinton was one of them, and Clarence Thomas was not. And because he was not, they had to destroy him. The left hates Republicans not because of what they are, but because of what the left *thinks* they are. What the left thinks is this: Republicans are "objectively" racists and reactionaries.

The idea of being "objectively" something—especially if it is retrograde—is a time-honored concept of the left. When Lenin ordered the liquidation of the kulaks,[25] he didn't mean that particular individuals should be punished for particular acts they had committed. In Lenin's eyes, being a kulak was itself a crime. To own land made one "objectively" an exploiter.

Though Democrats obviously don't intend to put Republicans before firing squads (other than verbal), they view Republicans the same way. They are convinced that Republicans are defenders of exploiters, racists, and oppressors, and that—whoever they may actually be—objectively, Republicans stand in the way of a better world.

This conclusion flows inexorably from progressives' belief that if the left can accumulate enough power, they can remake the world. Progressives think they can use the powers of government to end poverty, racism, sexism, pollution, war, and even bad habits like smoking cigarettes. The only thing that prevents them from accomplishing these noble ends is the Republican Party, which stands in their way. Republicans, in other words, are people who objectively oppose the happiness of mankind—if only because they won't spend the tax dollars necessary to buy it.

This refusal to go along with the program *in itself* makes Republicans like Bob Dole "evil." At least to Democrats like Bill Clinton. If you ever wondered why people who call themselves "liberals" are so intolerant and hateful towards those who disagree with them, this is the reason. For such people, politics is not a matter of pragmatic opinions about what will work and what won't. Politics is *who you are*.

The way progressives look at political conflicts is this: If you are a good person and a decent human being, you must be one of them. If not, you are probably a Republican.

However perverse it may seem, this attitude translates into powerful political advantage. If you are able to convince people that you care about them and your opponent doesn't—that you are on the side of the angels and he is in league with the devil—it doesn't really matter what his principles are or what his policy says or what kind of an individual he seems to be. People are going to believe you and not him. They will support you and they will distrust him.

This is the power of the left. It is what makes them so effective in political war. It is why nine of out ten African-Americans voted against George Bush, even though he worked hard on behalf of African-American children in Texas and would implement policies like vouchers that seven out of ten African-Americans support.

In the grand scheme that shapes its strategies and frames its arguments, the left divides the world into "us" and "them"—into victimizers and victims, oppressors and oppressed. Having so divided the world, the left then positions itself on the side of the victims and the oppressed. Morally, this puts them in the driver's seat. *They* are fighting for the weak; *you* are defending the powerful. *They* are on the side of the good; *you* are defending the bad.

In such a conflict, voters don't even need to know the details to know who should win. That is what gives Democrats their electoral edge. If Republicans want to beat the Democrats, they will have to turn this equation around.

A Winning Strategy

Democrats win elections because they understand a simple fact: the key to American politics is the romance of the underdog. Americans like the story of the little guy who goes up against the system and triumphs, a story about opportunity and fairness. To win the hearts and minds of the American voter, you have to tap the emotions the story of the underdog evokes.

America's heroes are all cut from this common cloth. Whether it's George Washington, Abraham Lincoln, Davy Crockett, Thomas Edison, Henry Ford, Amelia Earhart, Jackie Robinson, Ronald Reagan, or Colin Powell, the theme is always the same: the common man against the odds. America's political romance is *Mr. Smith Goes To Washington* to make things right. It is *Meet John Doe* who speaks for the voiceless. It is Luke Skywalker who saves the planet by using the good side of the Force to defeat the Empire. It is the odyssey of individuals who challenge power, overcome adversity, and rise to the top. Everyone in America thinks of themselves as an underdog and a hero. Just ask Bill Gates.

The cause of the underdog wins American hearts because it resonates with our deepest religious and moral convictions of doing good and helping others. And because it is America's own story. We began as a small nation standing up to the world's most powerful empire. We dedicated ourselves to the idea that all men are created equal. We are a nation of immigrants who arrived with nothing and made fortunes in a new world. This is the American Dream.

It's a story that will get you every time. But at election time, Democrats know how to wield it as a political weapon, and Republicans generally don't.

In deploying this weapon, Democrats use a version of the story that has a partisan edge. Through their grip on the media and academic culture, leftists have rewritten America's past. They have transformed it from an epic of freedom into a tale of racism, exploitation, and oppression. In their version, the American narrative is no longer a story of expanding opportunity, in which men and women succeed against the odds. They have turned it, instead, into a Marxist morality play about the powerful and their victims.

During the presidential election campaign, that's what the "hate crimes" issue was really about. It was not about punishing hate crimes, but about setting the stage for a morality play in which Republicans would be cast as the devil.

In staging their political dramas, Democrats invariably claim to speak in the name of America's "victims." Every Democratic policy is presented as a program to help these "victims"—women, children, minorities, and the poor. Simultaneously, Democrats describe Republican policies as programs that will injure the weak, ignore the vulnerable, and keep the powerless down.

Republicans play right into the Democrats' trap because they approach politics as a problem of management. To Republicans, every issue is a management issue—the utility of a tax, the efficiency of a program, the optimal method for running an enterprise. Republicans talk like businessmen who want a chance to govern the country so that it will turn a profit.

There is nothing wrong with instituting good policies and running things efficiently. But while Republicans are performing these Gold Star tasks, Democrats are busy attacking Republicans as servants of the rich, oppressors of the weak, and defenders of the strong.

Listen to Mario Cuomo describing Republicans at the 1996 Democratic National Convention: "We need to work as we have never done before between now and November 5th to take the Congress back from Newt Gingrich and the Republicans, because ladies and gentlemen, brothers and sisters, the Republicans are the real threat. They are the real threat to our women. They are the real threat to our children. They are the real threat to clean water, clean air and the rich landscape of America." Mario Cuomo knows the language of political war.

Democrats connect emotionally with people's fears and concerns. They do so, because they directly engage the myth of the underdog: "I will fight for you, against the powerful" is the populist mantra Al Gore used in the presidential race to good effect. Although Gore was himself part of the power elite, a *Business Week*/Harris poll taken right after the Democratic convention showed that three-quarters of the public agreed with his attacks on Big Oil, pharmaceutical companies, and HMOs.[26]

The appeal to help the underdog and defend the victim resonates with all Americans, not just Democrats. This is because Americans are a fair-minded people. Most successful Americans came from humble origins themselves. They want to help others. They want everyone to have the chance to succeed.

So do Republicans. But Republicans rarely connect their policies and principles to this political romance.

There's a good reason for this. Republicans are busy defending the real America against the left's attacks and the caricature they have constructed. Republicans know that America is still a land of opportunity and freedom, and that nobody in America is really "oppressed." (Otherwise, why would poor, black, Hispanic, and Asian minorities be desperately seeking to come here? Why wouldn't they be leaving instead?)

But politics isn't just about reality. (If it were, good principles and good policies would win every time.) It's about images and symbols, and the emotions they evoke. This is a battle that Republicans almost invariably lose.

In the romance of the victim, as Democrats stage it, Republicans are always on the side of the bad guys—the powerful, the male, the white, and the wealthy. It's easy to see how Republican patriotism plays into this trap. Defending America is readily misrepresented as an attitude that says: "I'm all right, Jack, so you should be too." Democrats relish the opportunity to smear Republicans as the selfish party. "You say that African-American voters in Florida who punched their ballots twice should have read the instructions? So, you think there's *no* racism in America?"

Democrats attack instinctively because they think of Republicans as mean-spirited and intolerant, in the pockets of the rich, looking for a way to pay no taxes. In each presidential debate Al Gore said something like this: "The problem is that under Governor Bush's plan [for a] 1.6 trillion dollar tax cut, mostly to the wealthy, under his own budget numbers, he proposes spending more money for a tax cut just for the wealthiest one percent than all the new money he budgets for education, health care, and national defense combined."

It does not really matter whether Gore's description of the Bush tax plan is accurate or not (and a lot of it is not). The *appearance* of the plan (and of all Republican tax plans) is that Republicans are the party of the wealthy who care more about themselves than those left behind. This is true even though George Bush labored hard, in his own plan, to provide greater percentage cuts to working Americans with lower incomes.

The reason, of course, is that Democrats have rigged the game before it starts. Through their control of Congress, Democrats designed the tax code to make it an unfair system of economic plunder. Under their code, the harder you work and the more jobs you create, the more you are taxed. Under their code, the bottom 50 percent pay only 5 percent of the government bill for services they are more likely to use. Therefore, *every* fair refund of a tax surplus can be maliciously portrayed as a tax cut for the wealthy at the expense of the poor. And that's the way Democrats portray Republican tax plans.

The reality is that a tax refund to the very rich does not affect lives of the rich at all. George Bush's tax refund would not enable one member of the super-rich to buy the yacht he couldn't afford, take the vacation he couldn't plan, or pay for the education he thought was too expensive. He can already pay for all that *without* the refund. Think about it—he's *rich*.

What a tax cut really affects is the investment capital of the rich— their ability to create jobs and wealth for other Americans. (Or did you think it was government that created those?) As Republicans know—but seldom say—the Democrats' progressive tax code actually works *against* poor and working Americans. Unfortunately, to appreciate this fact requires an understanding of the economic system that most Americans (and apparently all Democrats) lack.

Politics is about perception. The perception an across-the-board tax cut creates is of an unfair "giveaway" to the "haves," as opposed to the "have nots."[27] This may not fool all of the people all of the time, or even most of the people some of the time. But it does create a pool of resentment and envy—powerful emotions—that Democrats convert into a political *force.*

It is true that an increasing number of Americans are now stockholders in the corporate economy and, as a result, Democratic populism has built-in limits. But the political energies that class envy generates are still more potent in a campaign than the satisfactions of fairness and economic good sense, which Republicans defend.

For the Democrats, the romance of the victim stirs the souls of their supporters and energizes their base. Equally important, it provides the nuclear warhead of their political attack, which is even greater when the combustible elements of gender and race are added. Responding to this attack must become a Republican priority. Learning how to do this will provide the means for turning the political war around.

Going on the Attack

As I pointed out in *The Art of Political War*, in political combat the aggressor usually prevails. Aggression is advantageous because politics is a war of position. Position is defined by images that stick. By striking first you can define the issues and can define your adversary. Definition is the decisive move in all political wars. Other things being equal, whoever winds up on the defensive will generally be on the losing side.

Fortunately, Republicans can use the left-wing slant of the Democrats' attack against them. Contrary to the left's view, America is not a land of victims. It is a highly mobile society, with a mainly self-reliant citizenry that aspires upwards *through* the system, not against it. Republicans can also turn the Democrats' oppression myth around and aim its guns at *them*. In fact, using the romance of the underdog against the Democrats is the best way to neutralize their Marxist attack, for the most powerful forces obstructing opportunity for poor and minority Americans, the most powerful forces oppressing them, are the Democratic Party and its political creation, the welfare state.

There is really nothing new in this idea. Republicans already oppose the policies of the Democrats as obstacles to the production of wealth and barriers to opportunity for all Americans. What is new is the idea of connecting this analysis to a political strategy that will give Republicans a decisive edge in battle—that will neutralize the class, race, and gender warfare attacks of the Democratic left. Here are two examples.

Welfare. Democrats view taxes as contributions to charity. (Seriously. You should talk to a few Democrats if you doubt it.) Consequently, when Democrats designed a welfare system that cost taxpayers trillions, they considered it a double good deed. Welfare taxes benefited the poor and forced Americans to do the right thing.[28] Over the years, however, it became clear that government "charity" dollars were actually producing a social disaster—driving fathers from their children, bribing teenage girls to have children out of wedlock, subsidizing drug abuse, and destroying the work ethic of entire inner city communities.

To address the problem, Republicans proposed welfare reforms that would put recipients to work and get others off the rolls. Democrats said "No," and dug in their heels. They had to defend the vast patronage system that welfare created for government bureaucrats, social workers, and other beneficiaries who could be counted on to vote for the Democratic Party.

But Democrats also knew that the romance of the victim would work in their favor. When Republicans proposed welfare reform,

Democrats attacked them as mean-spirited and heartless. They said Republicans lacked compassion. They said Republicans were attacking the poor. They were *Nazis*.

Powerful moral images like this don't go away. They linger beyond the battle and resonate through future conflicts. In 1996, when Dick Morris persuaded Bill Clinton to sign the Republican welfare bill "or lose the election," the images of Republicans—anti-poor and uncharitable—stuck. Clinton won the election and presided over a Republican welfare reform, claiming it as his own. It is now part of his "legacy," while Republicans are still seen as mean-spirited and uncaring.

Republicans assisted in their own political undoing when they put the arguments for welfare reform in management terms. In proposing reform, Republicans did not call welfare mothers to Washington to testify against a system that was breaking up their families, destroying their children, and blighting their communities. They did not call Democrats "racists" for not caring about the destructive impact the welfare system had on inner-city populations. They did not call them "Nazis." Instead, Republicans argued that the welfare system was "wasteful" and "inefficient," that it "wasn't working" and that it was an impediment to balancing the federal budget.

But welfare is a human problem. It isn't about economic budgets. It is about the destruction of human beings. Republicans were not oblivious to the human reality of the Democrats' welfare nightmare. They spoke about it. But they did not attempt to speak in the name of the underclass, as the champions of the underclass, or to frame a moral indictment of the Democrats as the focus of their campaign. They did not invoke the romance of the underdog or use the language of victimization and oppression. They did not portray the Democrats as the enemies and oppressors of the poor.

As a result, the debate about welfare took place on Democratic turf, in Democratic terms. It became an argument about whether the government should spend more or less on the poor—on "charity." Republicans allowed themselves to be put in the position of arguing that government should spend less. Democrats inevitably wanted to spend more. When the debate was framed in these terms, it was easy for Democrats to portray Republicans as stingy, mean-spirited, heartless, and uncaring. Republicans did it to themselves.

If it is an argument about budgets, more money for welfare appears to be greater generosity to the poor. In fact it was just the opposite. The Democrats' welfare programs were destructive to the poor. More money spent on welfare was more money spent on a system that was blighting the lives of families and children.

Republicans should not have allowed the debate to be about government waste, about "welfare queens" rifling the public purse. They should have made it about government *harm*. They should have made it about government programs that *destroyed* the lives of poor and minority people (while allowing some to benefit unjustly). If Republicans had insisted on *those* terms, Democrats would be bearing the stigma today, and Newt Gingrich and the Republican congress would be seen as the heroes of minorities and the poor.[29]

Instead, the welfare system has been reformed and millions of poor people have been liberated from the chains that Democrats forged. But because Republicans failed to stick the Democrats with responsibility for the suffering their policies caused, Bill Clinton and Al Gore have been able to claim credit for a welfare reform they resisted and that half their party opposed. And Republicans have lost a political issue.

Education. Another issue even more powerful than welfare is education. Democrats are regularly billed as the "education party." How is that possible? There is a human tragedy enveloping America's inner cities. Twelve million poor children, mainly black and Hispanic, are trapped in failing government schools that are teaching them nothing. As a result, they will never get a shot at the American Dream.

Virtually every school board and every administration in inner city districts is controlled by Democrats, and has been controlled by Democrats for over fifty years. Everything that is wrong with inner city schools that policy can fix, Democrats are responsible for. Democrats and their allies run the public school system for the benefit of adults at the expense of children. Put in the language of political war: *Democrats have their boot heels on the necks of poor, black, and Hispanic children.* But Republicans are too polite to mention it.

How bad *is* the inner-city school crisis? In Los Angeles, the school district recently defined the problem. Los Angeles officials had declared their intention to end the practice of "social promotion," which lets students who have failed move on to the next grade.[30] But in January 2000, the school district announced it would have to postpone the plan. The reason? A feasibility study showed that if the plan were instituted, officials would have to hold back 350,000 students—*half* the entire school population.[31]

Half the school population is learning nothing! This is an atrocity. It is no secret that these children are poor, Hispanic, and black, and that for them an education is the only chance they will ever have for a better life. But Democrat-controlled schools are teaching them nothing! They will never be part of the information economy. They will never get decent paying jobs. And the Democrats—who oppose the opportunity scholarships and school vouchers that would rescue them from this disaster—are doing everything in their power to keep poor children trapped in the very schools that are failing them.

It gets worse. Shortly after the school district announcement, the Los Angeles Teachers Union demanded a 21 percent pay raise for its members. The union leader announced that his members would strike if bonuses were given as rewards to individual teachers who actually raised their students' grades. That would be setting "teacher against teacher." That would be competition.

Democratic legislators fully supported the socialist union and its selfish demands. Once again, Democratic leaders pledged to fight to keep poor, black, and Hispanic children trapped in the failing schools. At the same time, they send their own children to expensive private ones. When Al Gore was asked why he opposed school vouchers for black children while sending his own son to a private school, he said: "If I had a child in an inner city school, I would probably be for vouchers too." He said, "Leave my children out of it." [32]

Where is the Republican outrage? Where are the Republican voices exposing this hypocrisy and holding the Democrats to account? Where is the Republican plan to liberate these children and get them an education?

In fact, Republicans do have such a plan. For years, conservatives have been building a movement to reform education and provide adequate schools to poor and minority children. Instead of running the schools on bankrupt socialist principles, these reformers propose to reward teachers and schools that do their job, and hold the others accountable. The main mechanism they propose for school reform is economic choice—putting the education dollar directly in the hands of poor parents. This will force inner city schools to serve their constituents instead of merely exploiting them. It will establish a connection between performance and reward without which no reform can succeed.

But instead of rushing to the barricades with moral indictments of the Democrats who defend the existing system, instead of stigmatizing them as enemies of reform and of the poor, black and Hispanic children who are languishing in them, Republicans do what?

They approach the problem timidly and discreetly. They distance themselves from conservative voucher movements and instead make legislative proposals that are modest and "reasonable." They put forward bills that are designed to win over members of the opposition.

But this ignores the reality of the system the Democrats have created, which provides billions of federal dollars to enrich adults and to secure their political loyalty at the expense of the children. Democrats will not become "reasonable" until the American people understand what they are doing! The only way this will happen is if Republicans make the Democrats' oppression of poor and minority children the focus of their political attack.

If Republicans do not frame the indictment of Democrats, no one is going to do it for them. They cannot depend on the media to do it. The media is in the hands of the cultural left. This is the principal reason why Republicans are perceived as lacking compassion (and Democrats are not) and as the party of the rich (while Democrats are not).

In real life, Democrats are both well heeled and mean-spirited. Their programs oppress the poor. They have used their power to create public housing slums that are breeding grounds for drugs and crime. They have weakened the criminal justice system, allowing predators to make war on the vulnerable and the poor. And they have destroyed the bottom rungs of the ladder of success for poor, black, and Hispanic children.

But don't expect the media to tell this story. The successes of the school choice programs that conservatives have created are not going to be trumpeted by left-wing editors and journalists. Instead, they will be spun as failures whenever possible. There will be no press crusades to document the depredations that Democrats have committed on the lives of poor children. No Pulitzer prizes will be awarded for exposing their crimes.

Consequently, Republicans must do their own work in indicting the oppressors and promoting an agenda that will liberate the oppressed. To do this, Republicans must come up with a program that is so big that it dramatizes the issues all at once, and the press cannot ignore it.

Last year, Congressman Jim Rogan did just that. He devised a plan to spend one hundred billion dollars over ten years on scholarships for the twelve million poor, black, and Hispanic children in Title 1 schools. The bill would provide a $6,800 scholarship (the average public school tuition) for each of these children to enable them to find a school that would teach them. The scholarships would be granted under a formula that restricts them to one-quarter of the students in a given school in any one year. In this way, classroom size would be reduced and spending per pupil increased.

If Republicans were to support such a bill they would frame the issue as it should be framed, change their public image overnight, cast the Democrats as heartless reactionaries, ram them up against the education unions, and drive a wedge the size of Texas through their urban-minority base. They probably won't. But whatever they do, Republicans must remember to:

- Think politics along with policy.
- Speak the language of moral indictment.
- Frame Democrats as oppressors of minorities and the poor.
- Use the romance of the underdog to win the American heart.

Epilogue: The Battle Ahead

Right after the Supreme Court stopped Gore's effort to overturn the election, Jesse Jackson warned: "We will take to the streets . . . we will delegitimize Bush, discredit him, do whatever it takes, but never accept him." Socialist union boss, Gerald McEntee, a Jackson cohort and Gore insider, told the *Wall Street Journal*, "There is going to be a lot of pressure on Bush. . . . I think he is going to find it very, very difficult [to govern]."[33] Chief Clinton-fundraiser and DNC chairman Terry McAuliffe also announced there would be no honeymoon, that Democrats would use the outrage over the Republican victory as an "opportunity" to mobilize their troops.[34]

In short, Democrats are already mobilizing a war to set the political agenda, to control the next Congress, and to win the White House in 2004. Bill and Hillary Clinton have already established their Washington base and are planning Hillary's presidential run. The "next battle" is not a future engagement. It is *now*.

If Republicans want to win the battle for the American future, they will have to pursue a strategy aimed at winning an American majority. This means the Republican Party will have to change.

Presently, Republicans are mainly a rural party, and mainly a white party. This does not mean they are also a racist party as Democrats so maliciously suggest. It is the Democrats who are the party of racial preferences and racial politics, who have cynically exploited the loyalty of their minority supporters to the detriment of their communities. (And Republicans should never let them forget it.)

It has been said of the electoral map, which indicates Republican majorities in red, that every red zone marks a county in which people can still leave their doors unlocked. It is among Republicans that the virtues of the American Founding are preserved and actively defended, and it is over these principles that the culture war is being waged. But the fact that Republicans are a rural party also means they will become a minority party if they do not begin to make greater inroads into urban and ethnic America.

No party can achieve a majority in America that does not embrace its diverse communities. Unfortunately, the ugly racial campaigns that Democrats and the media wage against Republicans re-inforce their structural isolation.[35] In the 2000 election, George Bush made a greater effort than any previous Republican to reach out to minority communities. Yet he was rewarded with an even smaller percentage of the African-American vote. Some Republican strate-gists have concluded that pursuing minority votes is a losing propo-sition. Instead, Republicans should concentrate on increasing their majority among white Americans.

Such a strategy, born of frustration, would be a dead end for the Republican Party. It would go against the very principles of the Re-publican cause. Democrats are the party that believe in racial cat-egories and "identity politics," that presume that individuals and their attitudes are determined by skin color and gender. Democrats are the party that insists that the laws and even the census should divide Americans by race, that makes the non-American end of the na-tional hyphen the part that is important. Democrats are the party of racial caucuses, racial quotas, and racial targets.

Republicans believe in inclusion based on individual merit and individual rights. They support the principle that everyone should be judged by a single standard. They insist that the "American" end of the hyphen should be the one that counts. Republicans are—and must be—the optimists of inclusion, defenders of the proposition that all are created equal, and that opportunity should be open equally to all *regardless of race, national origin, or creed*. If Republicans surren-der these core beliefs and accept the Balkanized future of the left, there will be no battle for America. It will all be over.

But even from a short-term political view, doing the right thing by minorities is also the smart thing. Whenever Republicans show their inclusiveness, they confound the intolerant image Democrats use to demonize them.

This image of intolerance deprives Republicans of the support of Americans who are not minorities and who otherwise would endorse the Republican agenda. Neutralizing the racial attack will greatly enhance Republicans' ability to pick up swing voters among inclusive whites and conservative Democrats. Americans are a generous and fair-minded people, and they will respond to a party that displays similar virtues.

Finally, Republicans should not abandon a fight they have hardly begun. Republicans have failed to hold Democrats responsible for the blighted lives of inner-city children who are trapped in failing government schools. The Republican Congress barely made the case that the welfare system is ruinous for poor and minority communities or that Democrats are mean-spirited and racist for defending it. Nor have they framed other social issues in these terms.

For example, Republicans haven't begun to attack the exploitive aspects of the Social Security system that Democrats want to preserve. The Social Security tax robs working people and their families of hundreds of thousands of retirement dollars they would get if allowed to put the money in ordinary savings accounts. The system prevents them from passing their present Social Security savings to their children. Because African-American males have shorter life expectancies, the system deprives them of *any* benefits from the Social Security taxes the government forces them to pay their entire working lives. That's government theft—a massive, discriminatory rip-off of working Americans. But Republicans are too polite to mention it.

The presidential election won by George W. Bush was a reprieve for Republicans and for the country. Republicans must recognize the reprieve as a gift and use it as an opportunity.

The Republican Party lost the popular vote, but held the Congress and won the White House. Gratitude should go to those who made this victory possible in a difficult year, above all to the strategist Karl Rove and the candidate George Bush. Without a superior war plan this victory would have been a defeat. Republicans should draw confidence from the fact that the same team is now in Washington looking to the future. They should focus on the fact that what you do in battle determines who will emerge the victor.

But Republicans should also consider the impression the election made on the losing side. Democrats are bitter, they feel mugged, and they taste Republican blood. Their thinking is this: *The Republicans have lost ground in the last three election cycles. We should have won this time. Next time, we'll make sure that we do.* Democrats will be thinking of nothing else but how to mobilize every resource, shape every legislation, spin every debate, exploit every news cycle to position themselves for the kill.

Therefore Republicans need to start preparing now. The presidency will provide George Bush with an opportunity to capture the caring issues and forge a majority for the conservative cause. To do this, he will sometimes tack to the center. Conservatives, who showed admirable discipline during the election, will be called on to do so again. The important thing is to remember what is at stake if the Democrats win.

Who are the Democrats? The Democrats are a party whose credo is: *Everybody does it.* Soliciting illegal campaign money from foreign dictatorships? *Everybody does it.* Using the White House for sex, and lying before grand juries? *Everybody does it.* Obstructing investigations into the subversion of the nation's security and the theft of its nuclear arsenal? *Everybody does it.* Playing the race card? *Everybody does it.* Breaking the unwritten law by which defeated presidential candidates concede (absent fraud) in order to strengthen the democracy and legitimize its authority? *Everybody does it.*

This attitude, which has become the hallmark of Democratic politics, is often described as "moral relativism." But "relativism" is too abstract a term to describe the problem correctly. "Everybody does it" is the common excuse of moral delinquents. In a national party, it reveals a lack of respect for the law, a lack of reverence for national tradition, a lack of concern for the security of the Republic itself.

What is at stake, finally, is our Republic: A nation dedicated to the proposition that all men and women are created equal before the law and God; that in this regard they will not be judged by color, creed, or origin; that government of, by, and for the people, shall not perish.

The Republic is not a given, but a uniquely self-conscious creation. Succeeding generations need to renew the faith in its covenant. "We are a welcoming country. We will always value freedom, yet we will not allow those who plot against our country to abuse our freedoms and our protections."[36] This is the way President Bush expressed the nation's security concern in the months after the World Trade Center attack.

The immigration issue and the stability of borders are two crucial aspects of the present fight against terrorism because they are ways the nation defines itself. Democrats want loose borders and lax citizenship requirements because they do not understand or fail to appreciate that America is a nation built on a set of political ideas rather than on common blood, language, or soil. America cannot survive without a common commitment to its founding principles by those who inhabit it. The task of creating—and assimilating— new citizens is also the task of protecting and preserving the nation.

Democrats show little regard for these facts. Democrats think that the nation exists as a constellation of resources that are simply given, and should—or even could—be available to all, regardless of their cultural attitude toward the American community or their commitment to sustaining it. But America can only survive if its citizens accept responsibility for its survival. Democrats' failure to appreciate the centrality of this problem lies at the root of their failure to be reliable trustees of the nation's security. To provide for the common defense is necessary because the American idea itself has enemies. Others envy our prosperity and freedom. Not our sins, but our success makes others hate us. Because we are successful and free, we require a vigilant leadership and a military ready and able to defend us. The most dangerous failing of Democrats is that they fail to recognize this. What must we expect from ourselves—from all American citizens—if the great experiment is to continue?

Defending this Republic and the principles for which it stands is a tall task for any one party. But it is a task that, until Democrats reform their party, Republicans will have to face. This means that national security must be kept at the top of the political agenda. Concern for the nation's security is the Democrats' great weakness and the Republicans' great strength. Republicans must win the electoral battle for the sake of the nation. But to do this, Republicans will first have to change their approach to the battle itself. They can no longer afford to regard politics as a business. Instead, they will have to embrace it as a cause.

III

The War Room
An Election Manual

Among Democrats, whether in the White House
or on Capitol Hill, whether big pooh-bahs or lowly
staffers, they say the same things in the same words.
Whether its "tax cuts for the rich" or "it doesn't rise
to the level of impeachment," they are all on the
same page. Republicans aren't even in the same
book. When they come on the air, they sound as if
this is the first time they have ever thought about
what they are going to say. They all fumble for
different words.

Thomas Sowell

INTRODUCTION

A BASIC TACTICAL RULE OF WARFARE is to start your campaign
with an artillery barrage that pins your opponent down.
While he is scrambling to defend himself, you can proceed
with your attack. A familiar reality of Republican battlefields is that
our opponents almost always fire their artillery at us first, and our
troops are almost always down. This guide is designed to help Republicans rethink the way they conduct their political battles, so that
our side will be the one that almost always fires first.

I began this effort with a book called *The Art of Political War* in
which I outlined the six principles of the political battlefield:

1. Politics is war conducted by other means
2. Politics is a war of position
3. In political wars the aggressor usually prevails
4. Position is defined by fear and hope
5. The weapons of politics are symbols evoking fear and hope
6. Victory lies on the side of the people

If the Republican Party is to become a majority party, it must reposition itself on the side of the underdog—of women, children, minorities, working Americans, and the poor. The Republican agenda of lower tax rates, school vouchers, private Social Security accounts, respect for constitutional order, opposition to race preferences, and maintenance of a strong national defense would immensely benefit the American people. And therefore it must expose Democrats as the party whose policies and programs oppress them.

Republican policies would liberate ordinary working people from the heavy tax burdens, failing government school systems, racial quotas, exploitative Social Security arrangements, leniency towards criminals, and weak national defense policies, to which the Democratic Party is ideologically wedded.

It took a twelve-year Republican campaign to end the Democrats' welfare system that has destroyed inner-city families and created a dependent and dysfunctional underclass in every major urban setting in America. It took years of Republican agitation to create the tougher government attitude towards law and order that has driven down crime rates. It took thirty years of Republican efforts to force reductions in tax rates and oppressive government regulations, to balance budgets and to impose checks on government spending which have helped to fuel the greatest boom in economic history. It took a Republican dedication to rearm America in the 1980s and stay the course of Cold War containment to force the collapse of the

Soviet empire, to liberate its captive peoples, and achieve the prosperity and peace that followed.

All these policies have been beneficial to poor and minority Americans and working Americans, and to all Americans. But Republicans have not reaped the political benefits that the vindication of their policies and the failure of Democratic programs should have earned them. Democrats led by Bill Clinton—a man who disgraced the Oval Office, who fought balanced budgets, who twice vetoed welfare reform, and who has put his nation's security in jeopardy—have been able to retain executive power and remain competitive in congressional contests because they understand the art of political war better than Republicans do.

PART I: THE 2000 CAMPAIGN

1. THE BOOM AND THE 2000 CAMPAIGN

THE DEMOCRATS' ATTACK. Clinton's 2000 State of the Union Address will be the script for every Democrat running for office this year (2000). Republicans need to pay attention. Here is the Democrats' pitch: Things have never been better. The economy is booming. Unemployment is low. "My fellow Americans, the state of our union is the strongest it has ever been."

THE REPUBLICAN RESPONSE. The best response is often an attack. Ask not how the Dow is doing. Ask how the American people are doing. Ask how our children are doing. Ask how our families are doing. Ask how Americans' faith in their government, the cornerstone of our democracy, is doing after eight years of Clinton-Gore abuses and corruption. Ask how our faith in ourselves is doing: What do we see, as a nation, when we look in the mirror?

Republicans' first instinct will be to claim credit for the economic boom. Low marginal tax rates (Reagan), deregulation (Reagan), balanced budgets (Gingrich) and welfare reform (Gingrich) are indeed more responsible for the economic boom than the big government policies of Clinton and the Democrats. But politics is not about reality. Politics is about perception. In a sound-bite world an argument over details will have no impact on voters. People do not have the time or the attention span to follow the arguments. If they understand the economy, they will know that the digital revolution and the Internet are the main engines of this prosperity.

A cardinal rule of politics that Republicans habitually forget is: *Don't get lost in the nuances of policy and the details of government.* It's good to remind voters that Democrats fought welfare reform, opposed balanced budgets, and want to raise taxes every chance they get. But these charges will not be decisive. In an election campaign, promises will fall like rain from candidates' lips. Democrats will try to convince voters they've reformed. In swing districts, Democrats probably voted—out of sheer self-preservation—*for* balanced budgets and *for* welfare reform. Instead of arguing a case that can never be won, argue one that can: the mess that Clinton and Gore have left behind. The first priority of every Republican candidate must be to puncture the happy balloon.

THE CASE OF EDUCATION. It's true we're entering a "new economy," as President Clinton said. But half our children will never get there. They are condemned to ignorance by government schools that Democrats and special-interest unions created and control. Democrats and the pro-Democrat unions control every major urban public school system in the country and have done so for seventy years. The school systems in New York, Chicago, Boston, Los Angeles, Washington, D.C., Baltimore, St. Louis, Houston, Dallas, San Francisco and

Oakland are all controlled by Democrats and the far left. There are no major urban school boards controlled by Republicans. And these are the schools which are failing to teach our minority and poor children, and denying them a shot at the American dream. The Democrats' failed education policies have deprived these children of a future and put the nation's own future at risk.

The GNP may be soaring, but what about the American people? What about the children? Thirteen million American children are living below the poverty line. Five hundred thousand babies have been born to teenagers in the last year. Two million children have committed felonies. Twelve thousand have committed murder. Our education system, the ladder of hope for poor and minority Americans, is broken. Test scores are down for all ethnic groups, especially African-Americans and Hispanics. The Clinton-Gore solution is to change the tests and lower the standards. Technically, in fact, test scores are up. But that's because in 1995 the SAT college-entrance scoring system was changed to "boost the typical student's score by nearly 100 points." This is a typical Clinton era scam run on America's children, especially poor and minority children. The uneducated and the inadequately educated, no matter what their test scores, are not going to have access to the high-tech economy or get a shot at the American dream.

In January 2000—the first month of the new millennium—the Los Angeles Unified School District dropped a plan to end "social promotion," a standard policy under which children who actually fail their grade are promoted anyway. The plan was dropped when the school district received a report on what ending the policy would mean in practical terms. According to the report, the district would have to hold back 350,000 children! This is *half* the student population of Los Angeles.[1] By the school district's own admission, they are learning *nothing*. This is a social catastrophe. This is an atrocity committed by Democrats against children who are mainly poor, Hispanic, and black.

A statewide ranking by the Democratic governor of California further showed that 88 percent of the state's students were performing below state standards.[2] This is not just a California problem. It is a national crisis. In Maryland, the state has taken over one hundred public schools in which 90 percent of the children are performing below the minimum standards set by the school district itself. Guess which kids these are. They are poor, Hispanic, and black.

DEMOCRATS ARE RESPONSIBLE. Democrats have controlled the education system of nearly every major urban area in America for half a century. They control the education system now. Al Gore's promise to the voters is to spend billions of taxpayer dollars to build more government schools, which means more schools that will fail. Democrats like construction dollars because they provide patronage and jobs for adults that Democrats can use to buy more votes. But government schools don't work. That's why Democrats like Al Gore and Al Sharpton send their own children to private schools. If Democrats like Al Gore are elected, poor and minority kids will never have a shot at the American dream. America will become two nations. Crime and social chaos will follow.

REPUBLICANS HAVE A SOLUTION. Republicans support opportunity scholarships for poor children. This means putting education dollars directly in the hands of parents who will find schools that work and know which schools don't. Republicans want to give poor and minority children opportunity scholarships that will rescue them from failing and dangerous government schools. Republicans want to give them the chance to go to schools that are safe and that will give them the opportunity to learn. Al Gore, Bill Clinton, Ted Kennedy, and Jesse Jackson send their own children to private schools because they care enough to give their children the best education they can afford. Unlike Democrats, Republicans care enough about poor children to want them to have the same options to choose their schools that Al Gore's children have.

THE REPUBLICAN MESSAGE. We are entering a new millennium. But Democrats are still clinging to the political and educational past. Democrats want to expand a system that pays off their friends but has failed our children. Republicans care about what is happening to our children. Republicans want to restore hope to our inner cities. Republicans want to rebuild the ladder of opportunity for America's poor. Republicans are the party of the future, the party of reform, and the party of hope. For thirty years, Republicans pushed welfare reform and balanced budgets while Democrats resisted. For more than ten years Republicans have pushed voucher programs and opportunity scholarships which will empower poor and minority parents and give them the choice that others have. Republicans want to give poor children who are not being taught by the Democrats' government schools a shot at the American dream. Elect Republicans to make America a place where there can be liberty and justice and prosperity for all.[3]

2. LEARNING FROM HILLARY CLINTON

THE DEMOCRATS' ATTACK. When Hillary Clinton launched her Senate campaign, her announcement revealed that she understood the art of political war. This was the refrain that highlighted her speech: "*I'll be on your side* in the fight for a real increase in the minimum wage.... *I'll be on your side* ... for equal pay for every woman in every job. . . . *I'll be on your side* in the fight . . . [to ease] the marriage penalty." Her conclusion: "If you put me to work for you, I'll work to lift people up, not push them down."

The Republican Response. Remember that "in war there are two sides, friends and enemies. Your task is to define yourself as the friend of as large a constituency compatible with your principles as possible, while defining your opponent as their enemy wherever and whenever you can."[4]

Lesson 1: *Be a Friend.* "I'll be on your side" is a simple phrase, easy to remember. It defines the political battle as a war between somebody out there (Republicans, the rich, racists, religious zealots)— and you, the voter. "I'll be on your side." already implies that someone is against you and that I will be your friend in the battle. Al Gore had his own version of this mantra: "I'll fight for you."

Lesson 2: *Name the Enemy.* The promise "If you'll put me to work for you, I'll work to lift people up, not push them down" tells you just what your enemies have in mind. *They* want to push you down. *They* are your *oppressors.* A Republican would have said "I will vote to end the marriage penalty" and would leave out the part about being "on your side." That's because Republicans see this issue (and every issue) as a *management* problem. How to manage the tax system. How to manage social problems. How to provide government support for marriage, since marriage is an important social institution. The Republican Policy Committee came up with a slogan that expresses the Republican attitude: "Republicans target the problems; Democrats target the politics." But if you don't win the political battle, you don't get to target the problems.

In political war, it's never a management problem. It's about the enemies of marriage (*your* marriage) and what I as your candidate will do to stop them. Republicans are analytic when they talk about social problems. They speak to the head. Democrats are emotional. They speak to the heart. Republicans need to speak to the hearts of voters and not only their heads.

LESSON 3: *Speak to the Heart.* Unfortunately, Republicans usually ignore that it's a war and that they are under attack. When Republicans address the marriage penalty issue, therefore, they don't seem to be talking about anyone's marriage. They talk about marriage as an institution instead. That's why people say Democrats speak to the heart, while Republicans speak to the head. "I will vote to end the marriage penalty" doesn't engage the voters' passions. It doesn't strike fear into voters' hearts or alert them that they have enemies. Mrs. Clinton's formula does. *"I'm on your side. They're your enemies."*

LESSON 4: *Take the High Road.* Who are these enemies? For left-wing Democrats like Mrs. Clinton, the answer is: Republicans and their corporate masters. Mrs. Clinton doesn't have to say this. Her allies in the press will do that for her. Her constituencies (liberals, socialists, left-wing unionists, radical feminists) know who the enemy is. Her mailers and attack ads will dot the i's and cross the t's.

But Mrs. Clinton knows that as a First Lady and senatorial candidate, she has to look high minded and statesmanlike, even though her message is a mean-spirited and mendacious attack on Republicans as enemies of women, working Americans, and poor people. She said, "I am on your side and will fight Republicans who are working against you." Republicans want to *"push people down."* (Democrats will raise you up.) Republicans are oppressors—or the tools of oppressors. But she never has to use the word "Republican." She only has to say "they." That is the basic Democratic message. It's vicious. It's false. But it works.

Because Mrs. Clinton didn't use the word "Republican" or specify the enemy, no one can accuse her of a mean-spirited attack. (Of course, it helps to have lots of friends in the media to protect you from such labels, and to do your dirty work for you.) Republicans have to work harder to achieve the same effect. Sometimes you will have to name the enemy as "Democrats" or "liberals" or (what they really are) "leftists." But be careful when you do.

Republicans need to learn from Democrats how to frame the issues according to the principles of political war. It *is* a war. When you enter the war zone, you need to be psychologically prepared and you need to define the battlefield: It is always about *them* as the enemy of the people, and you as the people's friend. "I am on your side" is a good line for Republicans when going into political battle.

THE REPUBLICAN MESSAGE We are on your side. They are pushing you down. We want to give your children a choice in education. They want to keep your children in failing government schools. We want to give you control over your Social Security funds. They want to keep your money in government accounts. We want to give you tax relief. They want to take more cash out of your pocket to pay for more big government programs.[5]

3. RACE: THE DEMOCRATS' DIRTIEST WEAPON

THE DEMOCRATS' ATTACK. "The real enemy [is] the right-wing extremist Confederate flag–waving Republicans who are trying to roll back the progress we have made." These are words that Al Gore spoke to a mainly African-American audience in Harlem, on President's Day, February 22, 2000. Get used to it. The race card is the dirtiest weapon in American politics. But it is the Democrats' weapon of choice.

For example, the Jesse Jackson–Al Sharpton demonstration against the Confederate Flag in South Carolina just before the Republican primary was no coincidence. It was the first calculated shot in the 2000 campaign. It was part of the plan by the Al Gore–Al Sharpton Democrats to race-bait Republicans to defeat them in November.

THE REPUBLICAN RESPONSE. The first rule in political combat is that you can't stop an attack with a denial. If you are on the defensive in politics, you are losing the battle. Therefore, the second rule is: You have to meet an attack with a counterattack, and it must be of equal or superior force. Republicans should strike first when they can, expose the Democrats' strategy of race baiting, and neutralize it with a countercharge like this:

Democrats are conducting a racial witch-hunt. They are doing it to divert attention from the fact that they have betrayed minority children and trapped them in bankrupt school systems, denying them a shot at the American dream. They are doing it to divert attention from the fact that they are supporting a government Social Security system that robs African-Americans of their retirement incomes.[6] The Confederate flag may or may not be a racist symbol. But those Democratic policies are racist facts.

In their charges against Republicans over the Confederate flag, Democrats are conducting a *racial witch-hunt*. The Democratic attack is not about real racists or real racism; it's a witch-hunt to smear the Republican Party. It's a political lynching. It's *racial McCarthyism*. It was Democrats, not Republicans, who put the Confederate flag on the South Carolina State House (which is still occupied by a Democrat). The Confederate symbol also flies over Al Gore's state of Tennessee and Bill Clinton's state of Arkansas. But the Jesse Jackson–Al Sharpton protestors are not calling these Democrats racists.

This is a politically motivated witch-hunt against Republicans. It is not about racism. It is about smearing Republicans for what Democrats themselves have done. It's about covering up the Democrats' own policies that hurt minorities and the poor.

Racist Democrats put the flag up in 1962. Republicans overwhelmingly voted to end segregation (while Democrats like Al Gore's father voted to defend it). Nobody in his right mind thinks that George Bush or John McCain or the Republican Party wants to restore slavery or segregation today. Yet they are being attacked as though they are racists. This is nothing but a smear campaign against honorable men and women. This is a witch-hunt. It is racial McCarthyism. The Al Gore–Al Sharpton Democrats are pursuing the politics of division to smear Republicans and poison the body politic.

THE REPUBLICAN MESSAGE. Democrats need a captive African-American vote or they will lose their hold on all three branches of government. That's why they want to scare African-Americans into thinking that Republicans are racists. They want to keep the African-American vote in their pocket. Sixty percent of African-Americans want their children to have the right to get out of the failing government schools in which Democrats have trapped them (70% of African-Americans between the ages of 26 and 35 support government vouchers). Republicans want to liberate and empower African-American children by giving them scholarships to go to the school of their choice. The race card is the Democrats' weapon to stop them. Republicans want to give African-Americans control over their own Social Security and allow their savings to be inherited by their survivors. Democrats want government to keep it all.

There are no Republican racists running for president, so the Al Gore–Al Sharpton Democrats need to invent some. Racial name-calling is far too prevalent in our political culture. This hurts our democracy, and it hurts minorities. When Democrats use the term "racism" as a club to beat their political opponents, its moral seriousness is diminished, and real racists are the beneficiaries. The Democrats' racial McCarthyism hurts minorities and hurts our democracy. Democrats should disband the verbal lynch mob and stop the racial witch-hunt now. [7]

4. The Selfish Party

The Democrats' Attack. "The Republicans are proposing *risky tax cuts*."

The Republican Response. The Democrats *support selfish tax schemes* (They want to keep your money—and spend it.) Democrats want to give your tax money to bureaucrats. Republicans want to refund your tax money to you. It's a tax *refund*. Call it that.

Democrats Are the Selfish Party. What the surplus means is this: The Democrats' big government schemes took too much money from you. Now Democrats want to keep it so they can spend it on bureaucrats and destructive government schemes like welfare, which gave people a little money but asked nothing of them in return. The result was the destruction of the work ethic and millions of welfare dependents living at minimum levels, until Republican reforms restored the work idea and, with it, dignity to the poor. Republicans want to give your surplus tax payments back to you—to *you*. In Bill Clinton's last State of the Union address before the 2000 election, he included forty-eight new spending programs on his agenda. Al Gore has forty-eight others up his sleeve. How many more people's lives are they going to ruin by throwing government money at them?

It's Not a Surplus. It's an *Overpayment*. The IRS took more from you than the government needed. That's why there's a "surplus." You overpaid! But when it's about *your* money and *their* pockets, Democrats always twist the truth. They raised your taxes higher than necessary (in fact, higher than ever). Instead of saying, "We're sorry, here's your money back," they say, "We can't do that. It would be a 'giveaway' to the rich." This is the old "bait and switch" game. The truth is: *You* overpaid and *Washington* got rich. It's a *refund*. (Call it that, and it'll be harder for them to twist the truth.) It's time to take the money away from the bureaucrats and return it to the people who paid it. That would be *real* political reform.

The Democrats' big lie is that tax cuts—any tax cuts—are tax breaks for the rich. The truth: they're tax *refunds*, not "cuts." They're refunds, not "breaks." The Democrats aren't going to tell voters they want to keep their money. So, like Bill Clinton, they twist the truth. They say: "Republicans want to give the rich a tax break." It's not a tax break. It's a *refund*. The Democrats don't want to give you a refund of the money you overpaid. Democrats say: It's a Republican *giveaway* (a tax cut for the rich). There they go again, twisting the truth. It's a *giveback* (a tax refund for the people). Republicans want the government to give back your money. Democrats want to keep it and spend it.

"[Bush's] risky tax scheme gives 60 percent of all the benefits to the wealthiest 10 percent of the people." That's Al Gore twisting the truth. The Bush plan is not a "benefit" plan. It is a refund on a government bill that every tax-paying American *overpaid*. Under Bush's plan taxpayers would get back their overcharge on what they put in. Republican tax relief isn't about giving away. It's about giving *back*.

Gore doesn't want you to get your money back so he tells you someone else is getting it. That's twisting the truth. The wealthiest 10 percent of Americans paid over 60 percent of the taxes (actually

63 percent). That's why under the Bush plan they get 60 percent back. It's their overpayment. It's a *refund*. It's fairness. You get a refund on what you paid in. A tax cut is about protecting the people from a government rip-off. Democrats use the politics of envy to divide Americans so the bureaucrats can keep your money.

Where does your tax money go? It goes to bureaucrats. If the trillions spent on welfare went to the poor, they'd be rich. *It's tax money for the bureaucrats out of the pockets of the people.* Do we really need a president like Al Gore who wants to give your money to a bunch of bureaucrats, just because you overpaid his bill?

THE REPUBLICAN MESSAGE. You overpaid. It's your money. The Selfish Party wants to keep it and spend it. Republicans think you deserve a refund. Republicans want you to get your money back. Republicans put people first.[8]

5. THERE *Is* A DIFFERENCE

THE REPUBLICAN ATTACK. Whose Social Security plan will make your retirement really comfortable? Whose health plan is better for you? Whose education plan will give your children a chance to get ahead? Public policy can be complicated. Large government programs are extremely complex. They will drown you in numbers. Politicians can play fast and loose with those numbers. Is there any real difference between the programs the two parties are selling? There is. There is a big difference, and there is a way to tell.

Telling the difference between Republicans and Democrats is a matter of two words: *choice* and *trust*. "Choice" is the word of freedom. "Choice" is about whether you get to control your life. Republicans want *you* to have more control over your life. Democrats want *government* to have more control. That's because Democrats think they know what's good for you. That's why they want government to grow.

The second word is *trust*. "Trust" is a word of respect. If I trust you, I respect you. I regard you as an equal. If I trust you, I don't think I know better than you what is best for you. Republicans believe government was created *for* the people, to serve the people. Republicans trust people to know what is best for them. Republicans want to take power out of the hands of the government and put it in the hands of the people. The Republican Party is the party of individual freedom.

Democrats don't trust the people to know what's good for them. That's why they want mandatory *this* and government-controlled *that*. That's why they want to take as much tax money out of your pocket as they can. They think they know how to spend your money better than you do. The less a politician trusts you, the more power he wants over you. The more power government has, the less choices you have.

Take a look at the Democrats' programs. Every Democratic program puts more power in the hands of government, and less in yours. Every Democratic program trusts you less and trusts government more. Every Democratic program makes government more powerful. And makes you less free.

It's a matter of two words—*choice* and *trust*. Remember these words and you won't be confused by political doubletalk.

SOCIAL SECURITY. Both parties want your retirement to be secure. That's why both parties support plans to save Social Security. But Democrats want *government* to control their new plan. Republicans want *you* to control it as much as possible. That's why Republicans want to put part of your Social Security in private accounts that you control and that can give you even more security when you retire.

Democrats call this a "risky scheme." What they mean is, it's risky to give you some control over your future. That's because they don't trust you to make decisions for yourself.

PRESCRIPTION DRUGS. Both parties have prescription drug plans. But the Republican plan comes with a choice for you. It lets you decide which plan fits your needs. It puts more control in *your* hands and less control in the hands of government bureaucrats. The Democrats' plan is a government plan. They don't think you can be trusted to know what you need.

TAXES. Republicans want to lower taxes. The more of your money you keep, the more you can decide how to spend it. Democrats don't trust you to decide rightly. That's why, under the Democrats, government has grown so big. Democrats think government has to be there to make decisions for you. But the bigger government is, the smaller you are. Republicans want to cut the size of government. Because the smaller *government* is, the bigger *you* are.

THE REPUBLICAN MESSAGE. Elect leaders who trust you to know what you need. Elect a party that respects you. Vote Republican.[9]

6. GUILTY LIBERALS, INNOCENT GUNS

THE DEMOCRATS' ATTACK. We want stricter gun laws. Republicans don't. We care about the safety of our children, Republicans don't. Republicans care about the gun lobby.

THE REPUBLICAN RESPONSE. We want a cure for the killing in our streets. Democrats want a political fix. If stricter laws were the answer to crime, there would be no crime. Washington, D.C., has the strictest gun laws in the nation, but one of the highest murder rates in the world. Moreover, nearly half a million violent crimes are committed every year with knives. Do Democrats want to outlaw knives?

Republicans want to help Americans defend themselves. Democrats coddle criminals and refuse to enforce existing gun laws. Six thousand youngsters have been arrested for bringing weapons to school. Only thirteen have been prosecuted by the Clinton authorities. Instead of prosecuting criminals with guns, Democrats push phony gun-control remedies to raise their poll numbers. Democrats show more compassion for criminals who break gun laws than for law-abiding citizens who need protection. Democrats play politics with children's safety.

Al Gore has the Secret Service to protect him. Limousine liberals can afford private security companies and gated communities. *But what about poor people who don't have thousands of dollars for a private security system?* In a free country, they can purchase a handgun, for less than a television set. *A handgun is the equalizer that defends the poor from the predators on our streets.* Protection for a single working mother in a high-crime neighborhood is what she can put in her night table drawer. Democratic gun-control laws will make it harder for the poor in high-crime areas to obtain protection. Why should law-abiding citizens in dangerous neighborhoods be defenseless because Democrats want to drive up their poll numbers? Why should we make law abiding citizens lock the guns that defend them, when we don't lock up the criminals who do them harm? *The Democrats want gun laws for the comfortable at the expense of the poor.*

Attack First. Define the Issue. Once Democrats go on the attack, their battle is half won. If Democrats are allowed to frame the issue as passing laws against guns in order to make children safe, they already have the high ground. Less restrictions mean less safety for the children. Framed this way, it's a losing battle. Therefore, don't let them define the issue this way. Go on the offensive: The White House shamelessly exploited the shooting of six-year-old Kayla Rolland in Michigan to drive up its poll ratings. Kayla's first-grade killer lived in a crack house, used a stolen gun for the crime, and had previously stabbed another child but was put back in school. His father is a criminal and his mother is a drug addict. The White House is twisting the truth: The new trigger-lock law would not have saved Kayla's life. Why would a family of criminals observe a trigger-lock law? Did background checks stop them from stealing their guns? The people responsible for Kayla's death do not observe laws. They live to break laws. It's *typical liberal lunacy*: pass a new law to deter people who break laws that are already on the books.

The trigger-lock law is a v-chip for guns: it will be put on new guns, not the two hundred million already in use. The v-chip was supposed to protect children from television violence. Who uses a v-chip? Who even knows anyone who uses a v-chip? This is not a cure for the violence problem. It's Democratic snake oil. It's a political fix. How is the government going to enforce the law? Will the FBI come into your house to see that your triggers are locked? Are criminals going to lock the triggers on *their* guns? *If Democrats want to stop the killing, let them lock up criminals, not guns.*

CHANGE THE SUBJECT. REDEFINE THE ISSUE. Whenever Democrats bring up the gun issue, *change the subject*. Re-define the issue. "*Who is responsible for unchecked violence and what can be done about violent behavior?*" Expose Democratic policies as the source of the problem (the culture of irresponsibility, the lax attitudes towards enforcement). Be aggressive. Put a positive proposal on the table. Make *that* the focus of attention. Call for the punishment of the local authorities who failed to do their jobs and indirectly caused Kayla's death. Call for welfare reform to prevent the abuses that caused Kayla's death. Call for changes in the policies that govern violent students in schools. Make the debate about *these* issues rather than a trigger-lock law. Nail the Democrats for their exploitation of a child's death to advance their partisan political agendas.

Democrats focus on guns because it allows them to distract attention from their own responsibility for the violence in our streets. The destruction of the inner-city family through the welfare system, the failure to prosecute and lock up criminals, the failure to hold anybody accountable for anything—these are problems that liberalism has created and that are directly responsible for Kayla's death. Democrats do not want to look at the liberal social welfare workers and school officials and the lax law enforcement responsible for Kayla's death. Democrats don't want to focus on the criminal family responsible for the crime. That would be "blaming the victims."

THE REPUBLICAN MESSAGE. We care about the safety of law-abiding Americans, and that's why we defend their right to protect themselves. Democrats don't. A gun is a poor person's first line of defense. We care about our children's safety and that's why we want to enforce existing gun laws to lock up the criminals who break them.[10]

7. Democrats Put Americans' Security at Risk

THE REPUBLICAN ATTACK. Never before in our lifetimes has America been unable to field an army to fight a foreign war or defend itself from attack on its own soil. But eight years of Democratic defense cuts, national security leaks, and bungled foreign policy decisions have accomplished what no hostile power ever could. They have made America a paper tiger and exposed its citizens to devastating nuclear attack from powers as small and unpredictable as North Korea.

In eight years, the Democrats have cut the American military in half, slowed its modernization to a crawl, allowed staffing and readiness levels to sink to unprecedented lows, and pursued policies that have caused morale to plummet to an all-time. Not long ago, General Gordon Sullivan, a former chief of staff for the Army, told the secretary of defense that the U.S. Army was in a "perilous death spiral" under its present course.

Meanwhile, an arms race abroad is spiraling out of control. China has erased the twenty-year head start in nuclear, missile and satellite technologies that protected the United States before the Clinton-Gore team took over and squandered this advantage. According to U.S. intelligence services, more than twenty-five countries already possess or are acquiring nuclear weapons and the technologies to deliver them. These include the Chinese dictatorship and its outlaw allies, Libya, North Korea, Iran, and Iraq.

Clinton's foreign policies have destabilized the Indian sub-continent, where Pakistan and India ominously move towards war, and in the Strait of Taiwan where China issues nuclear threats to America and its ally. In Iraq, Saddam Hussein continues his buildup of chemical and biological weapons and is working to acquire nuclear warheads in the ruins of the Desert Storm victory that Clinton has undone. In the Balkans, ethnic cleansing continues in the aftermath of a conflict that revealed to military planners around the world that America could no longer put an army in the field of a shooting war.

Thanks to the reckless security policies of the Clinton-Gore White House, rogue states are building nuclear missiles and satellite surveillance systems with American know-how and American help. To make matters worse, for seventeen years Democrats have resisted both the development and the deployment of an anti-missile system that would provide a shield against just such attacks. The Clinton Administration's refusal means that American cities are no longer safe from missiles launched from China and North Korea and, perhaps in the near future, Iran and Iraq.

The American public has been lulled to sleep with false promises from Democrats that the world is no longer a dangerous place.

THE REPUBLICAN MESSAGE. For twenty years after the "anti-war" candidacy of George McGovern, the American people rejected Democrats for the White House because they did not trust them with the nation's military security. The one exception was Jimmy Carter, a naval officer elected in the aftermath of the Watergate scandal. The nation's security is Republicans' most important political responsibility and most voter-approved political issue.

It is time to make America's danger Americans' concern. If we do not begin to act now as a nation to restore our military power and defend our shores, the consequences for future generations may be too terrible to imagine.[11]

8. MOVE THE TARGET, EXPAND THE BASE

THE DEMOCRATS' ATTACK. Go for the Republican base, pick up the conservative center. We are the party of "fiscal responsibility," prosperity and prudence (pay down the debt) and family values ("families first"). We are the New Democrats. We have conservative values, but we *care* and they don't. That's why you should vote for us.

THE REPUBLICAN RESPONSE. Take away the compassion card. It's going to be much easier for Republicans to persuade voters that they care, than for Democrats to persuade voters that Al Gore and Dick Gephardt will hold the budget line and Republicans won't.

There are many ways to skin this cat. Both the Republican Congress and the Bush campaign are doing it well already. Focusing on policy issues like education, health care, and Social Security reform is exactly the right plan and has already put Democratic strategists in a tizzy. A softer, more caring Republican image puts pressure on Gore and the Democrats to attack. Their attacks make them look frenzied and mean. The dynamics work in Republicans' favor. But political images are created in many ways. Policy is only one of them.

Every Republican legislator and candidate should create a staff position for community outreach. Make a comprehensive list of the charities in your district—private, faith based, and public—that deal with inner-city problems. Contact every one of them. Make a regular schedule of visiting the programs. Listen to their problems. Ask how you can help. If they hold fundraisers, offer your help.

Because it is an election year, a low-key approach would probably be best. You don't want to appear to be exploiting new friends, and you don't need a photo-op for people to know that you are concerned. The network you build will lead to other opportunities to make public gestures and statements. You will learn about their problems. What you learn will become part of your speeches and agenda. You can organize public "hearings" to see what would help them. This program should be viewed as a long-term solution for ending Republicans' isolation from key sectors of the population, but with short-term benefits as well.

THE EDUCATION ISSUE. Education presents a tremendous opportunity for Republican breakthroughs—especially among African-American and Hispanic constituencies. One of the purposes of your field trips can be to visit church schools and other community attempts to remedy the catastrophic situation in inner-city public schools. Don't be dissuaded by consultants who say it's a waste of time. First, 70 percent of African-Americans between the ages of twenty-six and thirty-five support school vouchers. Second, every other minority in America is watching, along with independent voters. They will take your attitude toward these minorities as a measure of your true intentions. Almost every African-American parent feels their children are being betrayed by the public school system that Democrats control and defend.

The Bottom Line. In the long run, the Republican Party must become a party that reflects the diversity of the whole population. It is the only way for Republicans to become a majority party. It is the only goal compatible with Republican ideals.[12]

9. Republicans Are the Party of Reform

For twenty-five years, from 1969 to 1994, Democrats controlled both houses of Congress and relentlessly expanded the welfare state. For twenty-five years Democrats used your money for programs that destroyed inner-city families, promoted welfare dependency, and exploited poor and minority communities. For twenty-five years, no Democratic Congress passed a law to require balanced budgets or proposed reform for a welfare system that everyone could see didn't work. In fact Democratic congresses fought welfare reforms and balanced budgets, and attacked the Republicans who proposed them.

For twenty-four of those twenty-five years, Democrats used their control of Congress to spend more of your money than the taxman collected, and to put all of us deeper in debt. Democrats were perfectly satisfied to overspend their budgets forever and to waste the money you worked so hard to earn. They didn't care if big government programs led to teenage pregnancies and out-of-wedlock births. They didn't care that some Americans had become dependent on government handouts for life.

But in 1994, voters put Republicans in charge of Congress (for the first time since 1954), and changed all that. Republicans went to work to reform the welfare system and to bring wasteful government spending under control. Now there is a balanced budget and a government surplus. The national debt is shrinking and five million welfare dependents have gone back to work. That's what a Republican Congress did. That's what a Republican Congress can do.

DEMOCRATS ARE THE PARTY OF REACTION. Democrats didn't want to give up wasteful government programs they had created and that didn't work—even ones that were humanly destructive. Wasteful government programs provide government jobs for unions that support the Democrats. They increase the power of government bureaucrats who administer them (and vote for Democrats). So when Republicans proposed reforms, Democrats dug in their heels and went on the attack. They smeared the reformers as mean-spirited and reactionary. They called Republicans hard-hearted for wanting to change destructive programs. Some Democratic scaremongers even called Republicans "Nazis" for worrying about welfare children who had no fathers or futures, and for seeking to change the system that contributed to their suffering. If welfare was reformed, Democrats said, it would cause a million children to go hungry and even starve.

Democrats' solution to welfare problems was to demand more of your money for the same wasteful schemes. But once the voters no longer believed them, the Democrats lost the power to hold back the clock. Despite two Clinton vetoes and thirty years of Democratic attacks, Republicans were able to pass welfare reform.

Democrats call themselves "progressive." But words are cheap. (Bill Clinton can tell you that.) Some politicians will say anything to get elected. (Al Gore will tell you that.) By their deeds Democrats tell you they are afraid of change. Democrats' idea of progress is more of the same: more money out of *your* pockets, and more government pockets to fill. That's why Democrats are promising forty-eight new spending programs to add to your tax burden. That's why Al Gore's promises will cost you 1.9 trillion dollars if you decide to elect him.

The Party of Progress. You can put Republican actions in the bank. If Republicans had not controlled Congress the last six years, there would be no balanced budgets and no welfare reform. Five million Americans would still be living off your earnings, dependent on government, and having babies out of wedlock. Five million Americans would still be living off paychecks financed by your tax dollars. Five million Americans would never know what it is to stand on their own two feet.

The Republican Party is the party of reform. Democrats are the party of Big Government. Big Government is government that gets into your lives and pushes you around. It is government taking more of what you earn and using your money to tell you what to do. The Republican Party wants to give power back to individuals like you. It is the party of Lincoln and the party of progress. It is the party of a people that is free.[13]

PART II: THE NEW ADMINISTRATION
(before September 11)

1. First Blood

The Democrats' Attack. "I know a racist when I see one. Senator Ashcroft acts like a racist, walks like a racist, talks like a racist." This is from a press release by Representative Maxine Waters. Why hasn't Maxine Waters been hauled before the Ethics Committee for this unfounded, uncollegial, slander of a member of Congress?

With their attacks on conservative cabinet nominees of the new President, the Democrats have launched the next phase of the political war. Their agenda is to damage the Bush presidency and to prepare the ground for a Democratic victory in 2002. Republicans, but as usual are playing defense instead of going on offense.

Even when they are only insinuations, these attacks on Ashcroft as a "racist" and Gail Norton and Linda Chavez as "anti-gay" and "anti-Hispanic" or "anti–civil rights" (the NAACP's code words for "racist") are groundless, defamatory, and as bad as anything Senator Joe McCarthy was ever accused of.

Senator's McCarthy's targets were virtually all either members of the Communist Party or pro-communist fellow travelers. John Ashcroft is not a racist, and there is absolutely nothing in his record that would cause any reasonable person to draw that conclusion. Gail Norton is a libertarian and not in the least anti-gay. Linda Chavez taught the first Chicano studies program anywhere in the United States, at UCLA. These attacks aren't even guilt-by-association with organizations the government has designated "subversive" or "treasonous" as was the case in the McCarthy era. They are attacks on people who are guilty by association with policies the political left doesn't like.

THE REPUBLICAN RESPONSE. Attack the attackers. This is the only appropriate response to the Democrats' vicious campaign. Unless Republicans go on the offensive, the left will succeed in its objective, which is to damage the Bush Administration. Even if President Bush's nominees are confirmed (and they probably will be), the left will still have won a victory. If we continue to confine ourselves to defense (arguing only that "the record does not justify the accusations"), some of the charges will stick in the public mind. There will be a question mark over John Ashcroft's head, and he will be damaged and vulnerable to scurrilous innuendo every time he attempts to move a conservative agenda. The Bush presidency will be weakened. The time to stop the Democrat witch-hunters is now. The goal is to put a question mark over the heads of the witch-hunters themselves and damage *them*.

The only way to prevent a loss in the nomination battle is to go on the offensive. To accomplish this, question the legitimacy of the attacks, question the motives of the attackers, and question the propriety of the campaign that Democrats are encouraging and actively abetting. All three nominees should say: "This is the politics of personal destruction. This is character assassination. These unwarranted personal attacks—over what are really policy disagreements—show how empty are the Democrats' post-election promises of bipartisanship."

THE REPUBLICAN MESSAGE Disagreements over policy are obviously legitimate. But it is wrong—and destructive to the democratic process—to attack a person's character because of disagreements over policy. George Bush won the election. Now he has the time-honored privilege of appointing a team to carry out his policy. These underhanded, unwarranted, and malicious attacks on the character of his appointees are what we mean by the politics of personal destruction. This campaign is updated McCarthyism.[14]

2. How to Beat the Democrats on Energy (1):
The Rules of Engagement

1. REMEMBER: IT's A WAR. Politics is a war of position. In war there are two sides, friends and enemies. Your task is to define yourself as the friend of as large a constituency compatible with your principles as possible, while defining your opponent as the enemy whenever and wherever you can.[15]

In the energy battle, the Democrats—as usual—have observed this principle of political war. They have defined the enemy, before beginning the argument: It's "big oil." It's the "oil gougers." It's the "Bush oilmen." It's the "Grand Old Petroleum Party."[16] It's one big special interest conspiracy against consumers.

The majority of American voters are consumers. Very few of them are oilmen or friends of oilmen. Gallup reports that most Americans already blame the energy crisis on energy producers and foreign countries. The name-calling *is* the argument. With an attack like this, the Democrats don't need to even spell out a position, let alone articulate a policy.

How have Republicans defined *their* enemy in this battle? They haven't. As usual, they've forgotten the politics. They're too polite to name the enemy. And they're too busy talking about sound energy *policy* to notice that the Democratic opposition has already taken their heads off.

2. IT's THE POLITICS, STUPID! Republicans are good at public policy. Republicans were right about the cold war, right about tax cuts, right about welfare. And they're right now about the need for a comprehensive energy policy to increase production. So what? More than fifty million voters failed to figure these things out for themselves

(since Republicans have done such a poor job helping them) in time for the last election. Only 537 Floridians and one butterfly ballot prevented the party of bad policies and nasty politics from retaking the White House. Think about it! Remember: Smart politics and aggressive strategy will triumph over good policy almost every time.

3. In Political War, Sound Bites and Emotions Beat Arguments and Reason. "Class warfare," demonization of law-abiding businessmen and irresponsible partisan attacks on public servants like Vice President Dick Cheney are tactics that work. This is because the vast majority of the voting public is not paying attention, does not (and will never) understand the policy issues and, in any case, responds most powerfully to emotional appeals. A fundamental human reflex is to blame someone else for anything that goes wrong. (*They* did it.) A basic human emotion is to envy those who do better (wealthy oilmen, for instance). "The weapons of politics are symbols evoking fear and hope."[17] Remember: Two powerful forces—*fear* of enemies (big oil, politicians conspiring with special interests) and *hope* in friends (we will use government to defeat the oil conspiracy)—drive the political process.

Two reccommendations follow from this. First, define the Democrats as enemies of the people: Big Government Democrats and Environmental Extremists have put your destiny in the hands of foreign oil interests and dictators like Saddam Hussein and Mommar Khaddafi. Do you want to put your future in *these* hands rather than the care of George Bush and Dick Cheney? Big Government Democrats and Environmental Extremists want to risk your future, take away your freedom, and control your life. Don't let them.

Second, define Republicans as friends of the people and the people's freedom. Define yourself as a friend of the people through compassion and hope. Make the environment your issue by putting in the human element (we're part of nature too). Republicans want to defend the *human environment* against the reckless policies of Big Government Democrats and Environmental Extremists. A sound energy policy will preserve the *physical* environment but also protect the *human* environment. More energy supplies will mean lower prices and more freedom for the American people. More supplies and lower prices will mean more jobs and more power for the American people. Caring about the human environment means caring about the one resource that can protect all the others.

4. THE MEDIA IS AGAINST US. LEARN TO USE IT. The media is controlled by the political left. Don't expect Dan Rather to show the American people that Democrats have put their fate in the hands of Khaddafi or that the oil in Alaska can be retrieved without hurting the environment. Republicans should never embark on a new policy without an independent media campaign to educate the American people on the need for the policy. The media will never do it for us. They will spin every policy proposal against us. This time we failed to do our political job. We've let the Democrats attack us first. We need to mount our counterattack now. Next time, we need to attack first.[18]

3. HOW TO BEAT THE DEMOCRATS ON ENERGY (II): *Who Put the Lights Out?*

THE DEMOCRATS' ATTACK. The energy crisis is a conspiracy of Bush oilmen and their corporate cronies to gouge the American public by charging too much for energy. Oil company gougers put profits over people. They've got the Republicans in their greedy pockets. It's the Grand Old Petroleum Party.[19] We need government price controls so people can afford to buy the energy they need.

THE REPUBLICAN REPONSE. It's a *Democratic witch-hunt.* It's a *Democratic cover-up* for eight years of Big Government attacks on energy producers and the American public. The Democrats' solution—government controls—really means more power for government, less power for you.

In the 1990s, while energy demand soared, the Clinton White House made Americans dependent on foreign oil—on dictators like Saddam Hussein. Under pressure from environmental extremists, they closed coal mines. They blocked oil production. At one time, Americans produced 60 percent of the oil they used. But after eight years of Big Government controls imposed by Democrats, Americans now *import* 60 percent of their oil. There is no energy conspiracy to raise prices. Prices are going up because oil is scarce—thanks to Big Government controls. Utility companies are going bankrupt. Why would they conspire to do that? Price controls will mean reduced supplies. The only way to get more energy is to produce more energy.

THE COUNTERATTACK. *Who put the lights out?* Big Government Democrats and Environmental Extremists.

In California, extremists have blocked the development of new energy sources. They don't like coal. They don't like oil. They don't like nuclear power. As a result, California has been unable to a build a new energy plant in more than ten years while population has exploded and energy demands have risen more than 30 percent. That's why prices are going through the roof: there's not enough energy. Thanks to Big Government Democrats and Environmental Extremists, there are limited supplies in the midst of exploding demand. Big Government controls limit supplies. Environmental extremism demands extreme controls.

THE HUMAN ENVIRONMENT. Extremists have made us lose our sense of the balance between the human environment and the physical environment. Conservation is good. Protection of the environment is good. But the *human environment* needs protection too. Republicans care about the human environment. Republicans will protect human freedom and the quality of life.

EXTREMISTS' ALASKA SCAM. There are sixteen billion barrels of oil buried beneath a small patch of desolate Alaskan earth. As much oil as Saudi Arabia exports to the United States. Alaskan oil could mean hundreds of thousands of jobs for Americans. It could mean lower oil prices. It could mean more freedom for every working American family.

But Democrats say no. They say Republicans want to "punch holes in the Arctic tundra" and harm the environment. The big Democratic scam means more power for government less power for you.

The patch of Alaska that contains oil is no bigger than the Dallas-Ft. Worth airport. Alaska itself is twice the size of Texas. Building the Alaska pipeline—which environmental extremists opposed —has doubled the caribou herds, not destroyed them. The threat to the environment in Alaska by drilling for oil is non-existent. The threat to Americans by not drilling is huge.

THE DEMOCRATIC THREAT. Democrats want more Big Government control. They want caps on oil prices, which look good in the short run, but in the long run will reduce supplies and make prices higher. They don't want nuclear power; they closed up the coal mines in Utah; they don't want to drill for oil. Democrats say that all these controls will protect the physical environment. But Big Government control means control over you. It means control over your freedom. It means control over when and where you can drive your car. It means control over when you can turn on your air conditioning or heat, over whether you'll have a job. It means *your* environment is going to get poorer and less free.

THE REPUBLICAN MESSAGE. Protecting the physical environment sounds great. But what about the *human* environment? For eight Clinton years the Democrats didn't care about the human environment. While energy demands rose, they blocked the development of energy supplies. Now we have a crisis. Their solution is *more of the same*. More Big Government controls. This means less freedom now and bigger crises to come. The Democratic solution means *more power for government, less power for you.* The Republican solution is a solution that works: sensible development of energy supplies. Conservation of the human environment. A government that works *for* the people, not against them.[20]

4. How to Beat the Democrats on Energy (III): *Telling the Story*

Republicans are losing the war over energy and the environment. Every poll shows it. Seventy percent of the California public—where most of the political battle to date has been fought—thinks energy companies are responsible for the crisis and favors price controls (the Democrats' socialist solution).[21] We are losing because the Democrats are attacking us with images ("price gouging energy companies"), but we are opposing them with arguments ("it's about supply and demand") that soar over many voters' heads. If you don't think so, consider that 57 percent of California Republicans also support price controls.[22] We are losing because we haven't told the public that the Democrats and environmental extremists are waging a war against *them*—against their prosperity and freedom.

In politics, the weapons of battle are sound bites and images. Images are created by a story. The Democratic story is this: greedy oilmen who are gouging the public have Republicans in their pockets; Democrats are the friends of the people. Democrats will use your government to save consumers like you from the clutches of the greedy oil barons and their political pawns.

Fear is a powerful emotion. If Democrats are allowed to plant these fears in the hearts of the voting public, we will lose the 2002 elections. Count on it. Months into the energy battle, Republicans still have no story. Republicans answer Democratic attacks with negative policies (no government controls) and complicated analyses (if you cap prices, it will diminish supplies). That's why we're losing.

Here is a Republican story that is emotionally powerful and— more importantly—generates images of Democrats as bad guys. It's a story designed to help Republicans win:

Energy is freedom. You reach for your cell phone, you hop into your car, you flick on the air conditioning, and you connect to the Internet. Energy makes all this possible. But energy does more than that. Energy is required to produce everything that's made. Plentiful energy means cheap energy; cheap energy reduces the cost of everything. The cheaper energy is, the more you can buy. Energy is the basis of our prosperity. Plentiful energy is the freedom of all Americans to enjoy a good life.

California is now in the grips of an energy crisis. Supplies are short. Prices are skyrocketing. Businesses are failing. Even schoolrooms are going dark. But listen to what the Democratic governor of California, Gray Davis, has to say against the backdrop of rolling

blackouts in his state: "We are literally in a war with energy companies."[23] Gray Davis is at war with the companies that produce the
energy we need!

For more than thirty years, the American left—the Democratic
Party, the environmental zealots, and their media fellow travelers—
have been at war with energy producers. They have taken for granted
the freedom that energy provides, and they have waged a war on
those who make it possible.

The left has agitated and the Democrats have regulated and,
with the aid of a willing media, they have spread environmental panic
—and won. They have ensured that for twenty years no large petroleum refineries have been built in America. They have launched
alarmist attacks on the nuclear power industry and virtually throttled
it at birth. They have encouraged unwarranted fears about magnetic
fields and made construction of new power lines almost impossible.
They have inspired junk-science hysterics and slowed the building
of pipelines that deliver natural gas. In the name of a slip of wasteland the size of the Dallas-Ft. Worth airport, in a state that is twice
the size of Texas, they have blocked the development of Alaskan oil,
which would provide consumers with the equivalent of twenty years
of imports from Saudi Arabia.[24] For thirty years, the Democrats and
the left have choked off America's energy, and with it a significant
slice of Americans' freedom.

Now the chickens are coming home to roost. California leads
the nation in government regulation and environmental extremism.
As a result, in California energy supplies have become insufficient to
meet exploding demand. Prices are spiking, energy freedoms are
shrinking, and a crisis is at hand. What is the Democrats' response?
Continue the war.

Discussing the California energy crisis on FoxNews, top Democratic strategist Bob Beckel put it this way: "We're not going to have

an energy policy that's going to reward the oil companies."[25] Wow, that makes sense! The cause of the crisis is an energy shortage, but Democrats like Bob Beckel are not going to reward people for producing more energy! Instead they want price caps! Government controls! Was Bob Beckel talking through his hat or simply out of turn? In fact, he was talking the party line: "The Bush-Cheney energy plan is not a plan for America's future," Senate majority leader Tom Daschle announced at a recent press conference to attack the Administration proposal. "It is a page from our past. It relies almost exclusively on the old way of doing things, drilling more oil wells, burning more coal and using more natural gas."[26] What do Tom Daschle and the Democrats propose as an alternative to gas, coal, oil, and plutonium? Solar panels, perhaps? Windmills? As they say in Fargo, you betchya:

> *Tim Russert*: Over the next twenty years, U.S. energy demands will increase by 62 percent for natural gas, 33 percent for oil and 45 percent for electricity, according to estimates of the federal Energy Information Administration. How do you . . . maintain this country as the premier economic power in the world simply by conservation?
>
> *Tom Daschle*: Well, I wouldn't minimize conservation. We're 5 percent of the world's population. We have 30 percent of the world's energy demand. I think that's wrong. . . .
>
> *Russert*: Is drilling in the Arctic Wild Refuge dead?
>
> *Daschle*: Yes it is.
>
> *Russert*: How about an increase in nuclear power?
>
> *Daschle*: I don't think that this is the right time.

Here is the complete Gray Davis quotation cited earlier: "We are literally in a war with energy companies *who are price gouging us. Many of those companies are in Texas.*" It's Pearl Harbor in California! It's a sneak attack by Texas oilmen! And their cronies in the White House! "They sound like oilmen!" clucks the junior senator from California pointing her finger at the occupants of the White House. It's an oil plot from Texas. That's the Democrats' war cry.

The attack may be ludicrous but it works. Against a tale of conspiracy and stabs in the back, there is little room for rationality and common sense. Gray Davis himself received far more campaign contributions from big energy in California than did George Bush.[27] His own hired guns, Fabiani and Lehane, are on the payroll of the biggest energy utility in the state.[28] (The previous biggest energy utility was bankrupted by the current crisis. Some gouging!) Two experts at the Cato Institute have, in fact, looked into the question of whether the California problem was created by a conspiracy of Texans to charge ruinous prices the market could not justify. They checked the reports of the Federal Energy Regulatory Commission, and discovered that the legitimate price for power in January 2000, as the crisis unfolded, was twenty-seven cents a kilowatt-hour. The company operating the grid that supplies California with all of its power reports that in the same month it paid an average of twenty-eight cents per kilowatt-hour.[29] A one-cent price hike has obviously nothing to do with the California power crisis in which prices are spiraling astronomically higher than their normal levels (in fact seventy times their level last year[30]).

But we don't really need this evidence to know the Democrats are lying. How can there be massive price gouging unless there is a conspiracy to fix prices—a crime in the United States? But where are the grand juries, and what Democrat is actually charging *that*? Their accusations are pure demagoguery: all innuendo, no specifics.

This from the party that had to *see* the stain on the dress in order to be persuaded.

Attacking the energy companies is only half the Democrats' war plan. Attacking the President is the other. The president stands in the way of the Democrats' proposed "solution": government control of the price of energy ("price caps"). Government controls are a socialist scheme. Government controls on energy prices are exactly what caused the California crisis. First, the state of California placed such burdensome regulatory controls on energy production that a shortage resulted. Shortages mean higher prices. But high electricity bills are bad for politicians. So, in the face of rising demand, the state of California held down the retail price so California consumers had no incentive to save their power. That's why Pacific Gas and Electric went bankrupt. The government fixed the price the company could charge consumers while the scarce supplies made its own costs rise. It lost money with every price-controlled kilowatt-hour it sold, until it just went belly-up.

The government price caps that Democrats are now demanding will inevitably discourage new energy production—which is the only long-term solution to the problem. Government controls will also discourage conservation. If power is cheap, why should the consumer use less? As if the destructive proposal for price controls were not enough, California Democrats are also proposing state ownership of the means of transmission. Were Democrats asleep during the collapse of the Soviet empire? Apparently. The Democrat-sponsored legislation to enable the State of California to take over its power lines and get into the power business is proceeding rapidly in the state assembly.

The Democratic solution is no solution. Government controls will only create greater problems down the line. The Democrats are a party of the left; their solutions are big government controls—

socialist schemes that will cost taxpayers more money and will not work. The Democrats are a party that will say anything for political power. In order to gain and expand government power, they will divide Americans against each other, they will sacrifice America's prosperity, and they will make war on America's energy producers and the defenders of Americans' freedom.[31]

5. How to Beat the Democrats on Social Security (1): *It's Your Money. It's Your Life. Take Them Back.*

The Democrats' Attack. Republicans want to privatize Social Security. It's risky; it takes benefits away from working Americans to benefit the rich. It's "Welfare for Wall Street."[32] "The Wall Street crowd which was generous in its financial support to the Bush campaign likes this plan."[33] The stock market is a roller coaster. Under the Republican plan, "your Social Security savings [will be] riding up and down on the stock market." "That roller coaster ride would cause a lot of people to have heart attacks."[34] "President Bush wants to turn Social Security into Social Insecurity."[35]

The Democrats are like a broken Marxist record. They've got two lines: "It's scary" and "It benefits the rich." You always know what they're going to say. Since they are political reactionaries holding on to programs that are bankrupt, they really have no alternative to offer. That makes them an easy target. Attack them on the justice issue. Attack them on the fairness issue. Attack them for taking what rightfully belongs to the people (their earnings) and giving them back a sorry return.

The Republican Response. The Democrats want a Social Security program that is discriminatory and unjust, and that is going bankrupt besides. It steals the life savings of working Americans and gives back only half a loaf. Here's how it works: A worker who earns $34,000 a year and dies when he's sixty-seven loses $156,000 of his Social Security investment under the present Social Security system.[36] The average African-American working male dies at sixty-seven. He will pay money into the system all his life and never get anything back. It's a ripoff. It's a national scandal. It's government racism. It's time for reform.

Republicans want to give you control over your money and your future. The Democrats want government to control your life. That's why you're getting a raw deal. If you had control over the money that government takes out of your pocket for Social Security, where would you put it? Probably in a savings account. To Democrats, that's *"privatization."* Is it risky? Obviously not. If you put your Social Security taxes in a certificate of deposit at current rates (instead of having the government take them), you would earn twice as much as the government now promises to pay you—provided you live long enough to collect. If you were allowed to put all your Social Security savings in your own savings account, you would have tens of thousands of dollars more when you retire than you are going to get under the present system. And you would be able to pass that money to your children when you die. Under the present system, which Democrats want to preserve, your children get *nothing*.[37] The government gets it all.

Many Republicans will be tempted to focus on whether the Bush plan is risky or not. They will want to explain how the market works, and that there are financial instruments which carry almost no risk. These are good points, and one should have them ready to refer to in debate. But voters who understand the market are with you already. They will not be affected by the Democrats' scare tactics. Your real challenge is to reach voters who will be affected by the Democrats' attacks. You need sound bites, not lengthy analyses.

Therefore, emphasize savings accounts, which ordinary people understand. Use the example of savings accounts to close down the risk argument. Then hammer the Democrats for defending a system that rips off working Americans and cheats their children of the savings their parents have earned. It's a matter of justice. You have a right to control what you earned.

When they're engaged in political warfare (and not hosting high-dollar fundraisers) Democrats like to portray "Wall Street" as the enemy of working Americans and Republicans as the tools of big money capitalists. The Republican response should be that our Social Security plan is to give working Americans the same rights and opportunities as successful Americans already have. We want equal rights for working Americans to control their savings and their re-tirement futures, and to pass on their earnings to the next genera-tion. We are defending working Americans against the government bureaucrats who want to take their savings and use it for their own purposes.

Neutralize the scare factor by using the example of savings ac-counts. Emphasize the social justice issue. It's easier to present and understand the *injustice* of the present system and the justice of the reform plan than the economics of either. *We* are the reformers; *they* are the reactionaries. *We* want to give you control over your money; *they* want to take it away from you. *We* want to change the system so that you can have more opportunity and freedom; *they* want to pre-serve the old system, which gives you less.

Emphasize social justice because it engages the passions. And passion is what drives voters to the polls.[38]

6. How to Beat the Democrats on Social Security (II):
Faming the Issue

"Wall Street fans of privatization stand to make $240 billion over the next 12 years if Social Security is replaced by privatized individual investment accounts" (from the AFL-CIO website).

"The Wall Street crowd, which was generous in its financial support to the Bush campaign, likes this plan" (from the DNC website).

It is not surprising that the Democratic National Committee agrees with the socialist unions. Socialist unions finance the DNC's party operations, shape its campaigns, and supply the lion's share of its activists and ideas.

"Wall Street" is the symbol that Communists used to attack the market system. The Democratic Party has forgotten that the free market West won the Cold War. The federal government, municipalities of all sizes, and all government programs favored by the left also make money for "Wall Street" which finances their debt. If the Democratic position were argued consistently it would lead to the conclusion that government itself is bad and should be opposed. In fact, what the Democratic socialists really want is to eliminate the system of private enterprise and have the government fund—and politicians control—everything in sight.

The rest of us who are not saddled with the legacy of Marxist delusions understand that Wall Street and private enterprise are how things should work in a capitalist world. Small "d" democrats prefer a system in which Wall Street plays a significant role because this setup has provided more wealth to more people—to more formerly *poor* people—than any other system in the history of mankind. It is private corporations that made the liberation of the working poor possible. Only fanatics of the Seattle-Genoa sect will deny it.

One of those fanatics—Gerald McEntee, who is president of a government bureaucrats' union (AFSCME)—declared that the Bush reform plan was "Welfare for Wall Street." The leftist McEntee was a key Gore fundraiser and strategist in the last election. This illustrates the Democrats' problem. The Democratic Party is dependent on leftists like McEntee, so even though it feeds sumptuously off the capitalist teat, at election time it is still a prisoner of the socialist mind-set. Guided by the reactionary prejudices of the left, it acts in power as a mighty brake on social progress and social reform. Think of the Democrats' twenty-year war against Republican reformers over welfare. It was a futile effort to defend an indefensible system that did more damage to the inner-city poor, and to minority poor in particular, than any system has done to any group since the abolition of slavery.

Like the Bourbons, who learned nothing and forgot nothing, left-wing reactionaries are on the warpath again. This time they are out to thwart a presidential plan to reform the unjust and near bankrupt Society Security system. Democrats have dug in their heels to defend a program they created in the 1930s, which has become an epic Ponzi scheme for ripping off working people. There is no real money in the so-called Social Security Trust Fund—hence the "Ponzi" sobriquet—just a lot of government IOUs representing a promise that they will eventually pay you by taxing future generations. The problem is created because of the imbalance in generations. Too many retired "baby boomers," too few active earners to pay for them.

In order to understand the destructiveness of the Democrats' agenda, it is necessary first to clear away the ideological fog they have created to obscure and smother the Bush reform. The Commission overseeing the reform is, in fact, not a Wall Street–Republican cabal, but a strictly bipartisan group co-chaired by former

Democratic senator Pat Moynihan. The practical proposal to reserve 2 percent of individual retirement plans for private accounts is already a practice in social-democratic Sweden. These facts, of course, aren't enough to dissuade ideological storm troopers like the editors of the *Nation* from denouncing the plan as a "Social Security Heist" for the rich. But others should be more open-minded.

The idea behind the Bush proposal is to give working people control over their financial futures. Contrary to the Democrats' claims, this is not "welfare for the rich," but just the opposite: opportunity for the working classes. Rich people *already* have control over their financial futures through private plans that pay double—and more than double—what the Social Security system now offers. Unlike those who depend on Social Security, the rich get to control their retirement funds as personal assets and, therefore, to pass them on to their children. The Bush idea is really quite revolutionary: Let's give the working class the same privilege and power over their retirement funds that the "ruling class" has over its retirement.

Democratic big spenders and socialist ideologues like McEntee hate this. They hate it for the same reason that socialist bureaucrats hate all schemes that remove money from their control and put it in the hands of the people: it diminishes their own power. And that's basically what the Bush reform plan proposes to do. It will remove money from the control of government bureaucrats and put it into the hands of the people who earned it.

Since the left can't fight a program like this on the merits, it must resort to fear, which is its favorite tactic for manipulating the voters. "President Bush wants to turn Social Security into Social Insecurity," warns the DNC website. Bush's reform is "a dangerous privatization scheme. . . . Let him know you don't want him playing Russian roulette with Social Security." On the AFL-CIO website, the warning comes from a senior citizen: "'You don't trust Wall Street,' 82-year-old Florence Daniels told Reuters during the [union] rally. 'It goes up and down, up and down.'"

In TV spots against Republican Randy Forbes in Virginia's special election, Democrats used the visual of a roller coaster to dramatize the insanity of the Republican scheme. Seniors on camera were shot against a roller coaster backdrop and provided a Greek chorus:

Narrator: Did you know Randy Forbes wants to privatize Social Security?

Senior male: That's crazy.

Senior female: Oh, my goodness, no.

Narrator: Your Social Security savings riding up and down on the stock market.

Senior male: That roller coaster ride would cause a lot of people to have heart attacks.

Senior female: I'd have the pudding scared out of me.

So Republicans want to give old people heart attacks and scare them half to death. No wonder Democrats call them mean-spirited.

Fortunately, almost half the population is now invested in the market and thus financially sophisticated enough to know that this is hogwash. "Wall Street" is not a monolith, and there are plenty of investment instruments that are not as "risky" as a roller coaster ride (which, if you think about it, is not that risky either). A five-year certificate of deposit at your local savings bank will earn you 5 percent—twice as much as your present Social Security account. All that "privatization" means is that *you* control the money you put in your savings plan. Under the Bush reform, you could choose to put your Social Security funds in a savings account. If the entire account were privatized, instead of 2 percent, you'd be twice as well off when you retired.

The Bush reform plan is better than even this suggests, because it would allow you to pass the money your account accumulated to your loved ones when you die. In one or two generations, every working family could acquire the capital to become, well, capitalists. What happens now under the Democrats' plan? The government keeps it.

Having put the picture back in order, we can see what a colossal rip-off the present Social Security scheme actually is, especially for working people. Remember, if you're wealthy, the tax that underwrites the scheme is only an annoyance. It's not 12.4 percent of your income as it is for workers (that's because there's a cut-off after you've earned $80,000). It's an extra dollop in the tax bite the government is already taking out of your pocket. On the other hand, if you're wealthy, you're not even going to notice your Social Security check when it comes, because you have far better options for creating your own retirement nest egg—like investing in the market and making a conservative 8 percent (or *four times* the Social Security returns) for your efforts.

But if you don't have these options—if you're a working person of modest means—the Democrats' plan ensures that you are going to get cheated. And not just because the present system is heading for a cash crisis, which will eventually cost you 18 percent of your paycheck instead of the present 12.4 percent.

Terry Jeffrey is the editor of *Human Events* magazine. If Tom Daschle were asked to describe Terry Jeffrey, he would dismiss him as an extreme right-winger. In *Human Events*, Jeffrey fleshed out the present Social Security reality for African-Americans by imagining a man named "Bob," who was born in South Carolina in 1940, graduated from segregated schools in the 1950s, served in Vietnam in the

1960s, and got married and had two children in the 1970s. In 1998, Bob's wife died of breast cancer, and two years later he himself died of a heart attack.

For forty years the government had taken a healthy chunk out of Bob's pay before he could even deposit it in the bank. Under government rules Bob's employer was only required to tell him, however, that it took half of what it actually did take. By the mid-1980s, the chunk was 12.4 percent, but on Bob's paycheck it only said 6.2 percent. The Democratic framers of Social Security planned it this way to keep Bob from knowing what they were doing to him.

"Where did Bob's Social Security taxes go in those years?" asks Jeffrey. A good portion went to pay the current benefits of retired people. But "surplus" Social Security tax revenue—money that came in over and above what was needed to pay current benefits—was squandered by the members of a Democratic Congress to fund increased government spending for the purpose of enhancing their own power, prestige, and political invulnerability.

Among the projects the Democrats might have spent Bob's money on were Andrew Serrano's *Piss Christ*, a congressional pay raise, and a bailout of reckless New York bankers who invested in Mexican government bonds. "One place it didn't go was back to Bob, who wasn't a congressman, didn't patronize blasphemy, and was too shrewd to invest in the government of Mexico." It also didn't go to Bob's children, as it would under Bush's plan. Bob had paid the government more than $100,000 over his lifetime, possibly more than $200,000. This was more money than he had ever seen at one time while he lived. If Social Security were fully privatized, the money would go to his two children. Under the present system, it is just gone. Or rather it is gone to the congressional spenders. Bob's case is typical for one-third of all black men. They pay all their lives and die before they collect a dime. Under the Democrats' Social Security system, they lose what for them would be a fortune and get back exactly nothing.

What about the part of Bob's paycheck that went to provide benefits to current retirees? Here is Jeffrey's hypothetical example: "While Bob, at 60 was paying 12.4 percent of the last paycheck he earned to subsidize Social Security, a retired 70-year-old Lexus-driving white lawyer across town, who used to charge his clients $200 an hour and who has a stock portfolio worth $5 million, was receiving regular Social Security checks subsidized by Bob's current payroll taxes. The retired lawyer's habit was to pick up his checks at the Post Office on the way to the country club."

I have quoted Terry Jeffrey's example to show how topsy-turvy our political categories have become these days. The Democrats are defending a reactionary scheme that systematically robs black males and working people, bars them from the one chance they have to accumulate capital, and steals 10 percent of their hard earned income over the course of their working lifetimes. The Republicans are proposing a progressive plan to end this injustice, put power into the hands of working people, and return their hard earned money to them. Will they succeed? Only if the American people keep their heads clear of the ideological fog machine.[39]

7. HOW TO BEAT THE DEMOCRATS ON MISSLE DEFENSE[40]
One Missle Can Ruin Your Whole Day.

Joe Biden and the Democrats are preparing an attack on the President's missile defense program. This is no time for Republicans to play political defense. It is an opportunity for Republicans to go on the attack. It is an opportunity to take the battle into the urban centers that Democrats now control and that are now vulnerable (or soon will be) to enemy missile attack.

Don't spend too much political capital defending the policy aspects of missile defense. The issues are too complicated for voters to assess. They're too complicated for sound bites. But Republicans now control the White House bully pulpit, and voters *can* be made to understand that America is currently defenseless against a missile attack. Voters *can* understand the threat from China, North Korea, Libya, Iraq, and Iran. They *can* understand these nations cannot be trusted to keep arms agreements. They *can* understand the Clinton administration gave China our missile secrets.

Democrats have opposed missile defense for twenty years and kept America naked. Bill Clinton gave the Chinese the technologies that now threaten us. Democrats are derelict in their duty to protect the lives of American citizens. Particularly those who live in big cities that vote Democratic. This is the target. Go for it.

THE PITCH. North Korea is run by an unstable Communist dictator who has recently starved a million of his citizens (the official Korean figure is 250,000) to build a nuclear missile program, which can now reach the continental United States. The United States has no way to stop a North Korean missile from reaching its target. That is because the Clinton Administration refused to build an missile defense system. As a result, Los Angeles, San Francisco, and Seattle could be destroyed by a North Korean missile, tipped with nuclear warheads or carrying anthrax or chemical weapons.

In a few years, New York, Chicago, Boston, Baltimore, Washington, Detroit, Cleveland, St. Louis, Philadelphia, and other American cities will be vulnerable to nuclear, biological, and chemical weapons capable of killing millions of Americans. These missiles could be launched by North Korea or its patron, China, or by other rogue nations such as Libya, Iran, and Iraq.

But Joe Biden and the Democrats don't want America to have a missile defense. Why? It might upset the Chinese. It might upset the Russians. It might upset the French. If the Chinese and the Russians want to get upset because the American government wants to defend Los Angeles, New York, Chicago, and other American cities, let them. And let Joe Biden and the Democrats defend *their* policy of preventing America from defending itself against a missile attack.

Joe Biden and the Democrats place their faith in a strategy that says "Reduce weapons and all sides will feel more security."[41] Tell that to the Chinese and the North Koreans, who did not have nuclear missiles that could reach the United States until the Clinton Administration gave them the technologies to build such missles.

Where were Joe Biden and the Democrats in the 1990s, when the Clinton Administration transferred intercontinental missile technologies and satellite technologies to China (and therefore to North Korea, Libya, Iran and Iraq)?

Where were Joe Biden and the Democrats when the Clinton Administration was removing technology controls and selling super computers to China (and therefore to North Korea, Libya, Iran, and Iraq)?

An American president once said that America would be willing to bear any burden and pay any price to defend America and its freedoms. That president was John F. Kennedy. George Bush and the Republicans have kept his faith—the faith that a strong America is a beacon of freedom throughout the world.

Democrats have forgotten their first duty, which is to protect the safety and security of the American people. They have opposed missile defense for almost twenty years. They have kept America naked, while America's enemies have armed themselves with weapons of mass destruction and acquired the missile technologies necessary to deliver them.

Today the Republican Party is the party that puts American security first. Americans need to support their president and his plan to defend Americans by making America strong. Say no to the Democrats. Say no to the Chinese and the North Koreans. Say yes to an anti-missile defense.

PART III: THE NEW ADMINISTRATION
(after September 11)

1. TODAY IS PEARL HARBOR

The destruction of the World Trade Center, the attack on the Pentagon, the revelation to the whole world that even the White House is vulnerable—should be a wake up call to Americans.

This country is at war, and we are far behind in securing our citizens' safety. How was it possible to hijack four commercial airliners from major airports—one of them Dulles International—and to do so within a set time frame? How could obvious targets like the Pentagon and the World Trade Center be so undefended?

We know the answer. America is soft. America is in denial. America is embarrassed at the idea that it has enemies and must protect itself. America was so eager to cash in on "peace dividends" after the Cold War ended, that it has stripped itself of even prudent defenses. America is in denial that much of the world hates us and will continue to hate us. Because we are prosperous and democratic and free. Today's tragedies must be a wake-up call.

It's time to remember that the first duty of government is to provide for the common defense. That means it's time to spend the surplus on national security now. Beginning with a missile defense system that will prevent even bigger terrorist disasters in the future. It is time to dramatically increase our domestic counterterrorist and intelligence efforts and to step up the monitoring of all groups that have declared war on with the United States. It's time to tighten our security systems, beginning with airport checks. It's time to let the profiling of potential terrorists—and that does mean Islamic and Palestinian terrorists—outweigh the objections of the ACLU and other leftist groups. It's time for those on the political left to rethink their alliances with anti-American radicals at home and abroad. It's time for the President to identify the monsters who planned the day of infamy and then to carry out a massive military strike against them and any government who sponsored these acts. It's time for a new sobriety in America about what is at stake in the political battles with those who condemn America as an "oppressor" nation.

It's time for Americans who love this country to stand up in her defense.[42]

2. THE WAR WE ARE FIGHTING IS NOT NEW. OUR LEADERSHIP IS.

The fact that we are at war is not new. We have been at war for more than half a century with the radicals who hate America and hate American capitalism. The World Trade Center was the symbol of "Wall Street"—the Great Satan of the radicals' religion. It was the symbol of "globalization." That is why it was the prime target for these terrorist attacks.

This is a war that Communism started and that post-communist radicals are continuing. The radicals who hate America and America's freedom will never give up. They have to be defeated.

The September 11th tragedy was not the first time the World Trade Center was hit. In 1993, the same forces of terror detonated a bomb at the base of the towers that killed six people and injured one thousand. The architect of that bombing, Ramzi Yousef, was an Iraqi intelligence officer and was captured with plans for a coordinated series of hijackings and suicide crashes of U.S. commercial airliners. But no one in government took the plans seriously enough to prepare a defense.

CLINTON'S RESPONSIBILITY. President Clinton refused to recognize that we were at war; he did not alert the nation; he did not call us to arms; and he did not mobilize U.S. security forces to prepare the nation (or even the World Trade Center) against these attacks.

Instead of crushing Arafat and Hamas and their comrade Osama bin Laden, the Clinton Administration forced the Israelis into the Oslo "peace process," which legitimized the terrorists, provided them with billions of U.S. aid dollars, and gave them an army with tens of thousands of weapons.

Instead of preparing America for the war it was already in, the Clinton Administration pretended we were at peace. It acted as though America itself was the threat. Government security controls were removed on sales and transfers of high-tech instruments of war. Missile and satellite technologies and super computers were passed to China and thus to North Korea, Iran, Libya, and Iraq. Through these transfers, the Clinton Administration took away our military edge and disarmed our high-tech defenses.

THE INTELLIGENCE GAP. Why were U.S. intelligence agencies unable to provide warnings despite the large traffic of terrorist communications required to plan the September 11th attack? Because the Clinton Administration had given away the technology to encrypt such messages and make them invisible. These technologies included computer networks that cannot be monitored and spread-spectrum radios that change frequency and are impossible to penetrate. Our technological defenses were systematically disarmed by our own President.

The Clinton Administration also took steps to disarm our human intelligence defenses. In 1995, new "sensitivity" guidelines were issued for our intelligence agencies that gravely restricted their ability to gather information in countries where terrorists were based. Because an American leftist had been widowed by a "human rights violator" in Latin America who was employed by the CIA, the CIA was forbidden to use "human rights violators" as intelligence assets. This was like forbidding local law enforcement from using common criminals as informants. But common criminals do not bring down hundred-story skyscrapers, terrorists do.

After the CIA was hamstrung, the terrorist network bombed two of our African embassies. Our response was an impotent missile launched into the Sudan by Clinton (three days after Monica Lewinsky appeared before the grand jury). It destroyed a medicine factory and antagonized millions of Muslims around the world. Other missiles were launched into Afghanistan where Osama bin Laden had his camps and destroyed four mosques. More terrorist acts followed. The U.S.S. Cole was blown up in Yemen. A barracks containing our troops was bombed in Saudi Arabia. Nothing was done.

The Clinton Administration refused to recognize the threat, refused to mobilize the nation, refused to arm our security forces to the levels needed to defend us, refused to recognize that we were in a war, and refused to declare a policy to win it. The terrorists got the message: America is weak. The refusals put us in danger as a nation and made the tragedy of September 11th possible.

A New President Who Will Defend Us. But now we have a new president, and a new administration. "When I take action, I'm not going to fire a two million-dollar missile at an empty ten-dollar tent and hit a camel in the butt," this President told a group of senators, which indluded Hillary Clinton. "It's going to be decisive." With a new leadership, *our* war has begun. And we will win it.

The months ahead will be difficult ones, but they will also bring opportunities. We can be grateful that many Americans have now begun to appreciate what they have in this country and also what can be lost. Already there is a new unity, a new patriotism in the land. Already Americans are beginning to realize how lucky they are to have a president who believes in America and who is committed to winning America's war.

But we must not forget how slim the margin was by which this President was elected to lead us in our nation's crisis. We must not forget how deeply the forces that hate America have penetrated our institutions and weakened our national resolve. This is a battle we must fight together. It is a battle we lost in Vietnam. That loss led directly to America's weakness and the terrorist attack of September 11th. It is a battle we must not lose again.[43]

3. The Enemy Within

Representative Barbara Lee, Democrat of Berkeley, was the only member of Congress who refused to defend her country under attack. The *Los Angeles Times* calls Barbara Lee a "liberal" and compares her to "anti-war" dissenters of the past, most notably Jeanette Rankin who cast the lone vote in Congress against America's entry into the Second World War, and again after Pearl Harbor. "As a woman I can't go to war," she said, "and I refuse to send anyone else."

We are at war again, and it's time to call things by their right names.

Barbara Lee is not an anti-war activist; she is an anti-American communist who supports America's enemies and has actively collaborated with them in their wars against this nation.

I met Barbara Lee when she was working in city politics in Oakland, in the penthouse headquarters of Huey Newton, the infamous "Minister of Defense" for the Black Panther Party. Newton was a left-wing gangster at war with America, and Barbara Lee was his undercover agent in local government.

Barbara Lee later became a staffer in the office of Democratic congressman Ron Dellums. In this capacity she committed an act of betrayal that I am unable to describe as treason only because she was never prosecuted for it. At the time, Ron Dellums was the head of the House Subcommittee on Military Installations. He had top security clearance and carried on a one-man campaign to thwart U.S. foreign policy toward the communist dictatorship of Grenada.

U.S. security officials had identified the communist dictatorship as a threat because of the presence of large numbers of Soviet advisers and their ongoing construction of an airport that could be used for Soviet nuclear bombers. As the ranking Democratic member of the House Armed Services Committee, Dellums went to Grenada to conduct his own fact-finding tour. On his return he testified before the House Subcommittee on Inter-American Affairs that "based on my personal observations, discussion and analysis of the new international airport under construction in Grenada, it is my conclusion that this project is specifically now and has always been for the purpose of economic development and is not for military use. . . . It is my thought that it is absurd, patronizing and totally unwarranted for the United States government to charge that this airport poses a military threat to the United States' national security."[44]

What legislators did not know at the time was that Dellums had previously submitted his report to the communist dictator of Grenada for his prior approval and subject to any changes he or his military advisers chose to make. In other words, Dellums acted as an agent of the enemy in abetting his hostile designs against the United States. His emissary in this act of betrayal was Barbara Lee.

We know this from government documents retrieved by U.S. marines after Grenada was liberated by U.S. forces. One document was a love-letter from Dellums' chief of staff, Carlottia Scott (who was political issues director of the Democratic National Committee during the Gore campaign) to the Grenadian dictator himself. In the letter Carlottia Scott wrote: "Ron [Dellums] has become truly committed to Grenada, and has some positive political thinking to share with you. . . . He's really hooked on you and Grenada and doesn't want anything to happen to building the Revolution and making it strong. He really admires you as a person and even more so as a leader with courage and foresight, principles and integrity. . . . The only other person that I know of that he expresses such admiration for is Fidel."[45]

Another document liberated by the Marines contained the minutes of a Politburo meeting attended by the Communist dictator and his military command. "Barbara Lee is here presently and has brought with her a report on the international airport that was done by Ron Dellums. They have requested that we look at the document and suggest any changes we deem necessary. They will be willing to make the changes."

A third document liberated by the Marines was the diary of Grenada's communist minister of defense, who wrote: "The [Revolution] has been able to crush counter-revolution internationally. Airport will be used for Cuban and Soviet military."

Collaborating with a hostile power to conceal its military plans and subvert U.S. national security policy is treason. Why is this woman seated in the House?

The foes of free markets and free minds have not surrendered with the collapse of the Soviet empire. They are even bolder now that memories have faded, and they cannot be immediately linked to the crimes of Communism, which they encouraged and supported. But they are still here educating others to follow them. They are behind our own lines. They have burrowed into our schools, our churches, our media, and our government itself. And their message is always the same: *America is guilty; America is to blame.* In our war with terror, these are adversaries within that we ignore at our peril.[46]

IV

THE UNREPENTANT LEFT

I

An Open Letter to "Anti-War" Protesters

I AM A FORMER "ANTI-WAR" ACTIVIST who helped organize the first campus demonstration against the war in Vietnam at the University of California, Berkeley in 1962. I have written this as an appeal to college students not to join the so-called anti-war effort against America's battle with international terrorism.

The hindsight of history has shown that our efforts in the 1960s to end the war in Vietnam had two practical effects. The first was to prolong the war itself. Testimony by North Vietnamese military leaders such as General Vo Nguyen Giap and Colonel Bui Tin in the postwar years confirms that they knew that North Vietnam could not defeat the United States on the battlefield and counted instead on the division among our people at home to win the war for them. The Vietcong forces we were fighting in South Vietnam were destroyed during the Tet Offensive in 1968. They continued the war until their victory in 1975 because they believed their resolve was stronger than ours. They were correct. America gave up the fight in 1973.

In other words, most of the war (1968-1975) and most of the casualties in the war occurred because the dictatorship of North Vietnam relied on Americans to give up rather than pay the price necessary to win. The blood of hundreds of thousands of Vietnamese, and tens of thousands of Americans, is on the hands of the anti-war activists who encouraged the enemy to resist and prolonged the actual war.

The second effect of the war was to surrender South Vietnam to the forces of communism. This resulted in the imposition of a monstrous police state, the murder of hundreds of thousands of innocent South Vietnamese, the incarceration in "re-education camps" of hundreds of thousands more, and a quarter of a century of abject poverty that continues to this day. It also resulted in the genocide of two million Cambodian peasants at the hands of the Khmer Rouge who were armed and supported by the North Vietnamese communists. All this weighs heavily on heads of the so-called anti-war protesters of the 1960s, who divided Americans so effectively that their government could not protect Indo-China from its Communist fate.[2]

I say "so-called anti-war protesters," because, while many Americans were sincerely troubled by America's war effort, the organizers of this movement were radicals who supported a communist victory and an American defeat. Today the same people are organizing the campus demonstrations against America's effort to defend its citizens against the forces of international terrorism, barbarism, and anti-American hate.

Unlike the Vietnam War, this one is not ten thousand miles away and there is no political ambiguity about its nature. For the first time since Pearl Harbor, America itself is under attack. Our enemies have pronounced a death sentence against every man, woman, and child in America. Now is the time for decent Americans to stand up for each other and defend their country.

As a former protester, I have reason to understand better than most the importance of protecting freedom of speech and the right of citizens to dissent. But I also have reason to understand better than most that there is a difference between honest dissent and malevolent hate, between criticism of national policy and sabotage of the nation's defenses. In the 1960s and 1970s, in fact, the tolerance of anti-American hatred was so high that the line between dissent and treason was eventually erased. Along with thousands of other New Leftists, I was one who crossed the line between dissent and actual treason. (This story is told in my autobiography *Radical Son*. Only a handful of other "progressives," I regret to say, have been so candid as to own up to what they actually did).

I opposed my country for what I thought were the noblest of reasons: to advance the cause of "social justice" and "world peace." I have lived to see how wrong I was and how much damage we did— especially to those whose cause we claimed to embrace, in particular the peasants of Indochina who suffered grievously from our support for the communist enemy, but also to our own country. I came to see how precious are the freedoms and opportunities afforded by America to the poorest and most humble of its citizens. And I came to appreciate how rare these virtues are in the world at large.

Among the regrets I have from my radical years is that this country was too tolerant towards the treason of its enemies within. If patriotic Americans had been more vigilant in the defense of their country, if they had called things by their right names, if they had confronted us with the seriousness of our divisive agenda, they might have caught the attention of those of us who were well meaning, if utterly misguided. And they might have stopped us in our tracks.

I have written this for those of you who are out there today, full of righteousness, but who might live to regret what you have done.

2

The Ayatollah of Anti-American Hate

PART I: THE SICK MIND OF NOAM CHOMSKY

WITHOUT QUESTION, the most devious, the most dishonest and—in this hour of his nation's grave crisis—the most treacherous intellect in America belongs to one of America's most influential academics, MIT professor Noam Chomsky. On the 150 campuses where tenured radicals organized "teach-ins" against America's right to defend herself within two weeks of the September 11 attack; on the streets of Genoa and Seattle where "antiglobalist" anarchists have assaulted the symbols of markets and world trade; among the demonstrators at Vieques who wish to deny U.S. military forces their training grounds; and wherever young people manifest an otherwise incomprehensible rage against their country, the inspirer of their loathing and the instructor of their hate is likely to be this man.

There are many who ask how it is possible that our most privileged and educated youth should come to despise their own nation— a free, open, democratic society—and to do so with such ferocious passion. They ask how it is possible for American youth to even consider lending comfort and aid to the Osama bin Ladens and Saddam Husseins (or the communists before them). A full answer would involve a search of the deep structures of the human psyche. But the short answer is to be found in the speeches and writings of an embittered academic and his intellectual followers.

For forty years Noam Chomsky has turned out book after book, pamphlet after pamphlet and speech after speech with one message: America is the Great Satan, the fount of evil in the modern world. In Chomsky's demented universe, America is responsible not only for its own crimes, but for the crimes of others, including those of the terrorists who struck the World Trade Center and the Pentagon on September 11, 2001. Chomsky is the medium for all those who now search the ruins of lower Manhattan not for the victims and the American dead, but for the "root causes" of the catastrophe that befell them.

One little pamphlet of Chomsky's—*What Uncle Sam Really Wants*—has already sold 160,000 copies.[1] But this represents only the tip of the Chomsky iceberg. His venomous message is spread through tapes and cds, and on the campus lecture circuit where he is in extraordinary demand. He is promoted at rock concerts by superstar bands such as Pearl Jam, Rage Against the Machine, and U2 (whose lead singer Bono called Chomsky a "rebel without a pause"). He is the icon of Hollywood stars like Matt Damon whose genius character in the Academy Award-winning film *Good Will Hunting* invokes Chomsky as the ultimate authority for political insight.

According to the *Chicago Tribune*, Noam Chomsky is "the most often cited living author. Among intellectual luminaries of all eras, Chomsky placed eighth, just behind Plato and Sigmund Freud." On the web there are more chat room references to Noam Chomsky than to Vice President Dick Cheney, and ten times as many as there are to the Democrats' congressional leaders, Richard Gephardt and Tom Daschle. This is because Chomsky is also the political mentor of the academic left, the legions of 1960s radicals who have entrenched themselves in American universities to indoctrinate students in their anti-American creeds and who assign Chomsky's books to their vulnerable charges. The *New York Times* calls Chomsky "arguably the most important intellectual alive," and *Rolling Stone* magazine—which otherwise does not even acknowledge the realm of the mind—"one of the most respected and influential intellectuals in the world."[2]

In fact, Chomsky's influence is best understood not as that of an intellectual figure, but as the leader of a secular religious cult—the ayatollah of anti-American hate. This cultic resonance is even recognized by his followers. His most important devotee, David Barsamian, is an obscure public radio producer in Boulder, Colorado, on station KGNU. Barsamian has created a library of Chomsky screeds on tape from interviews he conducted with the master, which he has converted into pamphlets and books as well. In the introduction to one such tract, Barsamian describes Chomsky's power over his disciples in these terms: "Although decidedly secular, he is for many of us our rabbi, our preacher, our rinpoche, our pundit, our Imam, our sensei."[3]

The theology that Chomsky preaches is starkly manichean, with America as its evil principle. For Chomsky, no injustices, however great, can exceed those of America, while America is also the cause of evil in others. This is the Chomsky key to the mystery of September 11: *the devil made them do it*. The root causes of the attack were America's own crimes.

In every one of the 150 shameful "anti-war" demonstrations that took place on America's campuses in the two weeks following the disaster, Chomsky-like ravings provided the twin themes of those who agitated to prevent America from taking up arms and striking back in self-defence: Whatever atrocity has been committed against America, America has committed worse against others. America is responsible for the criminal attacks on itself.

In his first statement on Osama bin Laden's calculated strike on an office building containing thousands of innocent human beings, Chomsky's response was to eclipse it with an even greater crime he was confident he could attribute to former president Bill Clinton. This is how Chomsky's infamous and characteristically elliptical September 12 statement "On the Bombings" began: "The terrorist attacks were major atrocities. In scale they may not reach the level of many others, for example, Clinton's bombing of the Sudan with no credible pretext, destroying half its pharmaceutical supplies and killing unknown numbers of people (no one knows, because the U.S. blocked an inquiry at the UN and no one cares to pursue it)."[4]

Observe the syntax. The opening reference to the actual attacks is clipped and bloodless, a kind of rhetorical throat clearing for Chomsky to get out of the way so that he can announce the real subject of his concern—America's evil. The accusation against Clinton is slipped into the text, weasel fashion, as though it were a modifier, when it is actually the substantive theme itself. It is a message that says: Stop whining, America, at the injury that has been done to you. What else could you expect? Look at the horrors you have done to *them*. Here Chomsky exhibits his gift to the left, which is to make the victim seem an even more heinous perpetrator than the criminal.

In point of fact—and just for the record—Bill Clinton's decision to launch a missile into the Sudan, however ill conceived, was not remotely comparable to the World Trade Center massacre. It was, in its very design, precisely the opposite—a defensive response to an unprovoked attack and an attempt to minimize casualties in the process. Clinton's missile was, in fact, launched in reaction to the blowing up of two U.S. embassies in Africa by Islamic terrorists, the murder of hundreds of innocent people and injury to thousands, of mostly African civilians. In contrast to Clinton's response—and like the September 11 bombing—these acts were designed to maximize mayhem.

By contrast, Clinton's missile strike was shaped by a concern to prevent the loss of innocent life. The missile was fired at night, so that no one would be in the building when it was hit. The target was selected because it was suspected of being a factory producing chemical weapons, not a pharmaceutical plant. Far from being an exceptional outrage, Chomsky's malicious attempt to use this incident in order to diminish the monstrosity of the World Trade Center attack typifies his style of deceit. It is a telling measure of the anti-American dementia that infuses everything he writes and says.

The same psychotic hatred characterized the "historical" perspective he provided in an interview conducted a few days after the World Trade Center bombing. It was calculated to present America as the devil incarnate, a worthy target for the misguided forces of "social justice" all over the world. The atrocity was significant because it was the first time America itself—or as Chomsky put it, the "national territory"—had been attacked since the War of 1812. In Chomsky's calculus the attack on Pearl Harbor wouldn't count because Hawaii was a "colony" at the time. The fact that it was a benignly run colony and is now the proud state of a democratic union of course counts for nothing in Chomsky's twisted vision.

The significance was, of course, that the "Third World" was striking back at America for more than a century of attacks on *its* territory: "During these years [i.e., between 1812 and 1941], the U.S. annihilated the indigenous population (millions of people), conquered half of Mexico, intervened violently in the surrounding region, conquered Hawaii and the Philippines (killing hundreds of thousands of Filipinos), and in the past half century particularly, extended its resort to force throughout much of the world. The number of victims is colossal. For the first time, the guns have been directed the other way. That is a dramatic change."[5] Listening to Noam Chomsky, you can almost feel the justice of Osama bin Laden's cause.

But if you were one of the hundreds of thousands of young people who have been exposed to Chomsky's anti-American propaganda, if you had read, for example, *What Uncle Sam Really Wants*, you could extrapolate justifications for blind terror against the United States in all the years since Pearl Harbor as well. In *What Uncle Sam Really Wants*, you could learn that in the first battle of the Cold War struggle against the Soviet empire, "the United States was picking up where the Nazis had left off."

According to Chomsky, during the Cold War, American operations behind the Iron Curtain included "a 'secret army' under U.S.-Nazi auspices that sought to provide agents and military supplies to armies that had been established by Hitler and which were still operating inside the Soviet Union and Eastern Europe through the early 1950s."

According to Chomsky, U.S. support for legitimate governments against communist subversion in Latin America led to U.S. complicity by John F. Kennedy and Lyndon Johnson, in "the methods of Heinrich Himmler's extermination squads."

According to Chomsky, there is "a close correlation worldwide between torture and U.S. aid."

According to Chomsky, America "invaded" Vietnam in order to slaughter its people. Even after the last American left Vietnam in 1975, under Jimmy Carter and Ronald Reagan "the major policy goal of the U.S. has been to maximize repression and suffering in the countries [of Indo-China] that were devastated by our violence. The degree of the cruelty is quite astonishing."[6]

According to Chomsky, "the pretext for Washington's terrorist wars [he is referring to the attempts in the 1980s and 1990s to rescue the people of Nicaragua, El Salvador, Chile, Guatemala, and Iraq from the clutches of their totalitarian oppressors] was self-defense, the standard official justification for just about any monstrous act, even the Nazi Holocaust." [7]

In sum, according to the man some writer for the *New York Times* once called "arguably the most important intellectual alive," America *is* Nazi Germany and "legally speaking, there's a very solid case for impeaching every American president since the Second World War. They've all been either outright war criminals or involved in serious war crimes."[8]

What decent, caring human being who was persuaded to believe this would not want to see America and its war criminals brought to justice? Anthrax would probably be too good for them.

According to Chomsky—parroting his Marxist teachers[9]—what Uncle Sam really wants is to steal from the poor and give to the rich. America's crusade against communism was not a battle for human freedom, but actually a war "to protect our doctrine that the rich should plunder the poor."[10]

This is why, according to Chomsky, we have busied ourselves in launching a new crusade against what he regards as a mythic terrorism after the end of the Cold War. The end of the Cold War presented new problems for a predatory nation like America. In particular, "the technique for controlling the domestic population has had to shift . . . New enemies have to be invented. It becomes hard to disguise the fact that the real enemy has always been [the poor]— in particular, Third World miscreants who seek to break out of the service role."[11]

Underpinning this perspective on American policy is a cardinal Chomsky principle—that America is motivated by a fear that Third World peoples will seek to prosper on their own (outside the American empire). Those countries who threaten to succeed—in Chomsky's absurd perspective these include all Marxist governments—America regards as "viruses." During the Cold War, according to Chomsky, America's leaders were not really concerned with the expansion of Soviet and Chinese totalitarianism. "Except for a few madmen and nitwits, none feared [communist] conquest—they were afraid of a positive example of successful development." This prompts him to ask: "What do you do when you have a virus? First you destroy it, then you inoculate potential victims, so that the disease does not spread. That's basically the U.S. strategy in the Third World."[12]

No wonder they all want to bomb us.

Schooled in these big lies, taught to see America as the incarnation of Corporate Greed and politically a twin of the Third Reich, why wouldn't young people, with no historical memory, come to believe that the danger facing mankind lies in Washington rather than Baghdad or Kabul?

It would be easy to demonstrate how on every page of every book and in every statement that Chomsky has written the facts are twisted, the political context is distorted and even inverted, and the historical record is systematically traduced. Every piece of evidence Chomsky assembles and every analysis he makes is subordinated to the overweening purpose of his lifework, which is to justify an *idée fixe*—his pathological hatred of his own country.

It would take tedious volumes to rehearse every example, and there really is no need. Every Chomsky argument exists to serve the same repetitive end, transparent in every preposterous claim. Consequently, every refutation of a Chomsky lie exposes all the others. His invidious comparison of Clinton's misguided missile with the monstrous World Trade Center attack is good enough. (As the wittily astute Christopher Hitchens has remarked about this comparison, one obvious distinction between the two is that the terrorist missiles had innocent hostages packed inside them.)

The embarrassing aptness of the terrorists' targets provide an unremarked political problem for American radicals like Chomsky. They know better than to celebrate an event—the blowing up of Wall Street and the prime symbol of the "military-industrial complex"—that caused so many deaths. Yet the destruction of the World Trade Center and the Pentagon in fact represent the realization of their principal agitations and dreams. The destroyed edifices are the very symbols of the American empire with which they have been at war for fifty years. But it is a fact they cannot acknowledge in this moment of national tragedy.

In a memoir warmly profiled in the *New York Times* on the very day of the attack, the 1960s radical terrorist Bill Ayers recorded his personal joy at striking one of these very targets years before: "Everything was absolutely ideal on the day I bombed the Pentagon. The sky was blue. The birds were singing. And the bastards were finally going to get what was coming to them."[13] In the wake of September 11, Ayers—now a "Distinguished Professor of Education at the University of Illinois"—feverishly backtracked however, denying that these revealing sentiments of an "anti-war" leftist meant what they obviously did. Claiming now to be "filled with horror and grief," Ayers attempted to reinterpret his terrorist years as an effort to explore his own struggle with "the intricate relationships between social justice, commitment and resistance."[14] Sure.

Chomsky is so much Ayers's superior at lying that he works the same denial seamlessly into his account of the Trade Center bombing itself. On the day of the attack, the World Trade Center's Twin Towers were filled—as they normally would be—with bankers, brokers, international traders, and corporate lawyers, the hated men and women of the "ruling class." The very people who—according to Chomsky fanatics—run the "global order" in order to rob the poor in behalf of the rich. Before their fall, the Twin Towers were in fact the palace of the Great Satan himself. They were the "Belly of the Beast," the very object of Chomsky's lifelong, soul-devouring, self-righteous wrath. But, like Ayers and every other American radical, Chomsky is too clever and cowardly to admit this. He knows that in the hour of the nation's grief his joy would not only be unseemly but could be dangerous. And so he cynically conceals his true feelings and denies the very reality that took place in these unbelievable words: "The primary victims, as usual, were working people: janitors, secretaries, firemen, etc." As if this mendacity were too transparent, he then lards the lie with another cynical layer: "It is likely to be a crushing blow to Palestinians and other poor and oppressed people."

It is Chomsky's version of the old punchline about the *New York Times*'s end-of-days headline: "WORLD COMING TO AN END. POOR AND OPPRESSED TO SUFFER MOST." The very crassness of this attempt to convert the tragedy into yet another incitement to attack the wealthy tells us more than we probably care to know about Chomsky's standard of human concern.

Chomsky's message to his disciples—the young on our college campuses, the radicals in our streets, the moles in our government offices—is a call to action that needs to be heeded even by those who will never read his rancid works: "The people of the Third World need our sympathetic understanding and, much more than that, they need our help. We can provide them with a margin of survival by internal disruption in the United States. Whether they can succeed against the kind of brutality we impose on them depends in large part on what happens here."[15]

This is the authentic voice of the Fifth Column left. Disruption inside America is exactly what its external enemies seek, and what their terrorist attacks are designed to achieve, and they are also—and ominously—what Noam Chomsky and his treacherous disciples hope to provide.

PART II: THE METHOD OF THE MADNESS

ONE OF THE TYPICAL ILLUSIONS of the Chomsky cult is the belief that its imam is not the unbalanced dervish of anti-American loathing he appears to everyone else, but an analytic giant whose dicta flow from painstaking inquiry into the facts. Chomskyites who read part one of this essay, complained that, "there is not one single comment . . . that contradicts Chomsky's research." Moreover, the refutation of Chomsky was not attempted "by reasoned argument or detailing the errors of fact or logic in his writings and statements, but by character assassination and the trivializing of Chomsky's strongly held beliefs through accusations that they were unpatriotic."[16]

I confess to being a little puzzled by these objections. Having accurately described Chomsky's equation of post–World War II America to Nazi Germany, it did not actually occur to me that further "refutation" would be required. Chomsky's devotees might consider attempting a defense of their guru's sanity instead. On the other hand, the adulators of the MIT professor do share a group psychosis with those who once worshiped seers like Lenin, Stalin, and Kim Il Sung, also regarded in their day as geniuses of the progressive faith.

Now to the factual refutation.

Chomsky's little bestseller, *What Uncle Sam Really Wants*, draws on U.S. actions in the Cold War to portray America as the evil genie in world affairs.[17] As Chomsky believers are quick to point out, a lot of facts do appear in his text. In fact, they only appear to be facts in his text. A closer look shows that each has been ripped out of any meaningful historical context and then so violently distorted the result is as connected to the real world as the fantasies in Harry Potter's *Muggles Guide to Magic*.

In *What Uncle Sam Really Wants*, the bipolar world of the Cold War is portrayed as though there were only one pole, a distinction that renders every statement about the respective actors false. In the real world, the Cold War was about America's effort to organize a democratic coalition against an expansionist empire that conquered and enslaved more than a billion people. The Cold War ended when the Soviet empire collapsed and the walls that kept its victims locked up came tumbling down. In Chomsky's contrived world, the Soviet empire hardly exists. Not a single American action is seen as a response to a Soviet initiative.

This would be like writing a history of the Second World War without mentioning Hitler, or noticing that the actions of the Axis powers had any influence on its events. In Chomsky's malevolent hands, matters get even worse. If one were to follow the Chomsky method in analyzing World War II, one would list every problematic act committed by any element in the vast coalition attempting to stop Hitler, and would attribute them all to a calculated policy of the United States. One would then provide a report card of these "crimes" as if it were the historical record itself. The list of the worst acts of which the allies could be accused and the most dishonorable motives they may be said to have acted upon would provide the database from which America's portrait would be drawn. Using this method, even a moron could come up with a picture of America as the Great Satan.

What Uncle Sam Really Wants begins with America's emergence from the Second World War. It portrays the United States in contrast to its "industrial rivals," as having "benefited enormously" from the conflict—omitting from its account any mention of the 250,000 lives America lost, its generous Marshall Plan aid to those same rivals after the war, or for that matter, the role it played in the victory over Nazi Germany and the Axis powers. In this portrait, America in 1945 has no interest in rebuilding devastated nations, but is, instead, a wealthy power whose only aim is to profit from others' misery and aspire to world domination. "The people who determine American policy were carefully planning how to shape the postwar world," he asserts without evidence. "American planners—from those in the State Department to those on the Council on Foreign Relations (one major channel by which business leaders influence foreign policy)—agreed that the dominance of the United States had to be maintained."[18]

Chomsky never names the people who agreed that American policy should be world dominance, nor how they achieved unanimity in deciding to transform a famously isolationist country into a global power.[19] In Chomsky's political science, America has no internal politics that matter. Therefore, Chomsky does not acknowledge, let alone attempt to analyze, the powerful strains of isolationism not only in American policy, but in the Republican Party—in those days the very party of Wall Street and the Council on Foreign Relations businessmen who he claims exert such influence on American purposes. Above all, he does not explain why—if world domination was really America's goal in 1945—America disbanded its wartime armies overnight and brought its troops home.

Between 1945 and 1946, in fact, America demobilized 1.6 million military personnel. By contrast, the Soviet Union (absent as usual from Chomsky's narrative) kept its two-million-man army occupying the countries of Eastern Europe, whose governments it had already begun to systematically undermine and destroy. It was, in fact, the Soviet absorption of the formerly independent states of Eastern Europe in the years between 1945 and 1948 that triggered America's subsequent rearmament, the creation of NATO, and the overseas spread of American power. All these steps were designed to contain an ex-

pansionist Soviet empire and prevent a repetition of the appeasement process that had led to World War II.

These little facts are overlooked in Chomsky's text or contemp-
tuously dismissed ("Except for a few madmen and nitwits, none feared
[communist] conquest…".). Yet they determine everything that followed, particularly America's global military presence. There is no
historical basis for Chomsky's approach other than the desire to frame
his indictment of Uncle Sam. The events that led to the end of the
Cold War, on the other hand, have conclusively refuted Chomsky's
viewpoint and shown that the Cold War itself—the formation of
the postwar western alliances and the mobilizing of western forces—
were principally brought about by the Soviet conquest of Eastern
Europe. That is why the end of the Cold War came as soon as the
Berlin Wall fell, and the states of Eastern Europe were freed to pursue their independent paths. It was to accomplish this great liberation of several hundred million people—and not any American quest
for world domination—that explains American Cold War policy. But
there is no attempt to address these facts in Chomsky's pages. They
might as well never have happened.

Having begun the story of the Cold War with an utterly false
picture of the historical forces at work in creating it, Chomsky is
ready to carry out his scorched earth campaign against the democracy that has provided him with a privileged—and free—existence
for more than seventy years. "In 1949," Chomsky writes, "U.S. espionage in Eastern Europe had been turned over to a network run by
Reinhard Gehlen, who had headed Nazi military intelligence on the
Eastern Front. This network was one part of the U.S.-Nazi alliance."[20]

This smear, an exemplary display of the Chomsky method, is
breathtaking and worth a moment to consider. In less than a small
pamphlet page, Chomsky jumps from 1945 to 1949, skipping over
the little matter of the Red Army's refusal to withdraw its armies

from Eastern Europe, the swallowing of those independent regimes, and the establishment of Moscow-controlled police states in their stead. He has ignored the aggressive moves of the huge Moscow-directed communist parties of Italy and France agitating for the overthrow of their war-weakened governments and the absorption of both countries into the Soviet bloc. Instead of these matters, the reader is confronted with a small episode in the efforts of the U.S. to counter these threats by using an existing intelligence apparatus of the defeated German power.

The fact adduced—that the United States sought to draw on German intelligence expertise—can appear shocking in isolation from the larger realities. By introducing it out of the blue, Chomsky maximizes the shock. But he also grossly distorts it. First, Gehlen was an army intelligence officer and not a member of the ss or the Nazi Party. More importantly, the United States used Gehlen—not the other way around, as his devious syntax implies ("U.S. espionage ... had been turned over ... to Gehlen"). But even these distortions are insufficient for his malignant purposes, so he casually creates a really Big Lie by inflating what was a minor compromise of convenience into a major act of betrayal. Despite Chomsky's assertion, there was never a "U.S.-Nazi alliance." The United States had crushed Nazi Germany four years earlier, and by 1949—unlike the Soviet Union—had imposed a democracy on West Germany's political structure as a condition of a German peace. By contrast, East Germany, which remained under Soviet military control and political tutelage, remained a brutal, anti-Semitic police state.

Given these realities—whose significance a less dishonest writer than Chomsky might have weighed—the use of a West German military intelligence network with assets both in Eastern Europe and the Soviet Union was a reasonable compromise to defend the democratic states of the West and the innocent lives of the subjects of Soviet rule. Particularly since the Soviets were running a ruthless totalitarian empire almost identical in structure and method to Nazi Germany itself.[21] Spy work is dirty work as everyone recognizes. But far from being a "Nazi" taint on America, this episode was a necessary part of America's Cold War effort in the cause of human freedom. With the help of the Gehlen network, the United States kept Soviet expansion in check and eventually liberated hundreds of millions of oppressed people in Eastern Europe from the horrors of the communist system.

Chomsky describes all the postwar events not only without reference to the horrors of the Soviet empire or the eventual liberation that American policy produced, but as though the United States rather than having defeated Hitler, had instead made a pact to continue his regime: "These [U.S.] operations included a 'secret army' under U.S.-Nazi auspices that sought to provide agents and military supplies to armies that had been established by Hitler and which were still operating inside the Soviet Union and Eastern Europe through the early 1950s."[22] This typical Chomsky inversion of the truth—the restoration of democracy through American commitment—is as brazen as the propaganda the Kremlin distributed in those years, from which it is cynically cribbed.

The equation of American Cold War policies with Nazi Germany is the principle motif of Chomsky's account of the postwar era. Establishing a Nazi world order—with business interests at the top and the "working classes and the poor" at the bottom—was America's true postwar agenda. Therefore, "the major thing that stood in the way of this was the anti-fascist resistance, so we suppressed it all over the world, often installing fascists and Nazi collaborators in its place."[23] Such claims give conspiracy theories a bad name.

In 1947, a civil war in Greece became the first test of America's resolve to prevent the Soviet empire from spreading beyond Eastern

Europe. Naturally Chomsky presents the conflict as a struggle between the "anti-Nazi resistance" and U.S.-backed (and "Nazi") interests. In Chomsky's words, these interests were "U.S. investors and
local businessmen," and—of course—"the beneficiaries included Nazi
collaborators, while the primary victims were the workers and the
peasants."[24]

In reality, the leaders of the anti-communist forces in Greece
were not Nazis. On the other hand, what Chomsky refers to as the
"anti-Nazi resistance" was in fact the Communist Party and its fellow-traveling pawns. What Chomsky leaves out of his account, as a
matter of course and necessity, is the proximity of the Soviet Red
Army to Greece and the intention of the Greek communists to establish a Soviet police state should they win the civil war. Chomsky
ignores the enormously positive result of America's intervention. The
defeat of the Greek communist left paved the way for an unprecedented economic development benefiting all social classes and the
eventual establishment of a political democracy, which soon brought
democratic socialists to power rather than the capitalist servants of
American interests Chomsky's worldview would predict.

Needless to say, no country in which Chomsky's "anti-fascists"
won—and there were several—ever established a democracy or produced any significant betterment in the economic conditions of the
great mass of its inhabitants. These countries included Hungary,
Rumania, Czechoslovakia, Yugoslavia, Poland, Bulgaria, Albania,
Lithuania, Estonia, and Latvia, among others. These results of
Europe's civil wars put a markedly different color on every detail of
what happened in Greece and elsewhere, and how U.S. actions should
be judged.

The pivotal chapter of *What Uncle Sam Really Wants* is called
"The Threat of A Good Example." It is the Chomsky paradox with
which, as mentioned earlier, he proposes to explain America's dia-

bolical behavior in Third World countries. Chomsky prefaces his explanation with the paradox of America's alleged preference for atrocity when dealing with Third World leftists, which might seem uncharacteristic and unbusiness-like to anyone actually familiar with Americans and American institutions. "What the U.S.-run contra forces did in Nicaragua, or what our terrorist proxies do in El Salvador or Guatemala, isn't only ordinary killing. A major element is brutal, sadistic torture—beating infants against rocks, hanging women by their feet with their breasts cut off and the skin of their face peeled back so that they'll bleed to death, chopping people's heads off and putting them on stakes."[25] "U.S.-run" forces and "our terrorist proxies" do this sort of thing routinely and everywhere: "No country is exempt from this treatment, no matter how unimportant."[26]

There are no citations in Chomsky's text to support the claim either that these atrocities took place, or that the United States directed them, or that the United States was in any meaningful way responsible for them. Nor would it ever occur to Chomsky that these atrocities might be indigenous to the countries themselves (and the "proxies" involved), or that the atrocities might be carried out on both sides of any conflict occurring in them.

Chomsky then introduces his paradox, the "observation" that U.S. business is the evil hand behind all of America's foreign policies, yet many of those into which such atrocities are injected are not really important to these interests. "As far as American business is concerned, Nicaragua could disappear and nobody would notice. The same is true of El Salvador. But both have been subjected to murderous assaults by the U.S., at a cost of hundreds of thousands of lives and many billions of dollars."[27] The explanation is provided by the Chomsky paradox: "the weaker and poorer a country is, the more dangerous it is *as an example* [italics in original]. If a tiny, poor country like Grenada can succeed in bringing about a better life for its people, some other place that has more resources will ask, 'why not us?'"[28]

The Chomsky paradox—the pivot of his entire view of American foreign policy and postwar history—turns out to be particularly absurd. The logic goes like this: What Uncle Sam really wants is to control the world; U.S. control means absolute misery for all the peoples that come under its sway; this means the U.S. cannot allow any little country anywhere in the world to realize that there might be better ways to develop its resources than through free market institutions or by allowing U.S. investment. Take Grenada. "Grenada has a hundred thousand people who produce a little nutmeg, and you could hardly find it on a map. But when Grenada began to undergo a mild social revolution, Washington quickly moved to destroy the threat."[29] This is Chomsky's entire commentary on the U.S. intervention in Grenada.

In fact, something quite different took place in Grenada. In 1979, there was a coup in Grenada that established a Marxist dictatorship complete with a Soviet-style "politburo." This was a tense period in the Cold War. The Soviet Union had invaded Afghanistan, and communist guerrillas armed by Cuba were spreading their totalitarian influences in Central America. Then, in the early 1980s, Cuban military personnel appeared in Grenada and began building a new airport capable of accommodating Soviet nuclear bombers. Tensions over the uncompleted airport quickly developed between Washington and the Grenadian dictatorship. In 1983, in the midst of these tensions, there was another coup. This one was led by the Marxist minister of defense who assassinated the Marxist dictator and half his politburo, including his pregnant minister of education. The new dictator put the entire island—including U.S. citizens resident there—under house arrest. It was at this point that the Reagan Administration decided it was time to send the Marines to protect U.S. citizens, stop the construction of the military airport, and restore democracy to the little island.

Nor was the United States the only government concerned about the events in Grenada. The U.S. intervention was made at the formal request of four governments of Caribbean countries who feared a communist military presence in their neighborhood. Finally, a public opinion poll taken after the U.S. operation showed that 85 percent of the citizens of Grenada welcomed the U.S. intervention and America's help in restoring their freedom.[30]

There was no "threat of a good example" in Grenada. More importantly, there are none anywhere in the world of progressive social experiments. There is not a single Marxist country anywhere that has ever provided a "good example" in the sense of making its economy better or its people freer. Chomsky seems to have missed this most basic fact of twentieth-century history: Socialism doesn't work.

The example of Korea, a Cold War battlefield, provides as conclusive a case as one could expect. Fifty years ago, in one of the Cold War's early conflicts, the United States military prevented communist North Korea from conquering the anti-communist South. Today communist North Korea has achieved Chomsky's dream of being independent of the United States but—contrary to his paradox— is one of the poorest countries in the world. A million of its citizens have starved in recent years, even while its Marxist dictator was feverishly investing its scarce capital in an intercontinental ballistic missile program. In South Korea, by contrast, there are fifty thousand U.S. troops stationed along the border not—as Chomsky would maintain—to occupy it, but to defend it from a communist attack from the desperate North. For fifty years, nefarious U.S. businesses and self-interested U.S. investors have operated freely in South Korea. The results are interesting. In 1950, South Korea had a per capita income of $250 and was as poor as Cuba or Vietnam. Today South

Korea is an industrial power and its per capita income is $8,490, more than thirty times greater than it was before it became an ally and investment region of the United States—or as Chomsky would insist, an exploited "neo-colony" of American capitalism. Meanwhile, independent Vietnam's per capita income is $370, not much more than it was fifty years ago. America's protégé, South Korea, is not yet a full-fledged democracy but it does have elections, a multiparty political system, and an independent press that provides its people with information from the outside world. This is quite different from socialist North Korea's starving population whose citizens are ruled by a one-party state and have no access to information their dictator does not approve. Who do you think is afraid of the threat of a good example? Chomsky's friends or Washington's?

The "threat of a good example" is the same utopian nonsense that inspired the progressives of the last century to kill 100 million people. Soviet communism—which America's dedicated Cold Warriors finally vanquished—was an imperialist system that ruined nations and enslaved their citizens. But Chomsky—who spent the Cold War enjoying America's freedoms while relentlessly attacking America itself—still dismisses America's fear of communism as a mere "cover" for its own diabolical schemes. Far from acknowledging America's historic, progressive achievement, he explains the Cold War and one of its lost battles—the Vietnam War—this way: "The real fear was that if the people of Indochina achieved independence and justice, the people of Thailand would emulate it, and if that worked, they'd try it in Malaya, and pretty soon Indonesia would pursue an independent path, and by then a significant area [of America's empire] would have been lost."[31]

An exceptionally crude Marxist version of the domino theory, this was already transparently false by the time Chomsky came to write his little booklet. Contrary to his claims, America did leave Indochina—Cambodia and Thailand included—in 1973 and in 1975. For the next twenty-five years, Vietnam pursued an independent path, yet, no good example ensued. The communist utopia was as still-born in Vietnam as everywhere else. Todya, Vietnam is as poor as it ever was—one of the poorest nations in the entire world—and its people still suffer under the harsh rule of a primitive Marxist police state.

After its defeat in Vietnam, the United States withdrew its military forces from the entire Indochinese peninsula, something Chomsky, along with the rest of the left, had fiercely denied it would ever do. The result was that Cambodia was overrun by the Khmer Rouge—in other words, by the communist forces that Vietnam's communists along with Chomsky and the entire American left had supported until then. Freed from American military interference, the Khmer Rouge proceeded to kill two million Cambodians who, in their view, stood in the way of the progressive "good example" they intended to create. At the time, Chomsky earned himself a bad reputation by first denying and then minimizing the Cambodian genocide until the facts overwhelmed his case. Now, of course, he blames its killing fields on the United States.

Chomsky also blames the United States for the fact that "Vietnam is a basket case" and not a good example. "Our basic goal—the crucial one, the one that really counted—was to destroy the virus [of independent development], and we did achieve that. Vietnam is a basket case, and the U.S. is doing what it can to keep it that way." This is Chomsky's excuse for the failure of Vietnamese communism (which is no different from the failure of every communist state). It is the all-purpose leftist excuse.[32] *The devil made them do it*. As Chomsky knows, Vietnamese communists were Marxists. Marxism is a crackpot theory that doesn't work. Every Marxist state has been an economic basket case. So why not Vietnam's?

Take an illustrative counterexample: Cuba is a Marxist state that has not been bombed and has not suffered a war, but it is still an economic "basket case," poorer today than it was more than forty years ago when Castro took power in 1959. Then, Cuba was the second richest country in Latin America. Now it is the third poorest just before Haiti and Nicaragua (also ruined by Marxist fanatics). Naturally Chomskyites will claim that the U.S. economic boycott is responsible for Cuba's dramatic economic decline. *The devil made them do it.* But, this is just more tired commie claptrap. The rest of the world trades with Cuba, and has traded with Cuba all forty-plus years. Cuba is not only free to buy and sell goods to all of Latin America and Europe, but also to receive millions of dollars in aid in the process. Moreover, in the 1970s and 1980s the Soviet Union gave Cuba the equivalent of three Marshall Plans in economic subsidies and assistance—tens of billions of dollars for an island of less than ten million people.

Cuba is a fertile country with a tropical climate. It's failure is human and internal. It is poor because it has followed Chomsky's example, not America's. It is poor because it is socialist, Marxist, and communist and has wasted all the economic resources it has been given on delusional social schemes. Cuba is poor because the state is run by a sadistic lunatic, whose brain has been unhinged by years of sycophantic adulation inspired by serious police repression and legendary sunless prisons. Cuba is poor because in Cuba, America lost the Cold War. Its poverty is what Chomsky's vision would create for the entire world.

It is the communist-Chomsky illusion that there is a way to prosperity other than the way of the capitalist market that causes the economic misery of states like Cuba and North Korea and Vietnam, and would have caused the equivalent misery of Grenada and Greece and South Korea if America had not intervened militarily and stopped the Chomsky reactionaries in their tracks.

The illusion that socialism will provide a better future is not only the cause of mass poverty and death in the countries seduced by its followers, it is also the cause of the Chomsky cult. It is the illusion itself, the messianic hope, that creates the progressive left. This hope is a chimera, and it creates a worldview that is strictly Manichaean. Those who oppose socialism, Marxism, communism, Chomskyism, embody worldly evil. They are the party of Satan, and their leader, America, is the Great Satan itself. Chomskyism is, like its models, a religion of social hate.

Chomsky's great service to the progressive faith is to deny the history of the last hundred years, a history of progressive atrocity and failure. In the twentieth century, progressives in power killed one hundred million people in the attempt to realize their impossible dreams and made the lives of whole continents miserable and poor.[33] But as far as Noam Chomsky is concerned these progressive catastrophes never happened. "I don't much like the terms left and right," Chomsky complains in yet another ludicrous Barsamian screed *The Common Good*.[34] "What's called the left includes Leninism [i.e., communism], which I consider ultra-right in many respects. . . . Leninism has nothing to do with the values of the left—in fact, it's radically opposed to them."[35]

You have to pinch yourself when reading sentences like that.

The purpose of such Humpty-Dumpty mutilations of language is perfectly understandable. It is to preserve the faith for those who cannot live without some form of the communist creed. Communism is dead. Long live the Revolution. Communist catastrophes can have "nothing to do with the values of the left" because if they did, the left would have to answer for the evil it has done and confront the fact that it is intellectually and morally bankrupt as a move-ment. Progressives would have to face the fact that they killed one hundred million people for nothing—for an idea that didn't work.

And that now they're at it again.

The real "threat of a good example" is the American system, which has lifted more people out of poverty—within its borders and all over the world—than all the socialists and progressives collectively since the beginning of time. To neutralize this threat, it is necessary to kill the memory of American achievement along with the Ameri-can idea. This is, in fact, Noam Chomsky's mission in life, and his everlasting infamy.

3

A 1960s Terrorist Cult and 9/11

ON THE MORNING OF THE WORLD TRADE CENTER ATTACK, along with a million other readers of the *New York Times* including many who would never be able to read the paper again, I opened its pages to a large color photo that showed a middle-aged couple holding hands and affecting a defiant look at the camera. In an irony that could not have been more poignant, the article was headlined "No Regrets for a Love of Explosives." The couple pictured were Bill Ayers and Bernardine Dohrn, former leaders of the 1960s' Weather Underground, America's first terrorist cult. One of their bombing targets, as it happened, was the Pentagon.

"I don't regret setting bombs," Ayers was quoted in the opening line of the *Times* profile: "I feel we didn't do enough." In 1969, Ayers and his wife convened a "war council" in Flint, Michigan, whose purpose was to launch a military front inside the United States with the purpose of helping Third World revolutionaries conquer and destroy it. Taking charge of the podium, dressed in high-heeled boots and a leather miniskirt—her signature uniform—Dohrn urged the assembled radicals to join the war against "Amerikkka" and create chaos and destruction in the "belly of the beast." Her voice rising to a fevered pitch, Dohrn raised three fingers in a "fork salute" to mass murderer Charles Manson, whom she proposed as a symbol to her troops. Referring to the helpless victims of the Manson Family as the "Tate Eight" (the most famous was actress Sharon Tate), Dohrn shouted: "Dig It. First they killed those pigs, then they ate dinner in the same room with them; they even shoved a fork into a victim's stomach! Wild!"

Embarrassed today by this memory, but unable to expunge it from the record and unwilling to repudiate her radical past, Dohrn resorts to denial. "It was a joke," she told the sympathetic *Times* reporter, Dinitia Smith. She was actually protesting America's crimes: "We were mocking violence in America. Even in my most inflamed moment I never supported a racist mass murderer." In 1980, I conducted interviews with thirty members of the Weather Underground who were present at the Flint war council, including most of its top leadership.[1] Not one of them thought Dohrn was anything but deadly serious. Outrageous nihilism was the Weatherman political style. As soon as her tribute to Manson was completed, Dohrn was followed to the Flint platform by another Weather leader who ranted, "We're against everything that's 'good and decent' in honky America. We will loot and burn and destroy. We are the incubation of your mothers' nightmares."[2] Some joke.

It has long been a fashion among media sophisticates to ridicule the late J. Edgar Hoover and the FBI men who sought to protect Americans from the threats posed by radicals like Ayers and Dohrn in their "days of rage." But Hoover's description of Bernardine Dohrn as "La Pasionara of the lunatic left" is far more accurate than anything that can be found in Dinitia Smith's *Times* profile.

Instead of a critique of this malignant couple and their destructive resume, the *Times* provides a soft-focus promotion for Ayers's newly published *Fugitive Days*, a memoir notable for its dishonesty and the unreflective celebration of his malevolent exploits. Ayers' text wallows in familiar Marxist incitements and the homicidal delusions of 1960s radicalism, including the loving reprint of an editorial from the old socialist magazine *Alarm!* written by Albert Parsons, one of the Haymarket anarchists, whom the Weathermen idolized: "Dynamite! Of all the good stuff, that is the stuff! Stuff several pounds of this sublime stuff into an inch pipe . . . plug up both ends, insert a cap with a fuse attached, place this in the immediate vicinity of a lot of rich loafers who live by the sweat of other people's brows, and light the fuse. A most cheerful and gratifying result will follow. In giving dynamite to the downtrodden millions of the globe, science has done its best work."

In *Fugitive Days*, Ayers has written—and the *Times* promoted— a text that the bombers of the World Trade Center could have packed in their flight bags alongside the Koran as they embarked on their fatal mission. They might have underscored this passage: "Everything was absolutely ideal on the day I bombed the Pentagon. The sky was blue. The birds were singing. And the bastards were finally going to get what was coming to them."

"Memory is a motherf——r," Ayers warns his readers, in the illiterate style that made him an icon of the fringes of the New Left. It is as close as he gets to acknowledging that his account leaves World Trade Center size holes in the story of his criminal past. Among them is the story of how the Weathermen imploded in the year other Americans were celebrating the bicentennial of their nation. The revolutionary romance came to an end because the devotion of the terrorists to the tenets of the faith eventually led them into a series of brainwashing rituals and purges that decimated their ranks. None of this is remembered in Ayers's book. Nor is the passage of their closest comrades into the ranks of the May Nineteenth

Communist Movement, which murdered three officers—including the first black policeman on the Nanuet force during an infamous robbery of a Brinks armored car in 1981. The point of Ayers's omissions is to hide from others (and from himself) the real-world consequences of the anti-American ideas which took root in the 1960s and still flourish on the nation's college campuses today.

Today William Ayers is not merely an author favored by the *Times*, but a Distinguished Professor of Education at the University of Illinois. His Lady Macbeth is also a professor, the director of Northwestern University's Children and Family Justice Center. Their status reflects how fashionable was the culture of facile defamation of America on the eve of the September 11 attack.

President Bush has correctly defined the repulsive deed that has left thousands dead as an "act of war." It is a recognition postponed for almost a decade by an Administration infused with the attitudes of self-flagellation and moral equivalence, perfectly expressed on the day of the attack by the *New Yorker*'s John Lahr, who advised America to "Rush to Thought, Not to Judgment": "I fear the hysteria in the American character, which splits so easily into good and bad, which rushes to judgment rather than to thought. The terrorists have taken aim at the American government and American capitalism and brought them both—symbolically at least—down. America, from the point of view of the terrorists, has been humiliated and brutalized as they feel they have felt humiliated and brutalized by America."

The hysteria in the *American* character! This same character permitted fanatical America haters to bomb the World Trade Center not once but twice without instituting serious security controls at its airports. America the brutalizer! Osama bin Laden, our terrorist enemy, is not exactly one of the huddled masses. He is a Saudi prince. Sheik Abdel Rahman, the "spiritual" leader of the first World Trade

Center bombing is a sheik. Brutalization is not their problem. They *are* brutes. Like other radical zealots they are driven by religious fanaticism, confident that infidels are worthy of destruction. In Palestinian schools in democratic Israel, school children are taught by their teachers to chant "Destroy the heathen Jews." Not those who have injured them, but those who are not Muslims.

On the day of the World Trade Center bombing, I appeared on a Fox television program in San Diego and did my best to steer the discussion towards the steps America must take to defend herself, to strike back. But the host would have none of it. While thousands of Americans writhed in agony in the twisted steel of the Trade Center, she wanted to discuss the danger of American "hysteria," the "threat" that American prejudice might pose to Muslims in our midst. It did not even occur to her that if Americans were prejudiced in a way that made this issue pressing, these terrorists would never have been trained as pilots by American companies, housed in American homes, or ignored by American security agents at the airports where they hijacked airliners in order to convert them into bombs.

While the embers of the World Trade Center were still warm, we were treated to television images of college students attempting to shift the blame for the atrocity to American shoulders. The political friends of Bill Ayers and Bernardine Dohrn have been busily at work for the last two decades seeding our educational culture with anti-American poisons that could one day destroy us.

A visit to a well-traveled website "for the progressive community"—www.commondreams.org—reveals how profoundly America has been rejected, and how passionately its bloodthirsty enemies have been embraced, by significant sections of our population, even as we enter a life-and-death struggle with an enemy that wants so much to exterminate us:

- "Not only have we caused these events with our monstrous foreign policies but also with our complete disregard of our environment causing mortal damage to the Earth (Earth is a living being) and other species that co-exist with us."

- "My heart went out to all the people there as I sat watching, waiting ... and then sadness filled me, sadness that the foreign policy of this country has come back to haunt us; sadness that our government has been so arrogant that a lesson like this occurred. . . . It is U.S. policies of terror in other countries that have brought this down on us."

- "Our corporate entities not only run this country but have decimated many other small countries in ways we cannot even fathom. . . . This is a wake-up call America. It is time to change our ways."

- "We are reaping what we have sown. We will now have the dreaded opportunity to live in the same fear that our financial policies and military assistance have inflicted on others."

- "For fifty-six years Washington has successfully conducted mass murders."

- "The United States conducts itself as a terrorist organization throughout the world."

- "U.S. foreign policy has come home to roost today . . . we are reaping what we have sown."

America, the Great Satan.

Actually, these comments are merely lifted from bin Laden's friend, Saddam Hussein, whose response to the Trade Center attacks was as follows: "Notwithstanding the conflicting human feelings about what happened in America yesterday, America is reaping the thorns sown by its rulers in the world. Those thorns have not only bloodied the feet and the hearts of many, but also the eyes of people shedding tears on their dead whose souls have been reaped by America." Saddam then invoked a litany of misdeeds that could have come from a primer written by Noam Chomsky, Howard Zinn, or any number of familiar leftist professors: "There is no place that does not have a symbolic monument that shows America's criminal acts against these victims, whether in Japan that was the first to be seared by the nuclear destruction weapons boasted by America, or Vietnam, Iraq . . . or the criminal acts the U.S. is now perpetrating by supporting the criminal racist Zionism against our heroic Palestinian people."

This is the banal excuse of common criminals—*the devil made me do it.* "I don't think you can understand a single thing we did," explains the pampered Ayers "without understanding the violence of the Vietnam War." I interviewed Ayers twenty years ago, in a kindergarten classroom in uptown Manhattan where he was employed to nurture the minds of inner city children. Dressed in bib overalls with golden curls rolling below his ears, Ayers recounted his activities as a terrorist for my tape recorder. When he was done, he broke into a broad, Jack Horner grin and summed up the tale he had just told: "Guilty as hell. Free as a bird. America is a great country."

Bill Ayers is a scion of wealth. His father was head of Detroit's giant utility Commonwealth Edison, in line for a cabinet position in the Nixon Administration before his son ruined it by going on a rampage that to this day he cannot explain in a way a reasonable person might comprehend. It could be said of Bill Ayers that he was consumed by angers so terrible they led him to destroy his father's career. But in the ten hours I interviewed him, I saw none of it. What I saw was a shallowness beyond conception. All the Weather leaders I interviewed shared a similar vacuity. They were living inside a utopian fantasy, a separate reality, and had no real understanding of what they had done. Nor any way to measure it. Appreciating the nation to which they were born, recognizing the great gifts of freedom and opportunity their parents and communities had given them, distinguishing between right and wrong—it was all above their mental and moral ceilings.

4

The President's Pardoned Bombers

URING THE SUMMER DAYS, the Santa Monica promenade is a mecca for pleasure seekers and the curious. Its bricked sidewalks are crowded with Angelenos gawking at the antics of mimes, jugglers, and break-dancers who put on a good show that is also free. In August 2001, just before the World Trade Center bombing, I was taking a Saturday evening stroll with my wife past these sights, when I was given the opportunity to see one of Bill Clinton's infamous pardons in action—out of prison and back on the streets.

The last time I saw Linda Evans was thirty-two years before, in Berkeley, speaking to a packed hall of student radicals at the university. Evans was one of the leaders of the Weathermen, then a new radical sect that had taken over the national student organization SDS and destroyed it because it wasn't revolutionary enough. She had come to the university with fellow militant Ted Gold to recruit troops for the global race war the Weathermen believed had already begun. The only role white radicals could play in this war, they said, was to serve as a Fifth Column of saboteurs and terrorists inside the "belly of the beast," which is the way the left referred (and still refers) to America. White radicals were needed to blow things up, sow social chaos, and hasten "Amerikkka's" destruction (which is the way they spelled their country's name). "Vietnam is burning," Evans screamed at the audience. "It's only white skin privilege that prevents American cities from being burned too." Everyone present knew what this meant. Berkeley deserved to be put to the torch. Only our racism stopped us from lighting the match.

The year was 1969. A few months later, Evans and Gold disappeared from sight and into what the "communiqués" issued by their leader Bernardine Dohrn identified as the Weather Underground. The first of these communiqués was a formal declaration of war against the United States. Shortly thereafter, three of the Weathermen were blown up in a Greenwich Village townhouse while making a bomb filled with roofing nails which they intended to detonate at a dance at nearby Fort Dix. Ted Gold was one of the three. Months later, Linda Evans was arrested for transporting weapons and explosives in Detroit, and for crossing state lines to incite a riot. The charges were eventually thrown out on a technicality: the wiretaps that identified her had been unauthorized.

On her release, Evans resumed her anti-American activities as a self-styled fighter against "racism/white supremacy and Zionism" and as a supporter of communist movements in Central America. In a profile on a "political prisoners" support website, her activities in these years are described as "working to develop clandestine resistance, capable of conducting armed struggle as part of a multi-level overall revolutionary strategy." On May 11, 1985, she was arrested again, charged, and then convicted for acquiring weapons, fake IDs and safe houses, and of terrorist actions. Her targets included the U.S. Capitol Building, the National War College, the Navy Yard Computer Center, the Navy Yard Officers Club, Israeli Aircraft Industries, the FBI, and the New York Patrolman's Benevolent Association. In her possession were 740 pounds of dynamite. Evans was sentenced to forty years in prison.

But then her Clinton patrons intervened. The agent of her mercy was the blimpish New York congressman Jerry Nadler, one of President Clinton's staunchest defenders during the impeachment process and one of Senator Clinton's chief supporters during her election bid. Nadler appealed to Clinton and the President responded. As the last hours of the Clinton era expired, Linda Evans was freed. It was twenty-four years shy of her full sentence.

The serendipity that brought me into Linda Evans's presence a second time was a glance into the window display of the Midnight Special Bookstore, a radical haunt on the Santa Monica promenade, which featured anti-Bush posters and Noam Chomsky tracts, along with choice events on the progressive calendar. In the window display, I noticed an announcement that Evans would be presenting a film and talk that evening about "political prisoners."

When my wife and I entered the store, we saw that about thirty people had seated themselves on folding chairs in the back to watch the film, which was almost over. We sat through a sequence that featured Laura Whitehorn, a member of Evans's radical network who had been released on parole. At the conclusion of the film, which scrolled a long list of "political prisoners" still in jail, Evans herself appeared and asked the audience to form a circle around her. I had remembered her as a small, fiery, blond woman, with a pretty face hardened and flushed by revolutionary fervor. She was softer now, actually teary-eyed from watching the film of her comrades (as she referred to them) who were still in prison.

As she wiped her tears and apologized for the show of emotion, I noticed that the years had piled flesh on her petite frame giving her a roly-poly look and making her seem softer still. There was no hard edge to her voice as she began to explain how people were oppressed in prison and oppressed in America, and how their oppressors were white racism and imperialism. I wondered to myself how the other listeners squared this dark picture of things with the carnival of Saturday night revelers on the promenade. But Evans gave no thought to this cognitive dissonance at all. Instead, she pursued her tales of social woe, focusing on one of her comrades who had been denied even the ability to attend her prison pottery classes because of "the arthritis in her hands," as if this were yet another injustice inflicted by the System with which she was still obviously at war.

Her very solicitousness suggested the leader of a help group for the victims of unspeakable crimes who were ignored or forgotten by everybody else. In addition to cop-killer Mumia Abu Jamal, the most famous "political prisoner" on the list at the end of the film, Evans mentioned three comrades, in particular, who were in need of support. These were Sara Jane Olson, Jamil Al-Amin, and Kathy Boudin.

The very first questioner from the audience asked Evans what it was that these individuals had done to be singled out for such punishment. Evans seemed a little uncomfortable with the question from such an audience. In her answer, she singled out Olson and Brown because both had trials scheduled for the fall. Olson, she said, was accused of attempting to "fire bomb" a police car, hesitating over the words "fire" and "bomb" as though it was still an effort for her to lie about such things. In fact it was pipe bombs that Olson had randomly planted under *two* police cars, which would have killed the occupants if they hadn't malfunctioned first. "It didn't even go off," Evans griped, as though the failure to succeed in murdering one's victim absolved one for the criminal intent.

She proceeded then to the next level of excuse. After failing at this final revolutionary mission twenty-five years before, Olson had changed her name, which was really Kathy Soliah, and had lived as the wife of a doctor in Minnesota and raised three children. This fact was then used to underscore the sinister character of the state, which was so determined to prosecute her that it was charging her with complicity in *all* the crimes of the Symbionese Liberation Army whose soldier she had once been. Sara Olson's attorney, Shawn Chapman, who was in the audience, rose to second these observations. Neither she nor Evans ever got around to explaining, however, that this "liberation army" had assassinated the first black superintendent of Oakland's public schools with cyanide-tipped bullets and had murdered a female bystander in the course of a bank robbery, or that Sara Olson had publicly championed the crimes of the organization as acts of "social justice" at the time. If prosecutors had evidence linking her to the conspiratorial organization that planned such acts, it was perfectly legitimate for them to charge her for their consequences.

Evans then talked about Jamil Al-Amin, who had been known in the 1960s as H. Rap Brown. When arrested for killing a policeman, Brown, she pointed out, was an "imam" in a Moslem temple in Atlanta, a community worker who helped the drug addicted and the poor. She indicated that this was the reason the police had targeted him. "There was a shootout," she said, introducing the events that led to his arrest. Two police officers had gone to Brown's home at night with a warrant for traffic tickets. "Who arrests people at night for traffic tickets?" Evans asked in the most suspicious tone she could muster. One of the officers was killed in the "shootout" that followed. The surviving officer had reported that the fleeing gunman had been wounded and was bleeding. But when police tracked Brown three days later to another state, Evans said, he had no wound. Key facts that Evans omitted were that both officers were black, that they had not anticipated trouble and consequently were not wearing vests, and had been ambushed with a firearm that Brown owned and that was found in his possession. Evans did not attempt to explain why an innocent man should flee for three days until a massive manhunt tracked him down, or why the Atlanta police force, whose chief was a black woman in a liberal city whose mayor was also black, would want to murder or falsely imprison a community holy man whose name was H. Rap Brown.

When an elderly gentleman in a straw hat sitting near me asked Evans how she defined "political prisoners," she answered, "every prisoner in American jails is a victim of political circumstance." It was a common theme of the 1960s that divided the delusional world of radicals from everyone else's. Almost defensively, as though to maintain my own sanity, I thought first of the Night Stalker, a psychopath who had raped and murdered forty men, women, and children, and then of the recent front page saga of a fugitive who had been captured after killing his whole family with a knife. In Linda Evans's eyes, evil was a political circumstance called Amerikkka; and, more specifically, the "white" corporate power structure.

The separate reality of radicals, which made them unable to comprehend their own deeds, was made vivid for me in a *New York Times* story I read later about the parole appeal of Evans's third political prisoner, Kathy Boudin. The *Times* had run a series of stories on Boudin, doing everything possible to create sympathy for her as her appeal date approached. Like Sara Jane Olson, Boudin proposed herself as a "changed woman," who had been incarcerated almost as a matter of mistaken identity: "Today, her supporters say, Ms. Boudin is a different woman. During her 20 years in prison she has helped to create several innovative programs for AIDS victims, incarcerated mothers and inmates seeking to take college courses."[1] As part of its promotional effort on Boudin's behalf, the *Times* even ran a three thousand-word feature on her graduation from the college program she had created, which was funded by actress Glenn Close and *Va-*

gina Monologues author Eve Ensler among others. Boudin's boosters included the *Nation* magazine, numerous organizations advocating "prisoner rights" and "social justice" and, in general, the socially prominent and influential mandarins of the "progressive" elite.

Like her comrades, Kathy Boudin is—despite all these cosmetics of social uplift—a lifelong enemy of American democracy and a committed terrorist. She was part of the Weathermen team constructing the anti-personnel bomb whose explosion in the New York townhouse killed three of the guilty and prevented the loss of innocent lives. Far from renouncing her communist and terrorist past, Boudin is part of the same radical network that fuels Linda Evans' seditious projects and remains an integral part of the permanent revolution both signed on to in the 1960s. In the following decade, when Jimmy Carter was in the White House, Kathy Boudin joined a gang of black criminals calling themselves the May Nineteenth Communist Movement and became part of the getaway team in a $1.6 million robbery of a Brink's armored vehicle. The funds would have been used to finance a revolution to carve a "New Afrika" out of the United States.[2]

In the botched robbery attempt, an innocent Brinks guard and two Nanuet police officers were killed. Nine children ranging in age from two months to twenty-one years were left without fathers and with permanent wounds that are beyond the powers of the courts or Kathy Boudin to heal. One of the murdered officers was Waverly Brown, the first black policeman on the Nanuet force, whose hiring was the result of a lengthy civil rights struggle undertaken by blacks and whites in the Nanuet community. Yet, here is how Kathy Boudin explained to the *New York Times* her collusion in the cold-blooded killings of these men: "I went out that day with a lot of denial. I didn't think anything would happen; in my mind, I was going back to pick up my child at the baby-sitter's."

Susan Rosenberg was a comrade of Kathy Boudin and Linda Evans, a former Weather Underground bomber, a member of the May Nineteenth Communist Movement, and a participant in the Brinks robbery. Like Boudin, Rosenberg went to fancy private institutions, the Walden School and Barnard College and—as a 1960s radical—became part of a terrorist network called "The Family," which included the above organizations as well as the Black Liberation Army and the Red Guerrilla Resistance. On November 7, 1983, "The Family" bombed the U.S. Capitol in a blast that "ripped through a conference room near the Senate offices of then minority leader Robert C. Byrd." The bombers issued a war communiqué, explaining that, "we purposely aimed our attack at the institutions of imperialist rule rather than at individual members of the ruling class and government. We did not choose to kill any of them this time. But their lives are not sacred."[3]

Susan Rosenberg also participated in making possible the escape to Cuba of Joanne Chesimard, aka Assata Shakur, wanted in connection with the ambush assassination of a New Jersey state trooper. Shakur was convicted of the murder and was serving a life sentence when Rosenberg helped her escape. In 1984, Rosenberg was captured with Evans at a New Jersey warehouse where they were unloading the 740 pounds of explosives. She also was in possession of fourteen weapons including an Uzi submachine gun. As in the case of other leftwing murderers for political causes, Rosenberg became a progressive hero, supported by celebrity defenders of political criminals like Noam Chomsky and William Kunstler, both of whom actively lobbied for her release. Since she had been sentenced to fifty-eight years for her crimes, prosecutors decided not to pursue murder charges in connection with the killing of the three officers in the Nanuet robbery.

This proved to be a mistake. Like Evans, she gained the support of Congressman Nadler and, along with Evans, was pardoned by Clinton on his last day in office.

Linda Evans, Susan Rosenberg, Sara Olson, and Kathy Boudin are, in fact, part of the ongoing terrorist "Family," a community of political monsters who have regrouped—at least publicly—as an amnesty organization for "political prisoners." Although the *New York Times* and other left-leaning media are ready to portray them as idealists (*60 Minutes* performed the service for Rosenberg), these are not prisoners of conscience. They are prisoners without conscience, incapable of even a minimal accounting of what they willed and did fifteen or thirty years ago, or what—given the right circumstances— they would be willing to attempt in the future. The threat they represent lies not just in their monstrous deeds. It lies in the fact that their evil is protected by the mask of left-wing "idealism" they have adopted and that the left-wing media obligingly preserves for them. By consciously concealing their agenda behind a public aura of vulnerability and innocence and a desire for "social justice," they are able to manipulate real institutions of power in American society, and in particular in the Democratic Party, making the unsuspecting (but also the fellow-traveling) abettors of their malign intent.

For forty years, Linda Evans and a network of political comrades have inhabited an alternative reality that makes innocence seem criminal and their own criminality like nobility itself. They are supported in their delusions by an academic industry in anti-white, anti-capitalist, anti-male, anti-American ideologies and screeds. As in the days of the Weathermen, the supporters of their unholy war are recruited from college campuses. Three thousand benighted activists attended a conference this year at the University of California to protest the "prison-industrial complex." The event was organized by an academic hero, Angela Davis, a lifelong servant of communist police states while they existed, and a comrade of revolutionary criminals. In New York, a similar rally demanding the right of felons to vote was organized by the misnamed Center for Constitutional Rights and was addressed by such speakers as Democratic gubernatorial candidate Andrew Cuomo and television pundit Arianna Huffington.

The ideas behind this movement are the ideas of the anti-American, anti-globalization left. Their agenda is to attack legitimate law enforcement and to defame American justice as a system of racial oppression and—though they do not reveal this aspect to outsiders—to enlist the anti-social and the violent as a military vanguard. "Like the military/industrial complex, the prison industrial complex is an interweaving of private business and government interests. Its twofold purpose is profit and social control. . . . This monumental commitment to lock up a sizeable percentage of the population is an integral part of the globalization of capital." These sentences are taken from a pamphlet written by Linda Evans and her lover, Eve Goldberg, under the title *The Prison Industrial Complex and the Global Economy.*

As their pamphlet makes clear, the new radicalism is the old Weatherman race war brought up to date. Globalization is depicted as the white man's aggression against the non-white races of the world. It is American capitalism versus Third World victims. The prison networks, the "social justice" organizations, the anti-globalist protesters are the fifth column vanguards envisaged by the Weathermen, declaring war on the Empire and plotting to tear down its walls from within. "Tear Down The Walls" is actually the name of the next big mobilization of Linda Evans's army, an "International Human Rights Conference on Winning Amnesty For U.S Political Prisoners and Prisoners of War"—Mumia Abu Jamal, Kathy Boudin, and H. Rap Brown among them. The majority of the "political prisoners of war," the conference brochure explains, "are Black/New

Afrikans . . . .These political prisoners of war are women and men incarcerated because of their involvement in political activities which challenged the unjust nature of the U.S. socioeconomic system and its hegemonic policies around the world."

The conference was to be held seven months later at the end of March 2002, in the mecca of the revolutionary faith, Fidel Castro's Cuba, one of the last surviving communist police states. It is entirely fitting that the sadistic tyrant was himself to be the conference host having turned his unhappy nation into the world's oldest island prison.

5

Representative McKinney's Bizarre Mission

REPRESENTATIVE CYNTHIA MCKINNEY is a Georgia congresswoman whose district was originally gerrymandered so that
only a person who was black could be elected. The very as-
sumption of the gerrymandering—that whites would not vote for
blacks—was both racist and false, since all over the United States
and the south itself there were black representatives elected in majority white districts (the reverse unfortunately has yet to occur). Yet
McKinney fought to defend the racially drawn lines of her district
and insisted on the presumption that whites would not vote for her.
Conservatives took the government to court on the grounds that
creating racial voting districts violated the Constitution and in 1998
the Supreme Court supported their claim. The Court decided that
McKinney's district was unconstitutional and redrew its lines to include enough white votes to defeat her. In the next election, however, McKinney was re-elected, which seemed an apt vindication of
America's great civil rights triumph over its racial past.

Despite the racial generosity of her white constituents, McKinney
herself has not made the passage past racism into the twenty-first

century or, apparently, even managed to assimilate the idea of a two-party system that makes allowance for honest disagreement. "My impression of modern-day black Republicans," she told one reporter, "is they have to pass a litmus test in which all black blood is extracted."[1]

Despite her radicalism, McKinney is a member of the House Armed Services Committee and the ranking Democrat on the International Operations and Human Rights Subcommittee of the House International Relations Committee. Ten days before the attack on the World Trade Center, she presented a report to the United Nations World Conference Against Racism, Racial Discrimination, Xenophobia and Related Intolerance held in Durban, South Africa.

The Conference itself had become a center of controversy because the organizers of its agenda, a coalition of Arab theocracies led by Iran and assorted African dictatorships—including regimes guilty of some of the worst ongoing ethnic atrocities—decided that Israel, the Middle East's only democracy, and the United States should be the two nations condemned by the conference for their alleged racial abuses. Israel, a country with legal Arab parties and Arab members of its ruling parliament, which provides its Arab citizens with more civil rights than any Arab country, was to be denounced as "an apartheid, racist and fascist state" by UN conferees, while the United States which alongside England had led the world's fight against slavery was to be held up for reparations for a slave system that had been ended more than a hundred years before. The African states of Sudan and Mauritania, which were still practicing slavery, on the other hand, were to be exempted from condemnation or reparations, because they were Muslim and black.

Led by President Bush and national security advisor Condoleeza Rice, the United States refused to participate in this offensive farce and the event eventually collapsed. But a delegation of African-

American leftists led by NAACP chairman Julian Bond and members of the Congressional Black Caucus had traveled to Durban where they disgraced themselves not only by supporting the conference but by urging the UN to "highlight" American racism, and by suggesting that Colin Powell was not "really black" because he supported the White House boycott of the event. Human Relations subcommittee chair Cynthia McKinney then suggested to the press that the Bush Administration had adopted the boycott policy because the White House "is just full of latent racists."[2]

Exactly a year earlier, McKinney had held hearings of her Human Rights subcommittee on alleged U.S. abuses against minorities. The hearings were titled "Human Rights in the United States: The Unfinished Story, Current Political Prisoners—Victims of Cointelpro" and could only be described as bizarre.[3] The hearings provided the "factual" basis of the report that she and Congressional Black Caucus delegates then presented to the UN Conference on Racism. The delegates included International Relations Committee member and California radical Barbara Lee and ranking Judiciary Committee member John Conyers.

The McKinney hearings were little more than a show trial staged by radicals at war with the federal government. Almost all the witnesses assembled by McKinney were connected to terrorist groups of the 1960s, including the Weather Underground, the Black Liberation Army, and the Republic of New Afrika movement. All three were linked to the infamous Brinks robbery in Nanuet in which two police officers were murdered. The phrase "Victims of Cointelpro" referred to an FBI program that had been discontinued thirty years before. Making this the centerpiece of her investigation showed that McKinney's agenda was merely to provide an official stamp to the tired and discredited mythologies of the extremist American left.[4] The alleged "victims" of American injustice presented in the committee's report were the convicted killer of two FBI men, Leonard Peltier, convicted cop-killer Mumia Abu Jamal, convicted murderer Geronimo Pratt (subsequently released on a technicality), and convicted armed robber Dhoruba Bin Wahad, along with other assorted felons.

The level of the testimonies was established at the outset by McKinney's first witness, a woman named Nkechi Taifa, a law professor at Howard University and formerly an activist with the defense committee for the terrorist Republic of New Afrika group. She opened her remarks by reciting a poem she had written about Cointelpro, and the proceedings went downhill from there:

> COINTEL's got blacks in hell
> They open up our Mail
> Tap our phones and kick our bones,
> And railroad us to jail.

Another witness, warmly welcomed by McKinney as a political ally and a victim of American repression, was Laura Whitehorn, a recently paroled political bomber. Whitehorn was a member of the same terrorist "Family" to which Linda Evans and Susan Rosenberg belonged and had been convicted with them in an attempt to blow up the U.S. Capitol and the U.S. Naval War College in 1984, along with other government and corporate targets. Whitehorn had served fifteen years in prison before being paroled in 1999, after which, according to McKinney, she settled in New York where she was "working hard to free all political prisoners and prisoners of war"—that is, prisoners of the war their terrorist networks had declared against the United States.

McKinney's star witness was Kathleen Cleaver, daughter of a U.S. foreign-service officer who had rejected a privileged childhood in order to marry a convicted rapist named Eldridge Cleaver and join the Black Panther Party. As minister of information for the Panthers, Eldridge Cleaver participated in at least one self-confessed attempt to assassinate two police officers in 1968, a crime for which he served time after spending several years "in exile" in Algeria. Kathleen Cleaver is today a professor at the Cardozo School of Law in New York and a widely traveled campus speaker still railing against "racist Amerika," while defending the Panthers' many crimes as "revolutionary acts." In introducing Cleaver, Congresswoman McKinney attempted political humor, commenting, "Thank goodness she didn't follow in Clarence Thomas's footsteps."

The report McKinney presented to the UN Race Conference was titled "Cointelpro: The Untold American Story." It summarized the testimony of her committee hearing and came with grateful acknowledgments to academic advisers Howard Zinn, Ward Churchill, and Noam Chomsky.[5] To her UN hosts, McKinney explained, "[America is] not quite a democracy. And one of the things that makes it not quite a democracy is the existence of outfits like the FBI and the CIA." One wonders what her constituents and her Democratic colleagues on the House Armed Services Committee make of statements like that.

6

Scheer Lunacy at the Los Angeles Times

O<small>N A HOT AUGUST DAY IN</small> 1988, I was standing in the New Orleans Convention Center with my longtime writing partner, Peter Collier, when an old comrade unexpectedly crossed our path. Peter and I had known each other since the 1960s when we were both editors at the New Left magazine *Ramparts.* We were in New Orleans as speechwriters for Bob and Elizabeth Dole, part of our recent odyssey from the ranks of the left to the other side of the political barricade.

Suddenly, we noticed our former *Ramparts* boss, Bob Scheer, whom we had not seen in twenty years, since we had overthrown him in a palace coup, booting him out of the magazine. Scheer was covering the Republican Convention for the *Los Angeles Times,* whose "national correspondent" he had become.

For a beat or two, the three of us just stood there, eyeing each other at a distance that might have been forty paces, each trying to make up his mind whether to engage. "Hi Bob," I said, finally breaking the ice. But Scheer was not up for it. Taking a step towards the exit, he looked over his shoulder almost in the manner of drive-by, and fired in our direction the most crushing retort he could muster to everything we had become. "Deutscher was right," he said, and walked away.

It was vintage Scheer: smug, shallow, and intellectually lazy.

For 1960s veterans like us, Isaac Deutscher had provided the key to our continuing radical faith. A famed biographer of Trotsky and Stalin, Deutscher had explained the monstrosity socialism had become in a way that made it possible for us to retain our socialist beliefs. Deutscher described the Soviet Union as still encrusted with the tyranny of Old Russia, but transformed by socialist economics into a competitive world power. The scientific logic of socialism, he assured us, would soon transform the tyranny into a modern democratic state.

We had a New Left bon mot to sum up this Deutscherian vision. The first socialist revolution, we said, would take place in the Soviet Union. It was this hope that encouraged us to support the Soviet bloc and believe it was still "progressive" despite its totalitarian cast; and it was this hope that made us turn our backs on democratic America as reactionary and oppressive, despite its democratic "facade." Scheer's parting taunt to Peter and me expressed his belief that the reforms of *glasnost* and *perestroika*, then taking place under Mikhail Gorbachev, would transform the Soviet Union into a modern, democratic socialist state.

To the true believer, Gorbachev's reforms may indeed have looked like the transformation Deutscher had predicted, but the result was obviously anything but. A year after our encounter with Scheer, the Berlin Wall came crashing down and the Soviet empire with it. Its collapse revealed not the superpower of Deutscher's imaginings, but the pathetic shell of a Third World backwater, whose economic output was less than South Korea's. Contrary to Deutscher's vision, socialism had turned the Soviet Union into an economic wasteland. In

1989, after sixty years of Five Year Plans, the average meat intake of a Soviet citizen was less than it had been in 1913 under the Czar.

In a landscape devastated by the Marxism that progressives like Scheer continued to embrace, the new era of freedom meant only another round of poverty and despotism, albeit not nearly as bad as before. Deutscher could hardly have made a bigger mistake. He was wrong about the economic achievements of the Soviet past, which turned out to be little more than a Potemkin illusion, and he was wrong about the bright prospect of the Soviet future.

Scheer was wrong too, but his retro-Marxism had done nothing to impede his upward climb in the capitalist media world he loved to milk and despise at the same time. While Peter and I were doing our slow motion disengagement from the totalitarian temptation, Scheer, along with an entire generation of New Left intellectuals, was burrowing into the institutions they had tried to burn down and busily infiltrating the mainstream culture.

Scheer's own path to success was made a lot easier by his marriage to Narda Zacchino, one of the top editors at the *Times*. In 1976 he was made the *Times*'s national correspondent, a post he held for seventeen years before transitioning to his present role as all-purpose pundit and chief in-house columnist. His journalistic fronting for the Clinton White House even earned him a spot on Sidney Blumenthal's e-mail list of media friends. Scheer's power marriage at the *Times* helped to insulate him from scrutiny and created an ideal vantage within a profession that had become a left-wing redoubt. Among his many perks, Scheer was appointed to a visiting professorship on the faculty of the prestigious Annenberg School of Journalism at usc by its dean, a former Clinton official.

An aggressive sybarite even when I first met him forty years ago, Scheer had acquired a townhouse, a boat, pals like Barbara Streisand and Warren Beatty, and a first-name familiarity with some of the finest restauranteurs in town—all the while he continued his sancti-monious attacks on the ruling class in his columns in the *Times*. Nor had he lost the reputation for intellectual laziness first acquired among subordinate staffers at *Ramparts* who were conscripted to write his copy. In the early 1990s, I had lunch with a city editor at the *Times* who swore he had never seen anyone go so far on so little effort as Bob Scheer.

Two consequences flowed from this general approach to life. In 1961, Scheer published his first book—a celebration of Castro's revo-lution, co-authored with Maurice Zeitlin. But during the next forty years, Scheer managed to produce little besides a few collections of articles and a pamphlet. Periodically, notices did appear in the liter-ary gossip columns, announcing that he had received a six-figure advance to write a book on Gorbachev, or the official biography of Jane Fonda. But years passed and the books never came. The second result of this lassitude was the intellectual shallowness that charac-terized everything he did manage to complete.

Scheer's column on the power crisis in California—a story in his own journalistic backyard—affords sufficient evidence of the mal-aise. By general consensus, the California crisis was triggered by the unexpected convergence of at least four factors: (1) a thirty percent increase in the demand for electricity in one of the nation's fastest growing states; (2) a shortage of power sources due to environmental attitudes that had prevented the state from bringing online a single new power plant in fifteen years; (3) an increased dependency on power from other states in which demand was also rising; and finally, (4) a misguided legislative decision to half deregulate the industry, allowing utility companies to purchase power at market rates on the supply side of the equation, but maintaining regulatory controls on consumer prices on the demand side. By 2001, the cost of power to California's utilities was more than ten times what they were allowed to charge consumers who (because *their* price was fixed) lacked incentive to restrict demand. This put the utility companies on the verge of bankruptcy, unable to purchase additional power. Hence the crisis.

But to Scheer, such complexity was only a distraction from ideological clarity. This is how Scheer distilled the situation in a column mixing metaphors of Santa, Disney, and Frank Baum, in a hallmark style that might be described as Beverly Hills kitsch:

These Messes Are What Deregulation Gets Us
by Robert Scheer

> Capitalism is falling apart. . . . Yes, Virginia, we do need government regulation . . . because the market mechanism left to its own devices inevitably spirals out of control. Recognition of that reality has guided this country to prosperity ever since Franklin D. Roosevelt pulled us out of the Great Depression. But in recent decades, conservative economists and their fat-cat corporate sponsors have led us down the yellow brick road of deregulation. Getting government out of the market would free creativity and investment, leading us to the magic kingdom of Oz, where all would prosper. If anything went wrong, the wizard of Oz—a.k.a. Alan Greenspan—would make it all better.

Like the inscrutable reference to Federal Reserve head, Alan Greenspan, Scheer's column never actually got around to the facts of the case (nor did Roosevelt's New Deal "pull us out of the depression"). Instead his column provided a cook's tour of the author's anti-corporate prejudices along with many arcane irrelevancies off the top of the author's head, including the AOL-Time Warner merger and Europe's mad cow epidemic. Scheer's column concluded with a plea for "passage of the McCain-Feingold campaign finance reform" and "the revival of the consumer movement" to achieve "more, not less, regulation," Scheer's own solution to the problem.

I once asked an editor at the *Times* whether Scheer was, in fact, protected by its editorial powers from being held to the journalistic standards other writers were expected to observe. The editor replied, "Bob Scheer is anointed." It is this latitude, perhaps, that has made Scheer's capacity for ignorant mischief seemingly boundless, extending even to matters of the nation's security.

Over the last two years, Scheer has become the nation's leading defender of suspected atomic spy Wen Ho Lee, whom he has lauded as "an American Dreyfus" and about whom he has written a dozen columns—all proclaiming Lee's innocence, while portraying him as a victim of an anti-Asian conspiracy. Scheer has now been hired as "technical consultant" to an upcoming four-hour television whitewash of Lee. The mini-series is to be produced for ABC by long-time "peace" activist Robert Greenwald, whose last feature was an adoration of 1960s juvenile delinquent Abbie Hoffman, which closed almost as suddenly as it opened.

Is Wen Ho Lee guilty? The suspicions that he is are based in part on the fact he illegally removed four hundred thousand files from the nation's top nuclear weapons' lab during a period when the Chinese communist dictatorship—with whom he had contact—was systematically stealing the secrets of America's most sophisticated nuclear arsenal. Lee's response to the FBI investigation was also that of a guilty man. He destroyed files in his possession and repeatedly tried to break into the lab after his access was denied.

Since Scheer has been a leftist since the onset of the Cold War, his immoderate defense of an accused spy was reckless enough to surprise me. After all, every single communist spy identified by the FBI in the half-century since the Cold War began (the Rosenbergs, Morton Sobell, Joel Barr, Judith Coplon, William Remington, Alger

Hiss, etc.), had been proven guilty. At the same time, every one of those spies had been defended by progressives who claimed they were innocent. Why would Scheer want to expose himself to such embarrassment again?

The immediate context of the Wen Ho Lee case had been set by the Cox Committee Report on the theft of nuclear secrets, which was released in May 1999. The report had been approved by a bipartisan committee and concluded: "The espionage inquiry found Beijing has stolen U.S. design data for nearly all elements needed for a major nuclear attack on the U.S., such as advanced warheads, missiles and guidance systems."

Scheer's journalistic response to these disturbing facts about the nation's security proved to be no different than his approach to the California power crisis: Begin and end with an ideological premise; in between, stuff the column with half-baked information, unfounded accusation, and irrelevant asides. Scheer answered, with the following ludicrous dismissals, the findings of the bipartisan committee on the theft of nuclear secrets:

Our Secrets Are of No Use to Them
by Robert Scheer

Let's as those Apple computer ads implore, think different. There are no nuclear weapons secrets or, indeed, nuclear "weapons" for China to have stolen.

Scheer did not actually try to substantiate the claim that the United States had no nuclear weapons secrets (he just left it floating in the ether). But he did make a stab at the idea that there are *no* nuclear weapons: "Nuclear bombs are not actually weapons because, in today's world, they cannot be employed to win battles but can serve only as instruments of mass terror." (Think about that one for a moment.) The statement—and the entire column—showed an ignorance of deterrence theory astounding for a man whose personal website boasts that "from 1976 to 1993, he served as a national correspondent for the *Los Angeles Times*, where he wrote articles on such diverse topics as the Soviet Union, arms control, national politics and the military." A good thesis for a graduate student at the Annenberg School might be on what the *Times* editors could have been thinking when they allowed Scheer to occupy his position.

Having established that there were "no nuclear weapons secrets" to steal, Scheer found it relatively easy to reach the conclusion that the Los Alamos scientist Wen Ho Lee was innocent, notwithstanding his suspicious behavior. Drawing on years of training in the left, Scheer went on the offensive, identifying Lee as the hapless target of a racial witch-hunt. Two months later, Scheer wrote his first Wen Ho Lee column which began with the following subtlety: "The 'Chinaman' did it. The diabolical Asian has long been a staple of American racism, and it's not surprising that the folks attempting to whip up a new red espionage scare would focus on Wen Ho Lee."

In making these bizarre accusations, Scheer was obviously aware that any such witch-hunt against Lee would have to have been orchestrated by Lee's prosecutors—Attorney General Janet Reno, FBI Director Louis Freeh, and the local U.S. attorney on the case, who happened to be a former college roommate and close political friend of Bill Clinton himself. To make the persecution of Lee seamless, there would also have to be collusion on the part of Acting Deputy Attorney General for Civil Rights Bill Lann Lee, an American of Chinese lineage and a hypersensitive opponent of racial profiling.

All this did not cause Scheer to have second thoughts. Instead, he just plucked a more suitable culprit out of his journalistic hat. Actually two: the Republican head of the bipartisan nuclear secrets committee (to please radical fans) and the chief media rival to his own paper (to please editors at the *Times*). Wrote Scheer: "Facts evidently don't matter to those in Congress, led by Rep. Christopher Cox (R-CA), and in the media, where the august *New York Times* has acted as head cheerleader for those sounding the alarm of a Chinese nuclear threat."

The following day Congressman Cox responded. In a letter to the editor, he pointed out that the name Wen Ho Lee had actually not appeared in his Committee's report and that "neither I nor any member of the Select Committee had even heard of Wen Ho Lee when we completed our report in January." Cox further pointed out that when Energy secretary Bill Richardson actually fired Lee, calling him a man who had "massively violated our security system," Cox had issued a widely publicized statement criticizing the media's spotlight on Lee and saying that it was wrong, without proof, "to juxtapose him with some of the most serious crimes that have ever been committed against our military secrets."

The fact that the man whom Scheer falsely accused of persecuting Lee had actually defended him did not prevent Scheer from repeating the slander in a column the following month (September 14, 1999). "It's time to pronounce the Chinese nuclear weapons spy story a hoax," he repeated. Turning to the alleged witch-hunt of Lee, he said its rationale was provided by an investigation "led by an outraged Cox, who represents the more right-wing fringes of Southern California, eager to find a new evil empire as justification of a military buildup, once the staple of that region's economy."

In even more ungrammatical prose than usual, Scheer had managed to start a witch-hunt of his own, tarring Cox, a respected congressional leader, as a member of the farthest right fringe. Scheer's September 14 column, which was called "Time to Say Farewell to Spy Scandal," provoked a joint rebuttal from Cox and the ranking Democrat on the committee, Norm Dix, a liberal from Washington:

"[Robert Scheer's] column asserted four main 'facts'," their letter asserted, "each of them is false."

Five days before Scheer's column appeared, the National Intelligence Estimate, representing the consensus of the entire U.S. intelligence community, had been released. The estimate stated that China was ready to test a longer range, intercontinental missile than it previously had (this was one of the secrets that had been passed to the Chinese), which would be targeted primarily against the United States. This missile technology had been shared with Kim Il Sung's loony police state in North Korea. The letter also stated that the missile would be fitted with "smaller nuclear warheads—in part influenced by U.S. technology gained through espionage." It was the theft of a warhead, the w-88, small enough to fit into a missile, that Wen Ho Lee was suspected of stealing.

In the midst of Scheer's false claims and accusations (his articles continued into the following year), he got a break. On September 13, 2000, the government announced that it was dropping fifty-eight of the fifty-nine charges against Lee. President Clinton even volunteered an apology, as though some kind of injustice had been done. This didn't prevent Clinton, however, from flying to New Mexico the very next week to raise campaign money for Lee's prosecutor. The *New York Times* also apologized. Janet Reno and Louis Freeh did not. Freeh told a congressional committee: "The Department of Justice and the FBI stand by each and every one of the 59 counts in the indictment of Dr. Lee. Each of those counts could be proved in December 1999 [when Lee was formally indicted], and each of them could be proven today."

I wrote a column about Freeh's statement for *Salon.com* ("Wen Ho Lee's Reckless Defenders," October 3, 2000). In the article, I recalled an episode that had taken place when Peter and I were running *Ramparts*, after we had fired Scheer, in the early 1970s. We were planning to publish an article by a defector from an American spy program and thus to break the same Espionage Act that Wen Ho Lee had violated in removing secret files from the Los Alamos lab. In my column, I recalled how I had been advised by Charles Nesson, then, as now, a left-wing law professor at Harvard, on how to get away with the crime. Nesson advised us—with a cynicism that I will never forget—that since we lived in a democracy, in order to prosecute us for treason the government would have to prove in open court that we had damaged national security. In other words, it would have to reveal to the court and to our country's enemies far more than it would be willing to reveal. Hence, if we had the nerve to do it, we would most likely get away with what we were planning, which was to print national secrets in the pages of our magazine.[1]

I was sure that it was just this cynicism—use the privileges of American democracy to attack it—that lay behind the calculations of Wen Ho Lee's defense lawyers, and of course everything that Scheer wrote.

In my article for *Salon*, I even included some sentences about a Scheer column on Lee. Because I was convinced that Scheer's motivation in defending Lee and the Chinese communists was a bedrock of conviction that had not really changed in forty years, I put in the following sentence: "While we were divulging the secrets of America's electronic intelligence agency in the pages of *Ramparts*, Scheer was joining the Red Sun Rising Commune [in Berkeley] and becoming an acolyte of North Korean dictator Kim Il-Sung."

This sentence did not appear in the *Salon* article, however. A *Salon* editor had called Scheer before publication to ask him if the statement about his dalliance with Kim Il Sung was true. He said flatly that it was not. Even though I pointed out that I had already printed these facts in *Radical Son*, without contradiction from Scheer, and pressed for a change in the text that was already on-line, the editor remained adamant. Scheer had categorically denied that he was ever a supporter of Kim Il Sung, she said. Unless I had sourced proof to the contrary, they would not take my word against his.

I knew that I was right. When I called my old *Ramparts* co-editor Peter Collier, he reminded me that Scheer had taken a delegation from the Red Family commune to visit *Ramparts*, editor and Black Panther minister of information, Eldridge Cleaver, who was a fugitive in North Korea, having ambushed two San Francisco police officers and fled the country in 1968. The Red Family was a "guerrilla foco" that Scheer and Tom Hayden had formed. A member of the Scheer delegation, named Jan Austin, was a copyeditor at *Ramparts* and she came back with glowing tales about North Korean communism and Kim Il Sung's "Palace of the Children," and the gourmet spreads the government had laid out for them. Subsequently, a carton of the "Collected News Conferences of Kim Il Sung" had arrived, by mail, in the *Ramparts* office, and Peter and I had amused ourselves by opening one volume which began with a question to Kim, and was followed with a three hundred-page answer.

Thirty years is a long time, however, and even though I was familiar with Scheer's brazenness, I could not help but be shaken by the absolute character of his denial to *Salon*. Maybe Jan Austin's opinions were hers and hers alone. Thirty years *is* a long time, so what was at stake? What would Scheer have to hide but the embarrassment of youth? I let the incident pass.

A few months later, however, I had cause to mention Scheer in another *Salon* column, this one about the nomination of John Ashcroft for attorney general. Scheer had attacked Ashcroft, and since the nominee's past political opinions were an issue for his attackers, I thought it appropriate to bring up the political lineage of one of them as well. Again I was challenged by a *Salon* editor, and under pressure I agreed to drop my reference to Scheer's infatuation with Kim. But I was still sure that my memory was correct.

Then a funny thing happened. Peter had become the publisher of Encounter Books and sent me the manuscript of one of his upcoming titles. The book was *Commies: The Old Left, The New Left and the Leftover Left*, which is the autobiography of another old friend Ronald Radosh. I had not discussed these *Salon* incidents with Radosh, because he had been an East coast radical and I had no reason to think he had spent time with Scheer in his Red Family days. But when Peter asked me to read the manuscript of *Commies*, I came across the following passage:

> At the time [circa 1969], my friend Louis Menashe and I had a regular radio program on the Pacifica Network, a weekly political discussion show in which we interviewed Movement figures and engaged in political and theoretic discussion. Since Scheer was still considered an important figure on the Left . . . I got out my trusty, top-of-the-line SONY that WBAI had recommended we purchase, and began the interview. Scheer, however, said that he would talk on the record about only one topic—the only topic that mattered—the realization of the socialist utopia in Kim Il Sung's North Korea.
>
> For over two hours, Scheer talked and talked about the paradise he had seen during a recent visit to North Korea, about the greatness of Kim Il Sung, about the correct nature of his so-called *juche* ideology—evidently a word embodying Kim's redefinition of Marxism-Leninism in building Communism against all obstacles and with the entire world in opposition. . . At one point, I asked him incredulously: "Bob, do you really believe this crap?" Scheer responded with complete earnestness that he did—that Kim had charted out a path that other nations could and should take as an example of the art of the possible. . . . [Finally], the interminable interview ended, leav-

ing me recalling Woody Allen's famous words to Annie Hall's demented brother: "I have to go now. I'm due back on planet earth."

Me too.

But of course, this is not merely an episode of low comedy. It is a story that illuminates the state of American journalism, and of our country as well.

Scheer is currently working on a book about the Wen Ho Lee case.

7

Progressive Narcissism:
The Clinton Left[1]

THE SUBJECT IS HILLARY CLINTON as America's foremost left-wing politician. This is not an obvious idea to those leftists who identify themselves as radicals. Purists of the creed are likely to regard both Clintons as opportunists and sellouts. Hillary's embrace of Palestinian terrorism one day during her New York campaign for the Senate and her retreat under fire the next does not sit well with ideologues. But no political purist ever won an election. Moreover, the left is not, and has never been, a monolith, and its factions have always attacked each other almost as ferociously as their political enemies.

It is possible to be a socialist, radical in one's agenda, and moderate in the means one regards as practical to achieve them. To change the world, it is necessary first to acquire power. Transitional goals may be accomplished by stealth even more effectively than by frontal assault. Politics is never simple. A politics that appears too moderate to radicals may present even greater dangers to the unsuspecting. In 1917, Lenin's political slogan was not "Socialist Dictatorship, Firing Squads, and Gulags!" It was "Bread, Land, and Peace."

Yet Hillary Clinton perceived as America's first lady of the left is also not obvious to many conservatives. Since conservative politics is really about the defense of America's constitutional order, this is a far more significant myopia. Underestimating the foe on any battlefield can be fatal; the political battlefield is no exception.

The problem of perceiving Hillary is exemplified in a brilliantly etched and elegantly deconstructed portrait of Mrs. Clinton by former Reagan speechwriter Peggy Noonan. The focus of Noonan's book, *The Case Against Hillary Clinton*,[2] is not Mrs. Clinton's kitsch Marxism or her perverse feminism or her cynical progressivism. It is her *narcissism*. In this psychological nexus, Noonan finds the key to unlock Hillary's public persona. In Noonan's analysis, it is almost as though Mrs. Clinton's political beliefs were merely instrumental to her career, and as changeable as her famous hairstyles. "Never has the admirable been so fully wedded to the appalling," Noonan writes of Mrs. Clinton and her faithless spouse. "Never in modern political history has such tenacity and determination been marshaled to achieve such puny purpose: the mere continuance of Them."

The wit is razor sharp, but the point just wide of the mark. There are many unprincipled narcissists in politics. But there has never been a White House so thoroughly penetrated by the minions of the political left. Noonan's psychological characterization is surely correct. But if Hillary and Bill Clinton were unable to draw on the dedication and support of this left—if they were conservatives, for example—there would be no prospect of a continuance of Them.

Ever since abandoning the utopian illusions of the progressive cause, I have been struck by how little the world outside the left seems to actually understand it. How little those who have not been inside the progressive mind are able to grasp the cynicism behind its idealistic mask or the malice that drives its hypocritical passion for "social justice."

No matter how great the crimes progressives commit, no matter how terrible the futures they labor to create, no matter how devastating the human catastrophes they leave behind, the world outside the faith seems ready to forgive their "mistakes" and to grant them the grace of "good intentions."

It would be difficult to recall, for example, the number of times I have been introduced on conservative platforms as "a former civil rights worker and peace activist in the 1960s." I have been described this way despite having written a lengthy autobiography that exposes these self-glorifying images of the left as so much political deceit. Like many New Left leaders whom the young Mrs. Clinton once followed (and who are her comrades today), I saw myself in the 1960s as a Marxist and a revolutionary. What was idealistic about exploiting an issue like civil rights, for example, to achieve the destruction of the social order that made civil rights possible?

New Left progressives like Hillary Clinton and Acting Deputy Attorney General Bill Lann Lee were involved in supporting or promoting, or protecting or making excuses for violent anti-American radicals abroad like the Vietcong and criminal radicals at home like the Black Panthers.[3] We did this then—just as progressives still do now—in the name of social justice and a dialectical worldview that made this deception seem ethical and the fantasy seem possible.

As Jamie Glazov, a student of the left, has observed in an article about the middle-class defenders of recently captured 1970s terrorist Kathy Soliah: "If you can successfully camouflage your own pathology and hatred with a concern for the 'poor' and the 'downtrodden,' then there will always be a 'progressive' milieu to support and defend you."[4] Huey Newton, George Jackson, Angela Davis, Bernardine Dorhn, Sylvia Baraldini, Rubin "Hurricane" Carter, Mumia Abu Jamal, H. Rap Brown, Rigoberta Menchu, and many others have all discovered this principle in the course of their criminal careers.

There is a superficial sense, of course, in which we *were* civil rights and peace activists—and that is certainly the way I would have described myself at the time, particularly if I were speaking to an audience that was not politically left. It is certainly the way Mrs. Clinton and my former comrades refer to themselves and their pasts in similar settings today.

But they are lying. When they defend racial preferences now, for example, a principle they denounced as "racist" and fought against as "civil rights" activists *then*, even they must know it.

The first truth about leftist missionaries, about believing progressives, is that they are liars. But they are not liars in the ordinary way, which is to say by choice. They are liars by necessity, and often, therefore, without realizing that they are. The necessity for lying arises because it is the political lie that gives their cause its life.

Why, if you were one of them, *would* you tell the truth? If you were serious about your role as part of humanity's vanguard, if you had knowledge which others did not that would lead them to a better world, why *would* you tell them a truth they couldn't understand and that would only serve to hold them back?

If you believed that others could understand your truth, you would not think of yourself as part of a "vanguard." You would no longer inhabit the morally charmed world of an elite whose members alone can see the light and whose mission is to lead the unenlightened towards it. If everybody could see the same horizon and knew the path to reach it, the future would already have happened and there would be no need for the army of the saints.

That is both the ethical core and psychological heart of what it means to be a part of the left. That is where the gratification comes from. To see yourself as a redeemer. To feel anointed. To be among the elect. In other words: To be progressive is itself the most satisfying narcissism of all.

That is why it is of little concern to them that their socialist schemes have run aground, burying millions of human beings in the process. That is why they don't care that their panaceas have caused more human suffering than any injustice they have ever challenged. That is why they never learn from their "mistakes," why the continuance of Them is more important than any truth.

If you were active in the so-called "peace" movement or in the radical wing of the civil rights causes, why *would* you tell the truth? Why would you concede—even long afterwards—that no, you were never really a "peace activist," except in the sense that you were against America's war. Why would you draw attention to the fact that you didn't oppose the communists' war and were happy when America's enemies won?

What you were really against was not war, but American "imperialism" and American capitalism. What you truly hated was America's democracy, which you knew to be a "sham" because it was controlled by money in the end. That's why you wanted to "Bring the Troops Home." Because if America's troops came home, America would lose and the communists would win. And the progressive future would be another step closer.

But you never had the honesty—then or now—to admit that. You told the lie then to gain influence and increase your power to do good (as only the Chosen can). And you keep on telling the lie for the same reason.

Why would you admit that, despite your tactical support for civil rights, you weren't really committed to civil rights as Americans understand the meaning of the term—as rights granted not to groups but to individuals, not by government but "by their Creator"? What you really wanted was to overthrow the very Constitution that guaranteed those rights, based as it is on private property and the autonomous person—both of which you despise.

Since America is a democracy and the people endorse it, the left's "progressive" agendas can only be achieved by lying to the people. The unenlightened must be kept ignorant until the revolution transforms them. The better world is only reachable through deception of the people who need to be saved.

Despite the homage it pays to postmodernist conceits, despite its belated and half hearted display of anti-communist sentiment, today's left is very much the ideological heir of the Stalinist progressives who supported the greatest mass murders in human history, but who remember themselves today as civil libertarians—opponents of McCarthy and victims of political witch-hunts. (Only the dialectical can even begin to understand this logic.)

To appreciate the continuity of the communist mentality in the American left, consider how many cultural promotions of McCarthy's victims and how many academic apologies for Stalinist crimes are premised on the Machiavellian calculations and Hegelian sophistries I have just described.

Naturally, today's leftists are smart enough to distance themselves from Soviet communism. But the head of the Soviet Communist Party, Nikita Khrushchev, was a critic of Stalin forty years ago. Did his concessions make him less of a communist? Or more?

Conservative misunderstanding of the left is only in part a product of the left's own deceits. It also reflects the inability of conservatives to understand the religious nature of the progressive faith and the power of its redemptive idea. I'm sometimes asked by conservatives about the continuing role and influence of the Communist Party, since they observe quite correctly the pervasive presence of so many familiar totalitarian ideas in the academic and political culture. How can there be a Marxist left—even a kitsch Marxist left—without a Marxist party?

The short answer is that it was not the Communist Party that made the left, but the (small *c*) communist Idea. It is an idea as old as the Tower of Babel, that humanity can build its own highway to Heaven. It is the idea of a return to the Earthly Paradise, the garden of social harmony and justice. It is the idea that inspires Jewish radicals and liberals of a *Tikkun Olam*, a healing of the cosmic order. It is the Enlightenment illusion of the perfectibility of man. And it is the siren song of the serpent in Eden: "Eat of this Tree of the Knowledge of Good and Evil, and you shall be as God."

The intoxicating vision of a social redemption achieved by *Them* —this is what creates the left and makes the believers so righteous in their beliefs. It did so long before Karl Marx. It is the vision of a redemptive future that continues to inspire and animate them despite the still fresh ruins of their communist past.

It is the same idea that is found in the Social Gospel that impressed the youthful Hillary Clinton at the United Methodist Church in Park Ridge, Illinois. And it is the same idea that she later encountered in the New Left at Yale and in the Venceremos Brigade in communist Cuba, and in the writings of the New Left editor of *Tikkun* magazine who introduced her to the "politics of meaning" after she had become First Lady. It is the idea that drives her comrades in the Children's Defense Fund, the National Organization for Women, the Al Sharpton House of Justice, and the other progressive causes which for that reason still look to her as a leader.

For the self-anointed messiahs, the goal, social justice, is not about rectifying particular wrongs, which would be practical and modest— and therefore conservative. Rather, their crusade is about rectifying injustice in the very order of things. "Social Justice" for them is a world reborn, in which prejudice and violence and inequalities no longer exist. It is a world in which everyone is equally advantaged and lacks fundamentally conflicting desires. It is a world that could only come into being through a reconstruction of human nature and the social order. Even though they are too pragmatic and self-protective to name it anymore, the post-communist left still passionately believes in this totalitarian future.

But this new world that has never existed and never will, while the attempt to reach it can only bring back the gulags and graveyards we have come to know too well. The twentieth century has taught us that to attempt the impossible is to invite the catastrophic. But progressives have failed to learn the lesson, to make the connection between their utopian ideals and the destructive consequences that flow from them. The fall of communism has had a cautionary impact only on the overt agenda of the left. Its moral arrogance is not diminished.

No matter how opportunistically the left's rhetoric has been modified, no matter how generous the concessions it has made, the faithful cannot give up the belief in their mission to the future.

Because the transformation they seek is still total, the power they seek is total. No matter how many compromises they strike along the way. The compromises are themselves integral to the strategy of their mission. The transformation of the world requires the permanent entrenchment of the saints in power. Therefore, *everything* is justified that serves to achieve the continuance of *Them*.

In peggy noonan's psychological portrait, one can trace the outlines of the progressive persona I have just described. Noonan observes that the "liberalism" of the Clinton era is very different from the liberalism of the past. Clinton-era liberalism is manipulative and deceptive and not ultimately interested in what real people think, because "they might think the wrong thing."

That is why, observes Noonan, Hillary Clinton's famous plan that would have socialized American health care was the work of a progressive cabal that shrouded itself in secrecy to the point of illegality. Noonan labels Clinton-era politics "command and control liberalism," using a phrase with a deliberately totalitarian ring. But, like so many conservatives I have come to know, Noonan is finally too decent and too generous to fully appreciate the pathology she is confronting.

She begins her inquiry by invoking Richard Nixon's comment that only two kinds of people run for high office in America, "those who want to do big things and those who want to be big people." She identifies both Clintons as "very much, perhaps completely, the latter sort," and clinically examines their narcissism by way of unlocking the mystery of who they really are.

Regarding the husband, Noonan is probably right. I do not think of Bill Clinton as a leftist inspired by ideas of a socially just world, or as having even a passing interest in the healing of cosmic orders. He is more readily understood as a borderline sociopath. Fully absorbed in the ambitions of self, Clinton is a political chameleon who assumes the coloration of his environments and the constituencies on which his fortunes have come to depend.

Hillary Clinton is not so slippery. Despite the cynicism she shares with her husband, one can clearly observe an ideological spine that creates political difficulties for her that he would instinctively avoid. This is not to deny the force of her personal ambitions, or the power of her narcissistic regard. But these attitudes could also be expected in any member of a self-appointed elite, especially one like the left, which is based on moral election.

For this reason, it is difficult to separate the narcissistic from the ideological in the psychology of the political missionary. Do they advance the faith for its own sake, or because advancing the faith leads to their canonization? Do the Lenins of history sacrifice normal life in order to achieve "big things," or because they crave the adulation the achievement brings? It is impossible finally to answer the question. But we can observe that the narcissism of Stalin—exseminarian, Father of the Peoples, and epic doer of revolutionary big deeds—makes the Clintons' soap opera of self-love appear thin gruel.

Despite their life-long collaboration, Bill and Hillary are different political beings in the end. Indeed her marital rages provoked by a partner whose adolescent lusts put their collective mission at risk is probably a good measure of how different they are.

"In their way of thinking," Noonan writes of the Clintons, "America is an important place, but not a thing of primary importance. America is the platform for the Clintons' ambitions, not the focus of them." The implication is that if they were principled emissaries of a political cause, the ambition to do big things for America would override all others. Instead, they have focused on themselves and consequently have made the American political landscape itself "a lower and lesser thing."

They have "behaved as though they are justified in using any tactic in pursuit of their goals," including illegality, deception, libel, threats, and "ruining the lives of perceived enemies." They believe, she continues, "they are justified in using any means to achieve their ends for a simple and uncomplicated reason. It is that they are superior individuals whose gifts and backgrounds entitle them to leadership." They do it for themselves; for the continuance of *Them*.

But the fact is that they all do it. The missionaries of the big progressive causes, the Steinems, the Irelands, the Michelmans, the Friedans, and Hillary Clinton herself, all were willing to toss their feminist movement and its principles overboard to give Bill Clinton a pass on multiple sexual harassments and, in fact, a career of sexual predation that reflects utter contempt for the female gender. Indeed, the Clinton-Lewinsky defense that the feminists made possible can be regarded as feminism's Nazi-Soviet Pact. Their calculation was as simple as it was crude: If Clinton was impeached and removed, Hillary would go too. But she was *their* link to patronage and power, and they couldn't contemplate losing *that*. Their kind was finally in control, and the conservative enemies of their beautiful future were not. There was nothing they wouldn't do or sacrifice to keep it that way.

Almost a decade earlier—in the name of the very principles they so casually betrayed for Clinton—the same feminists had organized the disgraceful public lynching of Clarence Thomas. Despite fiercely proclaimed commitments to the racial victims of American injustice, they launched a vicious campaign to destroy the reputation of an African-American jurist who had risen, reputation unblemished, from dirt-shack poverty in the segregated south to the nation's high courts. They did it knowingly, cynically, with the intent to destroy him in his person and to ruin his public career.

Has there ever been a more reprehensible witch-hunt in American public life than the one organized by the feminists who then emerged as vocal defenders of the White House lecher? Was there ever a more sordid betrayal of common decency than this collective defamation for which no apology has been, or ever will be, given?

What was the sin Clarence Thomas committed to earn such judgment? The allegation—that he had talked inappropriately ten years previously to a female lawyer and made her uncomfortable—appears laughable in the post-Lewinsky climate of presidential gropings and borderline rapes that the same feminists sanctioned for their political accomplice. Thomas's real crime, as everybody knew but was too intimidated to confirm, was his commitment to constitutional principles they hated. They hated these principles because the Constitution was drafted with the explicit idea of thwarting socialist dreams—"a rage for paper money, for an abolition of debts, for an

equal division of property, or any other improper or wicked project"—
as James Madison wrote in *The Federalist*, Number 10.[5]

Peggy Noonan is right. The focus of Hillary Clinton's ambition
is not her country. But it is not merely herself either. It is also a place
that does not exist. It is the vision of a world that can only be realized when the Chosen accumulate enough power to destroy the world
we have.

That is why hillary and Sid Blumenthal, her fawning New Left
Machiavelli, call their own political philosophy the politics of "The
Third Way." This distinguishes their politics from the "triangulation" strategy that Dick Morris used to resurrect Bill Clinton's presidency. Morris guided Clinton, in appropriating specific Republican
policies towards a balanced budget and welfare reform as a means of
securing his re-election. Hillary Clinton was on board for these policies and in that sense is a triangulator herself. But "triangulation" is
too obviously tactical and too crass morally to define a serious political philosophy. Above all, it fails to project the sense of promise that
intoxicates the imaginations of political progressives. That is why
Hillary and Sid call their politics "The Third Way."

"The Third Way" is a term familiar from the lexicon of the left
with a long and dishonorable pedigree. It is the most ornate panel in
the tapestry of deception I described in the beginning of this essay.
In the 1930s, Nazis used "The Third Way" to characterize their own
brand of National Socialism as equidistant between the "interna-
tionalist" socialism of the Soviet Union and the capitalism of the
West. Trotskyites used "The Third Way" to distinguish their own
Marxism from Stalinism and capitalism. In the 1960s, New Leftists
used "The Third Way" to define their politics as an independent
socialism between the Soviet gulag and Western democracies.

But as the history of Nazism, Trotskyism, and the New Left have shown, there is no third way. There is the capitalist, democratic way based on private property and individual rights—a way that leads to liberty and opportunity. And there is the socialist way of group identities, group rights, a relentless expansion of the political state, diminished opportunity, and restricted liberty. "The Third Way" is not a path to the future. It is just the suspension between these two destinations—a holding pattern while the stigma of leftist disasters recedes. It is a bad faith attempt on the part of people who are incapable of giving up their socialist schemes to escape the taint of their discredited past.

Is there a practical difference in the modus operandi of Clinton narcissism and Clinton messianism? I think there is, and it is the difference between "triangulation"—a cynical compromise to hang onto power until the next election cycle and "The Third Way"—a cynical deception to ensure the permanence of *Them*. It is the difference between the politics of getting what you can and the politics of acquiring the power to change the world.

A capsule illustration of these different political ambitions can be found in the book *Primary Colors*, which describes, in thinly veiled fiction, Bill Clinton's road to the presidency in 1992. It is an admiring portrait not only of the candidate but of the dedicated missionaries—the true believing staffers and the long-suffering wife—who serve Clinton's political and personal agenda.

These functionaries—Harold Ickes and George Stephanopoulos are two examples—serve as the flak-catchers and "bimbo eruption"-controllers who clean up his personal messes and shape his image for gullible publics. But they are also the idealists who design his political message and who enable him to succeed.

It is *Primary Colors*'s insight into the minds of these missionaries that is striking. They see Clinton quite clearly as a flawed and often repellent human being. They see him as a lecher, a liar, and a man who would destroy an innocent human being in order to advance his own career (this is, in fact, the climax of the story). Yet through all the sordidness and lying, the personal ruthlessness and disorder, the idealistic missionaries faithfully follow and serve their leader.

They do it not because they are themselves corrupt. The prospect of material return or fame is not what drives them. Think only of Ickes, personally betrayed and brutally cast aside by Clinton, who nonetheless refused to turn on him, even after the betrayal. Instead, Ickes kept his own counsel and protected Clinton, biding his time and waiting for Hillary to make her move, then he joined her staff to manage her Senate campaign.

The idealistic missionaries in this true tale bite their tongues and betray their principles, rather than betray *him*. They do so because in Bill Clinton they see a necessary vehicle of their noble ambition and their chiliastic dreams. He, too, *cares* about social justice, about poor people and blacks (or so he makes them believe). They will serve him and lie for him and destroy for him, because he is the vessel of their salvationist hopes. Because Bill Clinton can gain the keys to the state, he is in their eyes the only prospect for advancing the progressive cause. Therefore, they will sacrifice anything and everything to make him succeed.

But Bill Clinton is not like those who worship him, corrupting himself and others for a higher cause. Unlike them, he betrays principles because he has none. He will even betray his country, but without the slightest need to betray it for something else—for an idea, a party, a cause. He is a narcissist who sacrifices principle for power because his vision is so filled up with himself that he cannot tell the difference.

But the idealists who serve him—the Stephanopouloses, the Ickeses, the feminists, the progressives and Hillary—*can* tell the difference. *Their* cyncism flows from the very perception they have of right and wrong. They do it for noble ends. They do it for the progressive faith. They do it because they see themselves as gods, as having the power—through correct politics—to redeem the world. It is *that* terrifyingly exalted ambition that fuels their spiritual arrogance and justifies their ignoble means.

And that is why they hate conservatives. They hate you because you are killers of their dream. You are defenders of a Constitution that thwarts their cause. They hate you because your "reactionary" commitment to individual rights, to a single standard, and to a neutral and limited state obstructs their progressive designs. They hate you because you are believers in property and its rights as the cornerstones of prosperity and human freedom, because you do not see the market economy as a mere instrument for acquiring personal wealth and stocking political war chests, but as both means and end.

Conservatives who think progressives are misinformed idealists will always be blindsided by the sheer malice of the left—by the cynicism of those who pride themselves on their principles; by the viciousness of those who champion sensitivity; by the intolerance of those who call themselves liberal; and by the ruthless disregard for the well-being of the poor on the part of those who preen themselves as their champions.

Conservatives are surprised because they see progressives as merely misguided, when they are, in fact, morally—even *ontologically*—misdirected. They are the messianists of a false religious faith. Since the redeemed future that justifies their existence and rationalizes their hypocrisy can never be realized, what really motivates progressives is an idolatry: their limitless passion for the continuance of *Them*.

Notes

Preface

1   Chris Matthews, *Now, Let Me Tell You What I Really Think* (New York, 2001), 72. Also remarks made at the Wednesday Morning Club, November 15, 2001.

1. How the Left Undermined America's Security

1   "A Nation Challenged; the Response; Planning for Terror But Failing to Act," *New York Times*, December 30, 2001. "If you understood al-Qaeda," Robert Bryant Deputy Director of the FBI, told the *Times*, "you knew something was going to happen. You knew they were going to hit us, but you didn't know where. It just made me sick on September 11. I cried when those towers came down." In fact, investigators had almost guessed where the enemy would strike. The report of the National Commission on Terrorism, published in 2000, had a picture of the Twin Towers in the cross-hairs on its cover.

2   Laurie Mylroie, *Study of Revenge: Saddam Hussein's Unfinished War Against America*, American Enterprise Institute (Washington 2000), 1

3   John Miller, "Talking With Terror's Banker," ABCNews.com, May 28, 1998.

4   *New Yorker*, September 24, 2001 (the comments were posted online on September 17).

5   The speech was made at Georgetown University on November 7, 2001. See the discussion below.

6   "Given my latest piece on Clinton's record on terrorism, I asked Dick Morris if he thought Clinton would be worried right now about what September 11 was doing to his legacy. Could Clinton be remorseful? Or angry? Or reflective? Morris's answer

239

took a while, since he hasn't spoken to Clinton in years. Here's a short version of his answer: 'The thing about Bill Clinton is that he never, ever, ever, ever, EVER, ever, ever, ever, ever, ever, EVER, blames himself.'" Andrewsullivan.com, January 11, 2001.

7   Christopher Hitchens, "Strangers in a Strange Land," *Atlantic Monthly*, December 2001: "October 6, the day immediately preceding the first U.S. counterstroke against the Taliban and Osama bin Laden, found me on a panel at the New York Film Festival. The discussion, on the art of political cinema, had been arranged many months before. But as the chairman announced, the events of September 11 would now provide the atmospheric conditioning for our deliberations. I thus sat on a stage with Oliver Stone, who spoke with feeling about something he termed "the revolt of September 11," and with bell hooks, who informed a well-filled auditorium of the Lincoln Center that those who had experienced Spike Lee's movie about the bombing of a Birmingham, Alabama, church in 1963 would understand that "state terrorism" was nothing new in America....I would surmise that audience approval of Stone's and hooks's propositions was something near fifty-fifty. Clapping and hissing are feeble and fickle indicators, true. At different times, in combating both Stone and hooks, I got my own fair share of each. But let's say that three weeks after a mass murder had devastated the downtown district, and at a moment when the miasma from the site could still be felt and smelled, a ticket-buying audience of liberal New Yorkers awarded blame more or less evenhandedly between the members of al-Qaeda and the directors of U.S. foreign policy."

8   Edward Rothstein, "Exploring the Flaws in the Notion of the 'Root Causes' of Terror," *New York Times*, November 17, 2001.

9   The anti-American crank, Gore Vidal, writing in *Vanity Fair*, was an exception.

10   Rothstein, ibid.

11   Rothstein, ibid. Cf. my discussion of these issues in David Horowitz, *The Politics of Bad Faith* (New York: Free Press, 1998).

12   John Miller, op. cit. For the camera—and the credulous—bin Laden also mentioned other "causes" such as the bombing of Nagasaki. Since the left's attacks on America have almost become a conventional wisdom, it is perhaps necessary to remind some that the Japanese imperialists were the aggressors in World War II, and had invaded China and Southeast Asia using methods that violated international norms, including some of the worst atrocities in the history of warfare. Since the Japanese are not Muslims, bin Laden's faux concern merely underscored his hypocrisy in even mentioning them.

13   "Bin Laden's Warning," October 7, 2001, BBCNews.com

14   Susan Page, "Why Clinton Failed To Stop Bin Laden," *USA Today*, November 12, 2001.

15   Thomas Powers, "The Trouble With The CIA," *New York Review of Books*, January 17, 2002.

16   But following the U.S. victory against the Taliban, the government of Yemen had second thoughts and began cooperating with Washington.

17   Page, op. cit.

18   Mylroie, op cit., 147

19   Ibid.

20   Ibid.

21   David Halberstam, *War In A Time Of Peace*, New York 2001, p. 20

22   March 9, 1975

23   Peter W. Rodman, *More Precious Than Peace: The Cold War and the Struggle for the Third World*, New York 1994, p. 185

24   Rodman, ibid.

25   Joe Klein, "Closework: Why We Couldn't See What Was Right In Front of Us," *New Yorker*, October 1, 2001, 45.

26   Kevin Cherry, "Clinton Assigns Blame," *National Review Online*, November 8, 2001.

27   Ibid.

28   Barton Gellman, "The Hunt for Bin Laden Part II: Struggles Inside the Government Defined Campaign," *Washington Post*, December 20, 2001. Dick Morris, "Why Clinton Slept," *New York Post*, January 2, 2002

29   Morris, ibid.

30   Ibid. Cf. also Gellman, op cit., who quotes a member of the Counter-terrorism Strategy Group of the National Security Council: "There was a lack of political will to follow through and allow investigators to proceed on the case [of the Muslim charities that were funding terrorists] . . . When I say political, I mean we can't have the public come out and saying we're bashing Muslims."

31   "Liberals felt that the civil rights of suspected terrorists were more important than cutting off their funds. . . . Everything was more important than fighting terrorism. Political correctness, civil liberties concerns, fear of offending the administration's supporters, Janet Reno's objections, considerations of cost, worries about racial profiling and, in the second term, surviving impeachment, all came before fighting terrorism." Ibid.

32   Klein, "Closework," op. cit., 47.

33   Dick Morris, *New York Post*, November 14, 2001.

34   Susan Page, "Why Clinton Failed to Stop Bin Laden," *USA Today*, November 13, 2001.

35   "U.S. Missed Three Chances To Seize Bin Laden," *London Sunday Times*, January 6, 2002.

36   Ijaz Mansoor, "Clinton Let Bin Laden Slip Away and Metastasize," *Los Angeles Times* December 5, 2001.

37   Ibid.

38   "US Missed Three Chances To Seize Bin Laden," op. cit.

39   Morris, op. cit.

40   For example, virtually every penny saved in Vice President Gore's showcase "reinventing government" program came from cuts in the military establishment.

41   Stephanie Gutman, *The Kinder, Gentler Military: How Political Correctness Affects Our Ability to Win Wars*, 2001.

42   The War in Afghanistan conducted by the Bush Administration relied on U.S. Special Forces, which had not been gender-integrated and on indigenous allies.

43   Paul Craig Roberts "Who's Responsible?" September 17, 2001, www.townhall.com

44 Thomas Powers, "The Trouble With The CIA," *New York Review of Books*, January 17, 2002; Gellman, Morris, op. cit.

45 Klein, "Closework," op. cit., 45.

46 House Amendment 276, to amend HR2330. Congressional Record, August 3, 1993 , H5692.

47 Terry Cooper, research paper on the Sanders-Owens amendment, supplied to the author. Cooper is an independent political consultant. Idem. H5692

48 Cooper, ibid.

49 Frank's amendment also allowed discretion in the nature of the cuts.

50 Cooper, ibid. "For a while it was renamed the National Security Committee. For the sake of simplicity, though, it's referred to herein as the Armed Services Committee. Similarly, the Defense subcommittee of the House Appropriations Committee, although for a period formally the National Security Subcommittee, is herein consistently called the Defense Subcommittee."

51 Cooper, Ibid.

52 Cooper, idem. at H5820

53 Ibid. . Idem at H2957

54 Ibid.

55 Klein, op. cit.

56 Ibid.

57 The details of the Clinton-Riady partnership are to be found in William Triplett III and Ken Timperlake, *Year of the Rat* (Washington, D.C., 2000). The book is based on the Burton and Thompson Committee hearings and interviews with national security officials.

58 Ibid.

59 *Wall Street Journal*, January 3, 2000

60 *Year of the Rat*, op. cit.

61 These included Senators Fred Thompson, James Imhofe and John Kyl, Representatives Dan Burton, Porter Goss, Curt Weldon, Joel Hefley, Tom Tancredo, Peter Hoesktra, Steve Buyer and Tillie Fowler, and members of the Republican congressional leadership such as Chris Cox, J.C. Watts and Tom DeLay.

62 Powers, op. cit.

63 Ibid.

64 Ibid.

65 October 1, 2001.

66 Powers, op. cit.

67 Beinart, ibid.

68 Reuel Marc Gerecht. Gerecht wrote under the pen name Edward Shirley.

69 *Ivory Towers on Sand: The Failure of Middle Eastern Studies in America*, published by the Washington Institute for Near East Policy, 2001.

70 Stanley Kurtz, "The Scandal of Middle East Studies," *The Weekly Standard*, November 19, 2001 Cf. also Martin Kramer, "Terroism? What Terrorism?!" *Wall Street Journal*, November 15, 2001.

71 Said's thesis was, in fact, an intellectual's version of Pol Pot's order to execute all Cambodians who wore glasses, because as readers they carried with them the bad ideas of the past. Pol Pot's perspective, in turn, was heavily influenced by Satrean Marxists on Paris's Left Bank, with whom he studied before embarking on his Cambodian crusade.

72 Kurtz, op. cit.(Emphasis added.)

73 Kramer, op. cit.

74 Kurtz, op. cit.

75 I am very familiar with this litany of CIA crimes now taught as a progressive catechism on American campuses, because as a leftist in the 1960s I wrote the first version of this black record myself *in The Free World Colossus*, which was published in 1965 as a history of the Cold War and became a kind of political bible for the anti-Vietnam movement. As veteran leftist Paul Berman begrudgingly wrote in the August 1986 issue of *The Village Voice*, I was one of the founders of the New Left "and the author of some of its most well-thumbed pages. Other writers figured larger in the awareness of the general public; but no one in those days figured larger among the leftists themselves." (cited in *Radical Son*, p. 359) For an example of how this anti-American message is spread on U.S. campuses today, see David Horowitz, *The Ayatollah of Anti-American Hate*, Center for the Study of Popular Culture, Los Angeles.

76 Beinart, op. cit.

77 Available at www.frontpagemagazine.com or from The Center for the Study of Popular Culture, Los Angeles, CA.

78 Peter Collier and David Horowitz, *Destructive Generation*, Summit Books, 1989, p. 161

79 Cal Thomas, "Will Liberal Democrats Keep U.S. Secrets Safe?" *Los Angeles Times*, February 14, 1991. Dellums replied in letter to the *Times*, March 5, 1991, accusing his political enemies of taking the quote "out of context." Wrote Dellums: "Their quote out of context printed and reprinted in various forums of my statement that we should 'dismantle every intelligence agency in this country piece by piece, brick by brick, nail by nail,' fails to include my call in the same sentence that 'if there was a need for us to rebuild such organizations that we rebuild them with civil liberties and civil rights and justice to people in mind." The response was as damning obviously as the quote. First it defended the statement that we should tear down our intelligence agencies by substituting a serious doubt that they should exist (not much of a retraction) and followed that with the completely disingenuous concern for civil liberties—in other words rights which are already respected by the CIA and other intelligence agencies and about which Ron Dellums has never shown a scintilla of concern when it comes to Communist police states like Cuba.

80 This phrase comes from a *Washington Post* report, R. Jeffrey Smith, "Energy Department Discloses 204 Secret Tests," 8 December 1993.

81 David Horowitz, *Who's Responsible for America's Security Crisis?* (Los Angeles, Calif.: Center for the Study of Popular Culture, 1999).

82 *Destructive Generation*, 168.

83   Michael Crowley, "The Dark Side of Patrick Leahy," The New Republic, November 8, 2001. Franklin Foer, "Sin of Commission," *The New Republic*, October 8, 2001 and Stephen F. Hayes, "Patrick Leahy, Roadblock: More Than Any Other Senator, He Has Stalled Anti-Terror Bills," *The Weekly Standard*, October 15, 2001; Jerry Seper, "Leahy Challenges Bush On Military Tribunals," *The Washington Times*, November 11, 2001.

84   *Los Angeles Times* January 28, 1993.

85   James Bornemeier, Wm J. Eaton, *Times* staff writers, "Pentagon Critic Gains Top Rank on Military Panel," *Los Angeles Times*, January 28, 1993.

86   A slogan of the campaign was "One, two, three, four, we don't want another war/five, six, seven, eight, win with Wallace in '48."

87   On the Soviet creation and control of the American Communist Party, see John Haynes and Harvey Klehr, *The Secret World of American Communism* (1996) and *The Soviet World of American Communism* (1998) two volumes in the *Yale Annals of Communism* series, based on the Soviet archives. On the Communist Party's control of the Progressive Party, see John Haynes, *Red Scare, Red Menace: Communism and Anti-Communism in the Cold War Era*, Chicago, 1996.

88   Radosh, *Divided They Fell: The Demise of the Democratic Party 1964-1996*, New York, 1996, 158-9.

89   These events are described in *Radical Son*, 160.

90   Ibid., 165-68.

91   How they accomplished this is described in Ronald Radosh's important book, op. cit Chapter 6: "McGovernism and the Captured Party"; cf. also Peter Collier and David Horowitz, *Destructive Generation*, and Steven Hayward, *The Age of Reagan: The Fall of the Old Liberal Order*, 1964-1980, New York 2001. On the subsequent cultural transformation of the old liberalism into new Democratic party leftism (or "modern liberalism,") see Robert Bork, Slouching Towards Gomorrah, New York, 1997.

92   Henry Mark Holzer and Erika Holzer, *Aid and Comfort: Jane Fonda in North Vietnam*, 2002.

93   These events are recounted in Radosh, op. cit., Horowitz, *Radical Son*, pp. 303-5; and Peter Collier, *The Fondas*, New York, 1991.

94   For instance, Michael Barone, *Our Country*, 508-9; Radosh, op. cit., 180.

95   The comment was made by Morris Abrams, civil rights lawyer and Democratic party activist. Cited in Steven F. Hayward, *The Age of Reagan: The Fall of the Old Liberal Order*, 1964-1980, New York, 2001, 542. Hayward describes how the Humphrey Democrats of the centrist Coalition For A Democratic Majority, were frozen out of foreign policy appointments. Ibid., 543.

96   Cf. Joshua Muravchik, "Why the Democrats Lost," *Commentary*, January 1985

97   Cited in Hayward, 535.

98   Waller R. Newell, "Postmodern Jihad: What Osama bin Laden learned from the Left," *The Weekly Standard*, November 26, 2001. Michel Foucault, perhaps the most influential social thinker among American academics "welcomed 'Islamic govern-

ment' as a new form 'of political spirituality' that could inspire Western radicals to combat capitalist hegemony." Foucault described Khomeni himself as "a kind of mystic saint." Ibid.

99 Hayward, op. cit., 559-60

100 Remarks As Delivered By President William Jefferson Clinton, Georgetown University, November 7, 2001.

101 David Horowitz, *Uncivil Wars: The Controversy Over Reparations For Slavery*, San Francisco 2001.

102 Andrew Sullivan, "AWOL President: Clinton's Legacy and 9/11," Salon.com January 11, 2002.

103 Ibid.

II. *How to Beat the Democrats*

1 David Horowitz, *The Art of Political War and Other Radical Pursuits*, Dallas, 2000. See also the website www.politicalwar.com.

2 Paul Gigot , "Why Dems Let Gore Fight On And On, And…" *Wall Street Journal*, December 1, 2000.

3 In the wake of Florida, the political leftists who dominate America's legal faculties came out en masse to attack the Supreme Court's resolution of the crisis Gore had created. Hundreds of leftist law professors including partisan media hounds like Alan Dershowitz signed a tendentious public advertisement condemning the Supreme Court's ruling. An examination by legal experts Peter Berkowitz and Benjamin Wittes in The Wilson Quarterly shows that the alleged arguments are almost exclusively contrived and pre-conceived political prejudices, without any attempt on the part of the critics to confront the legal issues themselves. Peter Berkowitz and Benjamin Wittes, "The Professors and *Bush v. Gore*," *Wilson Quarterly*, October 29, 2001.

4 Professor Bruce Ackerman a leftwing law professor at Yale is the figure most identified with this partisan, subversive and extra-legal (albeit fashionable) viewpoint. Ibid.

5 Al Gore's media campaigns were run by Bob Shrum, formerly Ted Kennedy's press secretary. Shrum had previously distinguished himself with a TV ad against the California anti-discrimination Initiative (Proposition 209), which featured hooded Ku Klux Klan members burning crosses. The voice-over in Shrum's ad, which was spoken by actress Candace Bergen, linked Newt Gingrich, Ward Connerly, California governor Pete Wilson and former Klan grand dragon, David Duke, as supporters of the measure, which the ad claimed would deprive blacks and women of their rights. The Proposition Shrum was attacking read as follows: "The state shall not discriminate against, or grant preferential treatment to, any individual or group on the basis of race, sex, color, ethnicity, or national origin in the operation of public employment, public education, or public contracting." Shrum used a similar ad to defeat Ellen Sauerbrey in a gubernatorial campaign in Maryland in 1998. The ad falsely painting her as a racist was so outrageous that Baltimore's African-American mayor Kurt

Schmolke, a Democrat, publicly dissociated himself from it. To Al Gore, on the other hand, Shrum's low character and ruthless tactics were reasons to hire him for a presidential run.

6   These principles are described in greater detail in *The Art of Political War and Other Radical Pursuits.*

7   "Hate Crimes"—as defined in the Democrat bills that Republicans oppose—are "thought crimes" and unconstitutional. One illustrative hate crime conviction that came before the Supreme Court involved Todd Mitchell, a 19-year old African-American who had seen Mississippi Burning with some friends. Mitchell was so upset by the film, that he said to his friends: "Do you all feel hyped up to get some white people?…There goes a white boy; go get him." But when his friends crossed the street to beat fourteen-year old Gregory Riddick into a coma, Mitchell got cold feet. "You should leave that boy alone," he said and refused to participate. Even though he didn't take part in the beating, Mitchell was sentenced to two years for the violence. Then he was sentenced to another two years for the "hate crime." Jeffrey Rosen, "Bad Thoughts," The New Republic, July 5, 1993

8   Of course, if Republicans win the center and retain their principles, they will move the "center" to the right.

9   *The Art of Political War & Other Radical Pursuits*, op. cit. The Rick Lazio campaign illustrates the penalty of ignoring this rule. Lazio lost his Senate race against Hillary Clinton by employing a strategy that was too negative, even attempting to link her to terrorists in the campaign's final days. The over-reach produced a fatal backlash. Hillary Clinton had astronomical negatives before the campaign even began. Lazio needed to give people a reason to vote for him, not against her.

10   Alan Bernstein, "Political Forecasters Sticking With Gore Despite All The Polls," Houston Chronicle, November 2, 2000 The prediction was made in July.

11   Kevin Sack, "Gore Urges Votes of Black and Labor Base," New York Times, 11/05/2000.

12   The phrase "three-fifths of a human being" refers to slaves not African-Americans. The three-fifths compromise was proposed by the anti-slavery framers who wanted to diminish the electoral power of the slave South. Under the compromise, slaves were to be counted as three-fifths of a person for the purpose of drawing congressional districts. (There were thousands of African-American free men, and even thousands of African-American slaveholders.)

13   Rich Lowry and Ramesh Ponneru, "Bush's Better Inclination," *New York Times*, October 25, 2000.

14   An exception were the Eisenhower years. But Eisenhower was a non-party-affiliated national war hero and was undecided about whether he would run as a Democrat or Republican until the last minute.

15   The exception was Jimmy Carter, a military man and a Southerner.

16   "Hardball With Chris Matthews," MSNBC, November 27, 2000.

17   As President, Clinton himself attended meetings of the Second Socialist Interna-

tional. I recently heard Henry Kissinger characterize these visits as inappropriate for an American president, since he attends them not as a party official, but as a head of state.

18 Cleta Mitchell, "How Democrats Wage Political War," *Wall Street Journal*, November 20, 2000.

19 Michael Kelly, "Saint Hillary," *New York Times Sunday Magazine*, May 23, 1993. See also David Horowitz, *Progressive Narcissism* below.

20 An illustrative case is the selection of Carlottia Scott as the political issues director of the Democrat National Committee in May 1999. Scott is the former mistress of the Marxist dictator of Grenada, and the former chief of staff for retired Congressman Ron Dellums (D-Berkeley), a radical whom Democrats made the head of the House Subcommittee on Military Installations with top security clearance. Every year during the Cold War, Dellums submitted his own military budget to Congress proposing to cut U.S. Defense spending by 75%. When the Marines liberated Grenada in 1983, they discovered a cache of Scott's love letters to the former dictator. In one of them she wrote: "Ron [Dellums] has become truly committed to Grenada….He's really hooked on you and Grenada and doesn't want anything to happen to building the Revolution and making it strong. He really admires you as a person and even more so as a leader…The only other person that I know of that he expresses such admiration for is Fidel." When Congressman Dellums retired in 1998, Bill Clinton's Secretary of Defense William Cohen awarded him the highest civilian medal the Pentagon can bestow.

21 Paul Begala, "Banana Republicans" www.msnbc.com, November 13, 2000.

22 Ronald Taylor killed three people in Pittsburgh; Colin Ferguson went on a shooting spree against whites and Asians on a Long Island commuter train. See the Politically Correct Hate Crimes Archives at www.frontpagemagazine.com for details.

23 Larry Elder, *The Ten Things You Can't Say in America*, New York 2000, 247.

24 George Stephanopoulos, *All Too Human*, New York 1999. Congressman Patrick Kennedy told Democrats in Pennsylvania, "All you need to do is look at Newt Gingrich, Trent Lott, Dick Armey, Tom DeLay…There's always been a fascist crowd in every society." Jeff Jacoby, "Vitriol From The Left," *Boston Globe*, December 28, 2000.

25 Land-owning peasants.

26 "The VNS exit poll showed Gore winning majorities of the vote on all the issues he emphasized as part of his populist approach; indeed, among voters who said issues, rather than 'qualities,' mattered most, Gore ran up a healthy lead of 55% to 40%." Ruy Teixeira, "Lessons for Next Time," The American Prospect, December 18, 2000.

27 Even speaking about the "haves" and the "have nots" provides a good example of how the left rigs the game through its control of the language we use. Seventy percent of American millionaires are self-made. It would be more accurate to speak of "the "dos" and the "do nots", the "cans" and the "cannots," the "wills" and the "will nots." But that would be blaming the "victims."

28 It was the same with their lawsuits against tobacco companies that lined the pockets

of the trial lawyers but failed to reduce teenage smoking. In the eyes of Democrats it was a good faith effort to get Americans to do the right thing, and it filled the coffers of the forces that do good (the Democrats).

29 Remember Reagan. Reagan resisted the Soviet Union and called it an "evil empire"— to liberals' everlasting consternation and dismay—and became a hero to the Soviet people when the Wall finally came down.

30 "Social promotion" is a scheme invented by progressives, in the name of "self-esteem," to deceive students– mainly poor, black and Hispanic– into believing that they are learning something when they are not. Instead of giving them "F's" and holding them back, progressive "educators" all over the country promote failing students until they graduate. It's only after graduation, when they go into the economy to look for a job and start a life that they discover they are functional illiterates and have been cheated of their opportunity.

31 *Los Angeles Times*, January 20, 2000

32 "Democratic Presidential Candidates Debate at Harlem's Apollo Theater," CNN, February, 21, 2000

33 www.drudgereport.com December 11, 2000; *Wall Street Journal*, December 12, 2000. McEntee was also a key organizer of the Seattle riots protesting free trade and the global market.

34 www.drudgreport.com December 20, 2000. "We'll give them the same honeymoon they gave us, which was nothing." Of course, this is a typical Democrat falsehood. Republicans did not challenge the legitimacy of Bill Clinton's victories in 1992 and 1996. They did not call them coups or thefts, nor did they seek to organize boycotts and other obstructions.

35 The media, for example, carried on a year-long campaign to discredit the death penalty and spread the impression that enforcement of the death penalty was racist. Since Texas is the foremost state in the Union upholding death-penalty law, this campaign had the (intended) effect of tarnishing Bush's credibility in the eyes of African-American and Hispanic voters.

36 Atlanta, November 7, 2001.

III. *The War Room*

1 *Los Angeles Times*, January, 20, 2000.

2 *Washington Post*, February, 3, 2000.

3 Vol.1, #3 Tuesday, March 7, 2000.

4 Prnciple 2, *The Art of Political War*.

5 Vol. 1, #3 Thursday, March 7, 2000.

6 The average African-American male dies within two years of becoming eligible to collect social security. Only the privatization programs that Republicans support and Democrats oppose will give him a better return on his investment.

7 Vol. 1, #1 February 29, 2000.

8 Vol. 1, # 9 Tuesday, March 27, 2000.

9   Vol. 1, #34 Thursday, June 22, 2000.

10   Vol. 1, #8 Thursday, March 23, 2000.

11   Vol. 1, #13   Tuesday April 11, 2000.

12   Vol. 1, #20 Thursday, May 4, 2000.

13   Vol. 1, #25 Tuesday, May 24, 2000.

14   Vol. 2, #1 Tuesday, January 9, 2001.

15   David Horowitz, *The Art of Political War and Other Radical Pursuits*, Dallas 2000, p. 11.

16   The DNC actually has created a website called Grand Old Petroleum. See www.grandoldpetroleum.com,

17   *Art of Political War*, 10.

18   Vol. 2, #2 Tuesday, May 21, 2001.

19   The DNC actually has created a website called Grand Old Petroleum party. See www.grandoldpetroleum.com.

20   Vol. 2, #3 Thursday, May 23, 2001.

21   Field Poll, reported in the *San Diego Union*, May 23, 2001.

22   Ibid.

23   CNN Live Event/Special, May 17, 2001.

24   Gregg Easterbrook, "The Producers," *New Republic*, June 4, 2001

25   Paula Zahn, The Edge, May 29, 2001.

26   Press conference, May 17, 2001.

27   San Diego Union-Tribune, May 25, 2001.

28   Fabiani and Lehane are on contract with Southern California Edison.

29   Jerry Taylor and Peter Van Doren, "The Bush-Davis Power Hour", National Review Online, May 30, 2001.

30   Gray Davis, weekly response on energy, May 19, 2001. www.democrats.org/news/featurs/feature051901.html.

31   Vol. 2, #4 Tuesday, June 5, 2001

32   Gerald McEntee, president AFSCME.

33   DNC website.

34   Democratic TV attack spot.

35   DNC website.

36   *Wall Street Journal*, July 19, 2001 .

37   Well, they get an $800 death benefit to pay for the funeral.

38   Vol. 2, #5 Tuesday, September 11, 2001.

39   Vol. 2, #6 Tuesday, June 5, 2001.

40   This *War Room* was actually written on Monday, September 10, 2001 and was never released.

41   *Los Angeles Times*, September 10, 2001.

42   Vol. 2, #7 Tuesday, September 11, 2001.

43   Vol. 2, #8 Tuesday, September 18, 2001.

44   Peter Collier and David Horowitz, *Destructive Generation: Second Thoughts About the Sixties* (New York, 1989), 162-63.

45 This and other documents can be found in *Grenada Documents: An Overview and Selection*, released by the U.S. Department of State and U.S. Department of Defense, Washington, D.C., 1984.
46 Vol. 2, #9 Thursday, September 20, 2001.

IV. The Unrepentant Left

2. The Ayatollah of Anti-American Hate

1   This is an edited version of a text that has appeared as an ad in 20 American college newspapers and as an op-ed in the *Los Angeles Times*, the *Minneapolis Star-Tribune* and the *Columbia Spectator* among other papers.
2   Norman Podhoretz, *Why We Were In Vietnam*, New York, 1982; Michael Lind, *The Necessary War*, New York, 1999; David Horowitz, *Radical Son*, New York, 1997.
3   Noam Chomsky, *What Uncle Sam Really Wants*, Tucson, 1986 (interviews with David Barsamian).
4   Ibid.
5   Noam Chomsky, *Propaganda and the Public Mind*, Interviews by David Barsamian, Cambridge, 2001, x. In the endpapers of this volume the *New York Times* is quoted praising Chomsky as "an exploder of received truths." *The Guardian* (London): "One of the radical heroes of our age…A towering intellect…" *The Times Literary Supplement*: "Chomsky's work … has some of the qualities of Revelations, the Old Testament prophets and Blake."
6   Available at www.zmag.org.
7   Interview, September 19, 2001. www.zmag.org.
8   *What Uncle Sam Really Wants*, 8, 18, 29, 31, 32, 56-58.
9   Chomsky, *Profit Over People*, New York, 1999, 102.
10 *What Uncle Sam Really Wants*, 32.
11 Chomsky has set up a smokescreen to the effect that he is really not a Marxist or a Communist, but a follower of obscure writers like Anton Pannekoek and Paul Mattick, and the anarcho-socialist Prince Peter Kropotkin. But since he has spent his intellectual life making excuses for (and defending) Stalinist regimes—Nicaragua's is only the most obvious—and now is Fifth columnist for Islamic fascists—only the terminally credulous would take his protestations seriously.
12 Ibid., 79.
13 Ibid., 82.
14 Ibid., 56-7.
15 Bill Ayers, *Fugitive Days*, New York, 2001, 256
16 Statement on the publisher's website, www.beacon.org.
17 *What Uncle Sam Really Wants*, 100.
18 Emails to the author.
19 Chomsky, op. cit., chapter 1, "The Main Goals of U.S. Foreign Policy."

20 Ibid., 7–8

21 What he does is to select quotes from isolated individuals and government documents that can be made to appear as though they lend credibility to his malicious
distortions.

22 Chomsky, op. cit, 8 (In other words, p. 2 of Chomsky's text).

23 Ibid., 8.

24 Hannah Arendt, *The Origins of Totalitarianism*, Harvest Books 1973.

25 Ibid., 14.

26 Ibid., 16.

27 Ibid., 21–22.

28 Ibid., 22.

29 Ibid., 23.

30 Ibid.

31 Ibid., 22.

32 Ibid., 23–4.

33 Ibid., 59.

34 Ibid., 59–60.

35 Noam Chomsky, *The Common Good*, Chicago, 1999 (Interviews with David
Barsamian).

3. *The 1960s Terrorist Cult and 9/11*

1 The interviews were for a history of the Weather Underground co-written with Peter
Collier for *Rolling Stone Magazine* that was subsequently included as the chapter
"Doing It" in our book *Destructive Generation*, New York 1989

2 Ibid.

4. *The President's Pardoned Bombers*

1 *New York Times*, April 20, 2001.

2 This story has been ably told in John Castellucci, *The Big Dance: The Untold Story of
Kathy Boudin and the Terrorist Family that Committed the Brinks' Robbery Murders*,
New York 1986.

3 This and other details in Barbara Olson, *The Final Days, The Last, Desperate Abuses of
Power by the Clinton White House*, New York, 2001, 21–23.

5. *Representative McKinney's Bizarre Mission*

1 Michael Barone, *The Almanac of American Politics*, Washington, D.C., 2001, 445.

2 "Show of Farce," *New Republic*, September 10, 2001.

3 www.house.gov/mckinney/news//if_000914_humanrights.htm. 1:25 PM Room 2000,
Rayburn House Office Bldg. Washington DC. Proceedings.

4 The most famous of the groups surveilled by COINTELPRO was The Black Panther Party a violent street gang, whose members were convicted of 349 felonies in the year 1969 alone. Cf. Hugh Pearson, *In the Shadow of the Panther*, New York 19DATE, David Horowitz *Radical Son*, and Edward J. Epstein, NAME of Book.

5 www.derechos.net/paulwolf/cointepropapers/coinwcar3.htm.

6. *Scheer Lunacy at the Los Angeles Times*

1 The full story is told in *Radical Son,*.

7. *Progressive Narcissism*

1 Originally given as a speech at a conference on Hillary Clinton in Washington D.C., April 7, 2000. The conference was co-sponsored by the Center for the Study of Popular Culture and the American Enterprise Institute.

2 Peggy Noonan, *The Case Against Hillary Clinton*, New York, 2000.

3 Specifically Hillary Clinton and Bill Lann Lee were involved in organizing protests at Yale in 1970 to defend Black Panther leaders who had tortured a black youth named Alex Rackley by pouring boiling water on his chest. Rackley was then taken out and shot in the head on Panther orders. The man who shot him, Warren Kimbro served four years for the execution-murder, was recruited into an affirmative action program at Harvard on release and subsequently became Dean at a Connecticut college. This story is told in my autobiography, *Radical Son*, New York, 1997.

4 Jamie Glazov in *The Salisbury Review*, Spring 2000. Soliah was a soldier in the Symbionese Liberation Army, a group that murdered Marcus Foster, the first black superintendent of Oakland schools and kidnapped Patty Hearst. Soliah, who has the support of several Democratic legislators and her Methodist? Church, is accused of setting a pipe bomb in a Los Angeles police car with the intent of murdering two officers of the peace. Jamie Glazov is also the author *15 Tips on How To Be A Good Leftist*, available from the Center for the Study of Popular Culture.

5 Cf. David Horowitz, *The Politics of Bad Faith*, New York 2000, 185.

Index

60 Minutes, 201
1960s
  anti-war movement of, 11-12
2000 election
  Bush, George and, x-xii
  Bush and, 86-88
  Democrats and, 51
  Gore and, 57, 60, 77-78, 86
  lessons of, 60-67
  political war and, 97-120
  Supreme Court and, 86
  See also political war

Abercrombie, Neil, 23
abortion, 53
Abzug, Bella, 42
Afghanistan, 10, 16, 30, 36, 44, 149, 178
Africa, 7
African-Americans
  Bush and, 55, 57-58, 73
  Democrats and, 106
  education and, 99, 117
  Social Security and, 141
  voter turnout and, 63
  See also race
aggression, politics and, x, 79-80
Al-Amin, Jamil, 196, 197

Alarm!, 187
Alaska, 125, 127
Albania, 176
Algeria, 208
Allah, 9
al-Qaeda
  fatwa of, 23
  Kenya and, 7
  September 11 and, 20
  Somalia and, 4-5, 9
  support for, 6
  Tanzania and, 7
  terrorist acts of, 4-5, 10-11, 39
al Shehhi, Marwan, 3
America
  Balkans and, 9-10
  in Cambodia, 12-13
  Cold War and, 170-76
  culture of, 7, 53
  democracy of, 18
  left and, 194
  racism in, 204-6
  slavery and, 18, 46
  Somalia and, 4-5
  terrorism and, 3-17, 188-91
  in Third World, 177
  in World War II, 171-76
  See also anti-American hatred
"America Come Home", 42

Annenberg School of
  Journalism, 211, 216
anti-American hatred
  Chomsky and, 160-69
  left and, 159
  social justice and, 159
  universities and, 160-61
  See also America; terrorism
AOL-Time Warner, 213
Appropriations Committee, 23
Arafat, Yasser, 148
  al-Qaeda and, 6
  PLO of, 12, 31
  terrorism and, 18-19
Arbenz regime, 34
The Art of Political War
  (Horowitz), 79, 95
Ashcroft, John, 120-122, 220
Asia, 12-14
Aspin, Les, 37, 39
Atlantic Monthly, 31
Atta, Mohammed, 3
Austin, Jan, 220
Awahiri, Ayman, 16
Axis powers, 171, 172
Ayers, Bill, 168, 169, 191
  1960s terrorism and, 185-89

Baer, Robert, 28

Baghdad, 167
balanced budgets
    Democrats and, 98
    political war and, 116-17
Balkans, 9-10, 19, 115
Baltimore, 98, 144
Baraldini, Sylvia, 225
Bardenstein, Carol, 35
Barnard College, 200
Barr, Joel, 215
Barsamian, David, 162
Bashir, Omar Hassan
    Ahmed, 16
Bay of Pigs, 34
Beatty, Warren, 212
Beckel, Bob, 13-31
Begala, Paul, 69-70
Beijing, 26
Beinart, Peter, 9, 30, 33, 34
Beirut, 6
Berger, Sandy, 11-12, 16
Berlin Wall, 60, 173, 210
Biden, Joe, 143-46
Big Government
    Democrats and, 64-65, 68
    energy and, 124-27
    Republicans and, 65
Big Oil, 76
bin Laden, Osama, 6, 20, 148
    attempted capture of, 16-17
    fatwa of, 23
    intelligence services and, 30
    September 11 and, 163
    slavery and, 46
    war aims of, 9-10
biological warfare, 13
Black Liberation Army, 200,
    206
Black Panther Party, 151, 208,
    225
Blumenthal, Sidney, 211, 234
Bollinger, Claude, 35
Bond, Julian, 205-6
Bonior, David, 22, 38, 42
Bono, 161
Bork, Robert, 54
Boston, 98, 144
Boudin, Kathy
    anti-American activities
        of, 196, 198-200
    "The Family" and, 201
    political prisoners and, 202

Bremer, Paul, 14, 47-48
Brinks robbery, 199-200, 206
Brown, H. Rap, 197, 198, 202,
    225
Brown, Waverly, 199
Bryan, William Jennings, 43
Buchanan, Patrick, 61
Bulgaria, 176
Burton, Dan, 25, 26
Burton committee, 26, 27
Bush, George W.
    2000 election and, x-xii,
        62-63, 86-88
    African-Americans and,
        57-58, 73
    "compassionate conserva-
        tism" of, 55, 63, 66-67
    defaming of, 54-55
    energy and, 131
    military and, 40
    national security and, 24,
        143, 145
    political war and, 56
    race and, 54-55, 106
    September 11 and, xii, 3, 4,
        8
    Social Security and, 54, 135,
        138-43
    stories of, x-xi
    taxes and, 108-9
    terrorism and, 8-9, 48
    tax plan of, 77-78
Byrd, Robert C., 200

Caddell, Patrick, 67
California, 100, 126
    energy crisis in, 127-33,
        212-13
Cambodia, 12-13, 43, 158, 180
campaign finance scandals,
    25-28
Cardozo School of Law, 208
Carter, Jimmy, 67, 199
    left and, 43
    military and, 36, 116
    Vietnam and, 165
Carter, Rubin "Hurricane," 225
*The Case Against Hillary
    Clinton* (Noonan), 224
Castro, Fidel, 34, 36, 182, 203,
    212

Cato Institute, 132
Center for Constitutional
    Rights, 202
Central America
    Cold War in, 38
    communism in, 14, 37, 194
    totalitarians in, 178
Central Intelligence Agency
    (CIA), 39
    Democrats and, 21
    hostility to, 28-31, 33-35
    language deficiency at, 33
    Latin America and, 149
    See also intelligence
        services
Chapman, Shawn, 197
Chavez, Linda, 121
chemical warfare, 13
Cheney, Dick, 124, 131, 161
Cherry, Kevin, 14
Chesimard, Joanne, 200
Chicago, 98, 144, 145
Chicago Tribune, 161
Children's Defense Fund,
    229
Chile, 166
China, 25, 26, 115, 116, 144,
    148
Chomsky, Noam, 191, 208
    anti-American hatred and,
        160-69
    political criminals and, 200
    refutation of, 170-84
Church Committee, 28
Churchill, Ward, 208
CIA. *See* Central Intelligence
    Agency
Cleaver, Eldridge, 207-8, 220
Cleaver, Kathleen, 207-8
Cleveland, 144
Clinton, Bill, 70, 87
    African expedition of, 7
    approval ratings of, xi-xii
    Arafat and, 18
    campaign finance scandals
        and, 25-27
    character of, 71-72
    Democrats and, 96
    economy and, 97-98
    education and, 100
    gun laws and, 112
    impeachment of, 52

left and, 231
national security and, 3-20,
  37-38, 45-47, 115-16, 144,
  148-50
"New Democrat" strategy
  and, 68
pardons of, 193-203
September 11 and, 8, 163
Somalia and, 5
taxes and, 107, 108
terrorism and, 3-20, 45,
  163-64
welfare and, 82
Clinton, Hillary, 42
left and, 223-37
narcissism of, 224
political war and, 101-4
politics and, 68-69
presidential run of, 87
Close, Glenn, 198-99
Cohen, William, 13-14, 24, 39
"Cointelpro: The Untold
  American Story", 208
Cold War, 17, 61
America and, 170-76
Chomsky and, 166-67
Grenada and, 178
intelligence services and, 29
Korea and, 179-80
Collier, Peter, 209, 219-221
Columbia University, 35
Combest, Larry, 23
Commerce Department, 26
*Commies: The Old Left, The
  New Left and the Leftover
  Left* (Radosh), 221
The Common Good
  (Chomsky), 183
communism
America's efforts against,
  11-12
in Central America, 14, 194
in Cuba, 229
in Korea, 220
in Latin America, 165
left and, 228-30
opposition to, 183
totalitarian doctrines of, 9
utopia of, 13
in Vietnam, 41, 158
Communist Party, American,
  40

"compassionate conserva-
  tism", 55, 63, 66-67
"Conference on Racism", 18
Congress, 51
Congressional Black Caucus,
  206
conservative majority, 62-63
Constitution, 53
Democrats and, 62
left and, 62, 233-34
racial voting districts and,
  204
Conyers, John, 206
Cooper, Terry, 22
Coplon, Judith, 215
Corporate Greed, 167
Coss, Peter, 23
Council on Foreign
  Relations, 14, 172
Counterespionage Groups, 29
Cox, Christopher, 26, 217
Cox Committee Report, 215
crime, 53
Crockett, Davy, 74
Crockett, George, 38
Cuba, 34, 178, 179, 182, 229
culture
of America, 7, 53
universities and, 35
Cuomo, Mario, 67, 76, 202
Czechoslovakia, 41, 176

Dallas, 98
Damon, Matt, 161
Daniels, Florence, 140
Daschle, Tom, 131, 141, 162
Davis, Angela, 202, 225
Davis, Gray, 129-30, 132
DeFazio, Peter, 23
defense. *See* national security
DeLauro, Rosa, 22
Dellums, Ron
as activist, 42
Grenada and, 151-52
intelligence services and,
  22, 23, 36-39
Democratic National
  Committee, 25, 26, 137, 152
Democrats
African-Americans and,
  106

attacks on Republicans by,
  69-73
balanced budgets and, 98,
  116-17
Big Government and, 64-
  65, 68, 124-27
campaign finance scandals
  and, 25-28
changes in, 67-68
Constitution and, 62
economy and, 97-98
education and, 82-86, 98-
  101
energy and, 123-34
Fifth Column Caucus of,
  35-39
gun laws and, 111-14
knowledge of, 67-74, 90-92
left and, 40-44, 68-69
military and, 19, 62
minorities and, 58
national security and, 20-
  28, 33, 40, 114-16, 143-46
political war and, 51-53
politics and, 90-91
race and, 20, 62, 87-89,
  104-7, 120-22
Social Security and, 109-11,
  134-43
tactics of, 63-66
taxes and, 98, 107-9
underdogs and, 74-79
voter turnout and, 63-64
welfare and, 80-82, 96, 98,
  118
See also left; political war;
  Republicans
Detroit, 38, 144
Deutscher, Isaac, 210
Directorate of Intelligence, 29
Directorate of Operations, 29
Dix, Norm, 218
Dodd, Chris, 38
Dohrn, Bernardine, 185, 194,
  225
1960s terrorist cult and,
  185-89
Dole, Bob, 58, 70, 73, 209
Dole, Elizabeth, 209
Drinan, Richard, 42
Duke University, 34

Earhart, Amelia, 74
economy, 17, 97-98
Edison, Thomas, 74
education
    African-Americans and,
        117
    Bush and, 66
    Democrats and, 82-86, 98-
        101
    Gore and, 84
    minorities and, 83-84, 99-
        100
    political war and, 116-17
    Republicans and, 82-86,
        96, 100-101
Egypt, 16
election campaigns. *See*
    political war
El Salvador, 38, 44, 166, 177
emotions, politics and, 55-56,
    124
Encounter Books, 221
energy
    Big Government and, 125-27
    California and, 212-13
    political war and, 123-34
Energy Information
    Administration, 131
England, 18
Ensler, Eve, 199
Environmental Extremists,
    124, 126-27
Espionage Act, 219
Esposito, John, 32
Estonia, 176
Ethics Committee, 121
ethnic cleansing, 9, 10
Evans, Linda, 202
    anti-American activities
        of, 193-98
    pardon of, 193-98

FAA. *See* Federal Aviation
    Administration
Fabiani, 132
"The Family", 200, 207
fascism, 9
FBI. *See* Federal Bureau of
    Investigation
fear
    Democrats and, 64-66

politics and, 57-58, 129
Federal Aviation Adminis-
    tration (FAA), 14
Federal Bureau of Investiga-
    tion (FBI), 14-15, 195, 218
Federal Energy Regulatory
    Commission, 132
Federalist, 234
Feingold, 214
Feinstein, Dianne, 14
Ferguson, Colin, 70
Fifth Amendment, 27
Fifth Column Caucus, 35-39
Flint War Council, 186
Florida, 3, 51
Foley, Tom, 39
Fonda, Jane, 42, 212
Forbes, Randy, 140
Ford, Henry, 74
Founding Fathers, 52, 53
FoxNews, 130
France, 174
Frank, Barney, 22
Frank amendment, 22, 23
Freeh, Louis B., 10, 216, 218
Freud, Sigmund, 161
Fugitive Days (Ayers), 187

Gates, Bill, 74
Gehlen, Reinhard, 173, 174, 175
Genoa, 160
Georgetown University, 8
Gephardt, Dick, 22, 116, 162
Germany, 166, 170, 172, 174, 175
Gertz, Bill, 27
Giap, Vo Nguyen, 157
Gingrich, Newt, 82, 98
glasnost, 210
Glazov, Jamie, 225
Gold, Ted, 193, 194
Goldberg, Eve, 202
Good Will Hunting, 161
Gorbachev, Mikhail, 60, 210,
    212
Gore, Al, 58
    2000 election and, 57, 60,
        62-63, 77-78, 86
    airline security and, 14
    balanced budgets and, 116
    Clinton administration
        and, 62

education and, 84, 100
gun laws and, 112
race and, 104
taxes and, 107, 108
underdogs and, 76
welfare and, 82
Gottemoeller, Rose, 37-38
government
    attitude toward, 3
    national security and, 146-47
    politics and, 98
Gramsci, Antonio, 61
Great Depression, 213
Great Satan, America as, 9,
    147, 161, 169, 171, 183, 190
Great Society, 62
Greece, 175-76, 182
Greenspan, Alan, 213
Greenwald, Robert, 214
Grenada, 151-52, 177-79, 182
Guatemala, 34, 38, 44, 166, 177
Gulf War, 18, 19, 115
gun laws, political war and,
    111-14

Haiti, 19, 182
Hamas, 14-15, 16, 148
Haq, Abdul, 30
Hart, Gary, 67
Hart, Senator, 24
Harvard University, 33, 34
hate crimes, 75
"hate crimes" legislation, 54
Hawaii, 164
Hayden, Tom, 41, 42-43, 220
Hezbollah, 16
Himmler, Heinrich, 165
Hispanics, 99
Hiss, Alger, 215
Hitchens, Christopher, 167
Hitler, Adolph, 40, 165, 171, 175
HMOs, 76
Hoagland, Jim, 11
Hoffman, Abbie, 214
Holland tunnel, 10
Holocaust, 166
Holtzman, Elizabeth, 42
"homeland security"
    campaign, 24
Hoover, J. Edgar, 186
hope, politics and, 58-59

House Armed Services
Committee
Dellums and, 37, 39, 151
intelligence services and,
22, 23, 36
McKinney and, 205
national security and, 27
House Democratic Caucus, 42
House International
Relations Committee,
205, 206
House Permanent Select
Committee on Intelli-
gence, 21-23, 31, 36, 39
House Subcommittee on In-
ter-American Affairs, 151
House Subcommittee on
U.S. Military Installa-
tions, 37, 151
House Subcommittee on
Western Hemisphere
Affairs, 38
Howard University, 207
Huang, John, 26
Huffington, Arianna, 202
Human Events, 141
Human Relations Subcom-
mittee, 206
"Human Rights in the
United States", 206
Humphrey, Hubert, 41-42
Hungary, 176
Hussein, Saddam, 28, 115,
126, 190-91

Ickes, Harold, 235, 236
Ijaz, Mansoor, 16-17
Il Sung, Kim, 170
immigration, 91
Indochina, 43, 158, 159, 165,
180-81
Indonesia, 180
intelligence services
civil liberties and, 17
Cold War and, 29
funding for, 21-23
lobbying against, 28-31
national security and, 148-50
September 11 and, 4
See also Central Intelligence Agency

Internal Revenue Service
(IRS), 108
"International Human
Rights Conference on
Winning Amnesty for
U. S. Political Prisoners
and Prisoners of War",
202
International Operations and
Human Rights Subcom-
mittee, 205
Iran, 16, 44, 145
Arab coalition in, 18
Islamic regime in, 36-37
Mossadegh and, 34
national security and, 115, 116
threat of, 144
U. S. weapons technology
and, 26
Iraq, 19, 28, 145, 148, 166
American bombing of, 7
Arafat and, 18
Gulf War and, 19
national security and, 115, 116
terrorism and, 7
U. S. weapons technology
and, 26
Iron Curtain, 165
IRS. *See* Internal Revenue
Service
Islam, 9, 10
Islamic charities, 15
Islamic Jihad, 16
Israel, 205
American support for, 18
government of, 12
root causes of terrorism
and, 6
Israeli Aircraft Industries,
194-95
Italy, 174

Jackson, George, 225
Jackson, Jesse, 86, 101, 105
Jakarta, 25
Jamal, Mumia Abu, 196, 202,
207, 225
Japan, 191
Jeffrey, Terry, 141, 142, 143
Jerusalem, 45
Jews, 45

Johnson, Lyndon, 62, 165
Joint Chiefs of Staff, 19
Jordan, 28, 29
Judiciary Committee, 206
Justice Department, 218

Kabul, 167
Kennedy, John F., 40, 67, 145,
165
Kennedy, Ted, 67, 100
Kenya, 7, 11, 17
Khaddafi, Muammar, 124, 125
Khmer Rhouge, 12-13, 158, 181
Khobar towers, 10
Khomeini, Ayatollah, 44
Khost, 30
Khrushchev, Nikita, 228
Khyber Pass, 29
Kissinger, Henry, 43
Klein, Joe, 14, 15, 21, 24-25
Korea, 179-80, 182, 220
Kosovo, 18
Kramer, Martin, 31
Kremlin, 40
Kunstler, William, 200
Kuwait, 7
Kyl, Jon, 14

Lahr, John, 188
Lake, Anthony, 12-13, 28
Langley, 28, 29
Latin America, 149, 165, 182
Latvia, 176
Leahy, Patrick, 14, 38-39
Lee, Barbara, 150-51, 206
Lee, Bill Lan, 216, 225
Lee, Wen Ho, 214-19
left
America and, 194
anti-American hatred and,
159
Chomsky and, 162
Clinton and, 231
communism and, 228-30
Constitution and, 53, 62,
233-34
Democrats and, 40-44, 68-
69
Hillary Clinton and, 223-37

left (cont.)
  media and, 85, 125
  national security and, 3-48
  progressives and, 223-28
  Republicans and, 72
  root causes of terrorism
    and, 6-7
  social justice and, 229-30
  strategies of, 74
Lenin, Vladimir, 72, 170, 223
Leninism, 183
Lewinsky, Monica, 7, 15, 17,
  19, 149
Lewis, John, 22, 71
"liberal", 53
Libya, 26, 115, 144, 145, 148
Lincoln, Abraham, 74
Lincoln tunnel, 10
Lithuania, 176
London *Sunday Times*, 17
Los Angeles, 98, 99, 144, 145
Los Angeles Teachers Union,
  83-84
Los Angeles Times, 39, 150
  Lee and, 214-19
  Scheer and, 209-12
Luntz Companies, 35

Madison, James, 234
Malaya, 180
Manson, Charles, 186
Marshall Plan, 171, 182
Marx, Karl, 229
Marxism, 69, 181, 183, 211
Maryland, 100
Massachusetts, 43
Matthews, Chris, xi
Mauritania, 205
May Nineteenth Communist
  Movement, 187-88, 199,
  200
McAuliffe, Terry, 86
McCain, John, 42, 106, 107,
  214
McCarthy, Joe, 121, 228
McCarthyism, 105-7, 122
McEntee, Gerald, 86-87, 138,
  139
McGovern, George, 66, 67
  foreign policy of, 41
  national security and, 116

presidential campaign of,
  12, 40-43
McKinney, Cynthia, 204-8
McVeigh, Timothy, 8
media
  conservative, 27
  left and, 85, 125
  liberal, 27
  national security and, 27-
    28, 33
  root causes of terrorism
    and, 7
Medicare, 71
Meehan, Marty, 23
Menashe, Louis, 221
Menchu, Rigoberta, 225
Mexico, 142, 164
Middle East, 14, 205
Middle Eastern studies, 31-32
Middle East Quarterly, 31
Middle East Studies
  Associations, 32
Midnight Special Bookstore,
  195
Miler, John, 6
military
  Democrats and, 19, 62
  economy and, 17
  expansion of, 40
  social experiments in, 18
Milosevic, Slobodan, 19
minorities
  Democrats and, 58
  education and, 83-84, 99-
    100
  political war and, 58
  Republicans and, 58
  as underdogs, 96
Modern Language Associa-
  tion, 31
Mogadishu. *See* Somalia
Morris, Deborah, 29
Morris, Dick, 15, 17, 70, 81, 234
Mossadegh, 34
Moynihan, Patrick, 139
Muslims, 10, 14, 19, 45

Nader, Ralph, 61
Nadler, Jerry, 195, 201
narcissism, progressives and,
  226

Nation, 139, 199
National Association for the
  Advancement of Colored
  People (NAACP), 54, 121
National Commission on
  Terrorism, 14, 47
National Intelligence
  Estimate, 218
National Organization for
  Women, 229
National Review, 28, 62-63
national security
  Bush and, 24
  Clinton and, 3-20, 37-38,
    45-47, 144
  Democrats and, 20-28, 33,
    40
  government and, 146-47
  intelligence services and,
    148-50
  left and, 3-48
  media and, 27-28, 33
  political war and, 114-16,
    143-53
  Republicans and, 13, 24, 28,
    38
  universities and, 31-35
National Security Agency
  (NSA), 30
National War College, 194
NATO. *See* North Atlantic
  Treaty Organization
Navy Yard Computer Center,
  194
Navy Yard Officers Club, 194
Nazism, 9, 235
Nazi-Soviet Pact, 233
Nesson, Charles, 219
New Deal, 66
New Left, 235
New Leftists, 159
New Republic, 9, 30
Newton, Huey, 151, 225
New York, 4, 98, 144, 145
New Yorker, 14, 24, 188
New York Patrolman's
  Benevolent Association,
  195
New York Times
  Ayers and, 168, 185-88
  Boudin and, 198, 199
  Chomsky and, 162, 166

CIA and, 33
Lee and, 218
political prisoners and, 201
root causes of terrorism
and, 8
*New York Times Sunday
Magazine*, 31
Nicaragua, 38, 44, 166, 177,
182
Nicholson, Arthur, 38
Nixon, Richard, 41, 43, 58, 231
Noonan, Peggy, 224, 230-32,
234
"No Regrets For A Love Of
Explosives", 185
North Atlantic Treaty
Organization (NATO), 172
North Korea, 26, 114-16, 144,
145, 148
Northwestern University, 188
Norton, Gail, 121
NSA. *See* National Security
Agency
nuclear warfare, 13

O'Leary, Hazel, 37
Oakland, 99, 151
Obey, Dave, 23
Oklahoma City bombing, 8,
15
Olson, Sara Jane
anti-American activities
of, 196-98
"The Family" and, 201
"On the Bombings"
(Chomsky), 163
Oreskes, Michael, 3
Orientalism (Said), 31, 32

Pacifica Network, 221
Pacific Gas and Electric, 133
Palestine Authority, 6
Palestine Liberation
Organization (PLO), 6, 31
Parsons, Albert, 187
Pashto, 30
Peace Now, 12
Pearl Harbor, 3-4, 158, 164
Pearl Jam, 161
Pelosi, Nancy, 22

Peltier, Leonard, 206-7
Peng, Li, 25
Pentagon, 3, 17
perestroika, 210
pharmaceutical companies,
76
Philadelphia, 144
Phillippines, 10, 14, 164
Phoenix Program, 34
"The Phony Islamic Threat"
(Said), 31
Plato, 161
PLO. *See* Palestine Liberation
Organization
Poland, 176
policy
in America, 7
politics vs., 55, 98
political war
2000 election and, 97-120
aggression and, x, 79-80
balanced budgets and, 116-
17
complexity of, 59-60
conservative majority and,
62-63
Democrats and, 51-53
education and, 116-17
energy and, 123-34
gun laws and, 111-14
Hillary Clinton and, 101-4
knowledge of enemy and,
51, 102-4
minorities and, 58
national security and, 114-
16, 143-46, 147-53
principles of, 95-96
race and, 54-55, 87-89, 104-
7, 120-22
Republicans and, 51-52, 89-
90, 95-97
Social Security and, 134-43
strategy and, 60-61, 87-88
taxes and, 107-9
underdogs and, 74-80
unity and, 61
voter turnout and, 63-64
winning and, 53-54
See also politics
politics
art of, 56
Democrats and, 90-91

emotions and, 55-56, 124
fear and, 57-58, 129
government and, 98
hope and, 58-59
identity, 88
perception and, 78-79, 98
policy vs., 55, 98
position and, 56
principles of, 55-60
stories and, x
task of, 68-69
victims and, x
See also political war
Pol Pot, 12-13
Potter, Harry, 170
poverty, 6, 73
Powell, Colin, 46, 47, 74, 206
Powers, Thomas, 28, 29
Pratt, Geronimo, 207
prayer, 53
prescription drugs, 111
Primary Colors, 235-36
Princeton University, 33, 34
*The Prison Industrial
Complex and the Global
Economy* (Evans and
Goldberg), 202
"progressive", 53
Progressive Party, 40, 42
progressives, 73
Democrats as, 119-20
left and, 223-28
narcissism and, 226
political conflicts and, 73
social justice and, 224-25

race
in America, 204-6
Democrats and, 87-89, 104-
107
government and, 73
political war and, 54-55, 87-
89, 104-7, 120-22
Republicans and, 69-70,
87-89, 96, 104-7
terrorism and, 6
See also African-Americans
"radical", 53
Radical Son (Horowitz), 159,
220
Radosh, Ronald, 221

Rage Against the Machine, 161
Rahman, Abdel, 188-89
Ramparts, 209, 212, 219
Rankin, Jeannette, 150
Rather, Dan, 125
Reagan, Ronald
  African-American vote and, 58
  Cold War and, 60, 178-79
  as hero, 74
  politics and, 67
  taxes and, 98
  Vietnam and, 165
Red Army, 44
Red Family Commune, 220
Red Guerrilla Resistance, 200
Red Sun Rising Commune, 219
Remington, William, 215
Reno, Janet, 216, 218
Republicans
  balanced budgets and, 116-117
  Big Government and, 65
  conservative majority and, 62-63
  Democratic attacks on, 69-73
  economy, 97-98
  education and, 82-86, 96, 100-101, 116-17
  energy and, 123-34
  "Gold Star", 54, 57
  gun laws and, 111-14
  minorities and, 58
  national security and, 13, 24-28, 38, 143-46
  political war and, 51-52, 89-90, 95-97
  race and, 69-70, 87-89, 96, 104-7, 120-22
  Social Security and, 89, 96, 109-11, 134-43
  strategy and, 87-88
  taxes and, 96, 107-9
  totalitarian threat and, 12-13
  underdogs and, 75-79, 96
  unity and, 61
  voter turnout and, 63-64
  welfare and, 80-82, 96, 119
  See also Democrats;

political war
Republic of New Afrika Movement, 206, 207
Reuters, 140
Riady, James, 25, 26
Rice, Condoleeza, 46, 47, 205
Richardson, Bill, 217
Robinson, Jackie, 74
Rochester Institute of Technology, 34
Rogan, Jim, ix, 85
Rolland, Kayla, 113-14
Rolling Stone Magazine, 162
Romania, 176
Roosevelt, Franklin, 3, 40, 66, 213
Rosenberg, Susan, 200-201
Rosenbergs, 215
Rothstein, Edward, 8
Rove, Karl, 66, 89
Rudman, Senator, 24
Rush, Bobby, 42
Russert, Tim, 131

Said, Edward, 31-32
Saigon government, 34
Salon, 170, 218, 219, 220
Sanders, Bernie, 21
Sanders amendment, 21, 23
Sandinista dictatorship, 38, 44
San Francisco, 98, 144
Saudia Arabia, 10, 16, 127, 130, 149
Scarborough, Rowan, 27-28
Scheer, Bob
  Lee and, 214-19, 222
  Los Angeles Times and, 209-12
  Sung and, 219-21
Schroeder, Pat, 23, 42, 212-13
Scott, Carlottia, 152
SDS, 193
Seattle, 144, 160
security. *See* national security
Seitlin, Maurice, 212
Senate Judiciary Committee, 38
September 11, 161
  al-Qaeda and, 20
  American response to, 8, 10
  Arabic operatives and, 20

bin Laden and, 163
Bush and, xii, 3, 4, 8
intelligence services and, 4
Pearl Harbor vs., 3-4
root causes of terrorism and, 162
terrorist networks and, 16
Serbs, 9
  in Kosovo, 19
sexism, 73
Shakur, Assata. *See* Chesimard, Joanne
Sharpton, Al, 100, 105, 229
Sidan, 16
slavery, 7, 8, 18, 46, 106
Smith, Dinitia, 186
Sobell, Morton, 215
socialism, 183
social justice
  anti-American hatred and, 159
  bin Laden and, 9
  left and, 229-30
  progressives and, 224-25
  Social Security and, 136
  terrorism and, 6, 8
Social Security
  African-Americans and, 141
  Bush and, 54, 66
  political war and, 109-11, 134-43
  Republicans and, 89, 96
  social justice and, 136
Soliah, Kathy, 225. *See* Olson, Sara Jane
Somalia, 4-6, 9, 16
Sontag, Susan, 6-7
South Carolina, 105, 141
Soviet Union, 13
  Afghanistan and, 44, 178
  collapse of, 21, 22
  World War II and, 172-76
Sowell, Thomas, 95
Spence, Floyd, 24
St. Louis, 98, 144
Stalin, Joseph, 34, 40, 41, 170, 210, 232
State Department, 16, 172
Stephanopoulos, George, 235
strategy, political war and, 60-61, 87-88

Streisand, Barbara, 211
Sudan, 19, 20, 46, 149, 163, 205
Sullivan, Andrew, 47
Sullivan, Gordon, 115
Sung, Kim Il, 218-21
Supreme Court, 86, 204
Sweden, 139
Symbionese Liberation
    Army, 197

Taifa, Nkechi, 207
Taliban, 30
Tanzania, 7, 11, 17
Tate, Sharon, 186
"Tate Eight", 186
taxes
    Democrats and, 98
    political war and, 107-9
    Republicans and, 96
Taylor, Ronald, 70
"Tear Down the Walls", 202
terrorism
    in 1960s, 185-92
    al-Qaeda and, 4-5
    America and, 3-17, 188-91
    Arafat and, 18-19
    bin Laden and, 16
    Bush and, 8-9, 48
    Clinton and, 3-20, 45, 163-
        64
    immigration and, 91
    Iraq and, 7
    Muslims and, 14
    root causes of, 6-7, 8-9, 41,
        45-47, 162-65
    social justice and, 6, 8
Third World and, 164-67
Tet Offensive, 157
Texas, 57, 73, 132
Thailand, 180
Third Reich, 167
"Third Way", 234
Third World
    America in, 177
    terrorism and, 164-67
Thomas, Clarence, 54, 71, 72,
    233
Thompson, Fred, 25, 26
Thompson committee, 26, 27

Tiananmen Square, 25
Tikkun magazine, 229
Tikkun Olan, 229
Time, 35
Timperlake, Ken, 27
Tin, Bui, 157
totalitarians, 9, 11-13
trigger-lock law, 113
Triplett, William C., III, 27
Trotsky, Leon, 210
Trotskyism, 235
Truman, Harry, 40, 41, 67
Turkey, 28
twentieth century, ideologies
    of, 9
Tytler, Alexander, 65, 68

U. S. Capitol Building, 194
U2, 161
Uganda, 7
underdogs, political war and,
    x, 74-80
United Nations (UN), 18, 205-
    206
universities
    anti-American hatred and,
        160-61
    CIA and, 30
    culture and, 35
    national security and, 31-35
    root causes of terrorism
        and, 7
University of California,
    Berkeley, 157, 201
University of Illinois, 168, 188
University of Michigan, 35
USA Today, 15
USS Cole, 11, 14, 149

Vagina Monologues, 199
Vance, Cyrus, 43
victims. *See* underdogs
"Victims of Cointelpro", 206
Vieques, 160
Vietcong, 225
Vietnam, 12, 34, 43, 141
    Cold War and, 179-80
    communism in, 41
    defeat in, 181

Vietnam War, 40, 157-58, 165
Vietnam War syndrome, 12
voter turnout, 63-64

Wahad, Dhoruba Bin, 207
Walden School, 200
Wallace, Henry, 40, 45
Wall Street Journal, 26, 27-28,
    51, 68, 86
Washington, D. C., 144, 98
Washington, George, 74
Washington Post, 11-13, 24, 47
Washington Times, 27
Watergate, 43, 52, 116
Waters, Maxine, 121
Weather Underground, 185,
    186, 193, 194, 200, 206
Weekly Standard, 28
welfare
    Clinton and, 82
    Democrats and, 80-82, 96,
        98, 118
    Gore and, 82
    Republicans and, 80-82,
        96, 119
"Whack-A-Mole" strategy,
    19
What Uncle Sam Really Wants
    (Chomsky), 161, 165, 170,
    176-77
Whitehorn, Laura, 195, 207
Woolsey, James, 16
World Conference Against
    Racism, Racial Discrimi-
    nation, Xenophobia, and
    Racial Intolerance, 205
World Trade Center attack,
    4, 5, 10, 15, 147
World War II, 171-76

Yale University, 229
Yemen, 11, 149
Yousef, Ramzi Ahmed, 5, 10,
    148
Yugoslavia, 176

Zacchino, Narda, 211
Zinn, Howard, 191, 208

This book was designed and set into type
by Mitchell S. Muncy,
with cover art by Stephen J. Ott,
and printed and bound
by Thomson-Shore, Inc.,
Dexter, Michigan.

The text face is Adobe Caslon,
designed by Carol Twombly,
based on faces cut by William Caslon, London, in the 1730s,
and issued in digital form by Adobe Systems,
Mountain View, California, in 1989.

The index is by IndExpert,
Fort Worth, Texas.

The paper is acid-free and is of archival quality.

31